ArtScroll Series®

Rabbi Nosson Scherman / Rabbi Meir Zlotowitz

General Editors

Touched

Published by
Mesorah Publications, ltd

by a Story
3

A new collection of inspiring stories
retold by the best-selling author of
Touched by a Story

RABBI YECHIEL SPERO

FIRST EDITION
First Impression … June 2005
Second Impression … June 2005

Published and Distributed by
MESORAH PUBLICATIONS, LTD.
4401 Second Avenue / Brooklyn, N.Y 11232

Distributed in Europe by
LEHMANNS
Unit E, Viking Business Park
Rolling Mill Road
Jarow, Tyne & Wear, NE32 3DP
England

Distributed in Australia and New Zealand by
GOLDS WORLDS OF JUDAICA
3-13 William Street
Balaclava, Melbourne 3183
Victoria, Australia

Distributed in Israel by
SIFRIATI / A. GITLER — BOOKS
6 Hayarkon Street
Bnei Brak 51127

Distributed in South Africa by
KOLLEL BOOKSHOP
Shop 8A Norwood Hypermarket
Norwood 2196, Johannesburg, South Africa

ARTSCROLL SERIES®
TOUCHED BY A STORY 3
© *Copyright 2005, by* MESORAH PUBLICATIONS, Ltd.
4401 Second Avenue / Brooklyn, N.Y. 11232 / (718) 921-9000 / www.artscroll.com

---

ISBN:
1-4226-0002-5 (hard cover)
1-4226-0003-3 (paperback)

Typography by CompuScribe at ArtScroll Studios, Ltd.

Printed in the United States of America by Noble Book Press Corp.
Bound by Sefercraft, Quality Bookbinders, Ltd., Brooklyn N.Y. 11232

מכתב ברכה מאת הרב דוד קוויאט

ר"מ בישיבת מיר

ורב דאגודת ישראל סניף חפץ חיים

ב"ה

י"ג מנחם אב תשס"ג

מכתב ברכה

לכבוד ידידי הרב יחיאל ספירא שליט"א, רבי בישיבת הק' חפץ חיים בבלטימור,

הנה בא לפני עלים מספרך אשר כתבת ושמו "נתרגש פון א מעשה" הנה כשמו כן הוא כולו ספורים יקרים המביא רגשות קודש להקוראים בו, מה שנחוץ זה למאוד לחזק האמונה וללמוד איך להתנהג באמונה ובמדות טובות כמו שעולה מהספורים. ולכן אברכהו שיצליח בספרו ושיהנו הקוראים בו,והשם יתב' יברכהו להרבות תורה ומוסר ויגדיל תורה ויאדיר.

ממני ידידו המברכו בכל לב

דוד קוויאט

Her Royal Majesty

– a dedication

ON SHABBOS MORNING, MY GRANDMA MRS. ELISSA Spero ascended to her deserved place — her heavenly throne. The following afternoon her loved ones tearfully escorted her to her final resting place, next to our Grandpa Herb, the man she so adored. Moments such as these always give one reason to pause, to introspect. Exactly how was it that our loving Grandma earned our love and admiration? Was it her smile? Her cheer? Her love? Ironically, we might discover the secret to her life hidden within the day she passed away — the day on which Hashem chose to call her home.

The 14th day of the *Omer.* Hidden discreetly beside the *Omer*-count appears a two-word combination. These are character traits of the Almighty, which we are taught to emulate and in turn master.

Providentially, the 14th day of the *Omer* carries the distinction of *malchus she'bigvurah*, loosely translated as royalty cloaked in strength.

We might suppose that royalty is something one is born into; it is neither learned nor taught. However, history teaches us otherwise. The monarchy of the Jewish nation was earned. It was secured by one woman, a woman who refused to let go ... of her mother-in-law, of all people! When Naomi urges Rus to go back home, Rus pledges her unwavering allegiance to her widowed mother-in-law, a tragic figure indeed. *Ki el asher teilchi eilech — Where you go, I will go. And I will never let go of you, no matter how much you try to convince me.* Because Rus understands what commitment, dedication — and yes, royalty — are all about.

Ein melech belo am — There is no king without a nation. Rabbeinu Bachya clarifies that royalty is not defined by how large one's palace is or how many horses one owns. Rather, it is forged through the undying commitment that one demonstrates to others. To *their* needs. And to their people.

Was Grandma beautiful? Most certainly so. An elegant lady? Never one finer. But selfless love was her crowning achievement. And it is that and that alone that allows one to become the *Eim Hamalchus* she was.

Strength is similarly misunderstood. It is not physical strength that defines gevurah. Rather, it is inner strength, like the incomprehensible self-control evident at the *Akeidah*, where Yitzchak personified absolute gevurah. Yitzchak was terrified. Not of dying. But rather, he was concerned that if he was not tied down properly he might move. *Va'atza'arecha (Bereishis Rabba 57:8)...*

Upon reading this word I had to look carefully. At first I assumed that Yitzchak was worried that Avraham might hurt him. That is what the logical assumption would be. But that is not what the word means. In fact, it is just the opposite. Astoundingly, Yitzchak, armed with only the *gevurah* in his soul, was afraid that he might move, cry out and cause *his father* pain. His concern was for his father and not for himself! This — more than anything else — exemplifies *gevurah*!

We have discovered *malchus* and we have learned of *gevurah*. But *malchus she'bigvurah* — that was Grandma. Her undying commitment to others. To her husband. To her children. To their children. To our successes. And more importantly, to our failures. Grandma, your very own throne for an *Eim Hamalchus* awaits you.

That *malchus she'bigvurah* was also what personified Grandpa Herb. Grandpa Herb was many things. A builder. A visionary. Imaginative and inventive. A maverick. But most of all — a *locheim milchemes Hashem*. Our Grandpa, our very own *melech*, could have sat back and enjoyed the fine lifestyle he had secured for himself and his family. But there was work to be done. Schools and yeshivos to be built. A nation to be tended to. And so he went out to battle, anchored by the gevurah of his queen.

Rus struggles. She lives alone, widowed, and almost completely forgotten. But she carries on. For she carries within her the seed of Mashiach. And eventually she finds it together with the *az* of Boaz. Rus' *malchus* unites with her husband's *gevurah*. Perfection achieved.

As we buried Grandma I could not help but notice Grandpa Herb's *matzeivah*, moved aside to make room for Grandma. On it the inscription stood proudly: *Ish she'ruach eitzah u'gevurah bo* — A man in whom a spirit of *gevurah* and vision shined; *venilcham b'oz milchemes Hashem* — and fought with *oz* battles for Hashem ...

Forty years ago that "*oz*" was handed to you, Grandma. *Oz vehadar levushah* ... And you carried that torch with grace, elegance and style. But most of all with *malchus* — in the truest sense of the word. Nothing was able to diminish your grace and beauty. *Vatitzchak leyom acharon* ...

And now we say good-bye to you, Grandma. We love you. We always have and we always will. The throne for the *Eim Hamalchus* awaits you. We will each try to learn from your glorious life. We will carry with us the memories and we will cherish them forever. And though you are no longer physically with us, you will continue to live on within each and every one of your loving family. Your legacy will endure. Through your children, grandchildren and great grandchildren. Through your smile and laugh and charm. Through your courage and strength. Through your love. We will carry you with us in our hearts forever.

Long Live the Queen ...

Foreword

I AM OFTEN ASKED HOW I CHOOSE THE STORIES TO INCLUDE
in the books. Why these and not others? The answer, I believe,
lies in the secret to a great story — and that is the element
of surprise. When we expect the main characters to behave one
way and they act otherwise, or when they are able to overcome an
impossible challenge, that makes a great tale.

The Talmud (*Avodah Zarah* 18a) recounts a compelling story.
Rav Chanina ben Tradyon once came to visit Rav Yosi ben Kisma.
During their visit Rav Chanina asked Rav Yosi, "*Mah ani lechayei
HaOlam Haba* — Am I worthy of meriting *Olam Haba*?" Rav Yosi
responded with a pointed question, "*Klum maaseh ba leyadcha?*
— Has a *maaseh,* a particularly challenging incident, ever come
your way?"

Rav Chanina then replied that indeed one had: One Purim
he had some of his own money, which he planned to use for the
Purim *seudah,* along with some money he intended to distrib-

ute to the poor. Inadvertently he gave the funds which he had designated for his Purim *seudah* to the poor people. He certainly could have sought restitution from the general *tzedakah* fund, but decided not to do so. When Rav Yosi ben Kisma heard this he responded, "If only my portion in the World to Come would be like yours."

This narrative is puzzling — almost bizarre! Rav Chanina had spent his entire life teaching Torah to others. In fact, he would eventually sacrifice his life for teaching the forbidden Torah and be burnt at the stake, as we read in the riveting account of the *Asarah Harugei Malchus* which we recite on Tishah B'Av and on Yom Kippur. Surprisingly, his *mesiras nefesh* to teach Torah is not the *maaseh* he chose in answer to Rav Yosi's question. Rather the *maaseh* he related is one that appears to be insignificant, a trivial story of mixed-up money. Is *that* Rav Chanina ben Tradyon's legacy?

The answer lies in the wording of Rav Chanina's question. *Mah ani lechayei HaOlam Haba.* I know that my actions deem me worthy of entering *Olam Haba.* But how do I know who I really am? Rav Chanina knew well what he had accomplished, the structures of Torah he had built. But he wanted to know: What have I truly become? *Mah ani*? What defines *me*?

This is the pivotal question of each and every person's life — the question we must all ask ourselves. *Klum maaseh ba leyadcha?* How have we reacted when life has thrown us detours and diversions, tragedies and misfortune? What has our response been to the adversity we have faced?

We hope we have all achieved the merits to enter *Olam Haba.* But when we look back on the edifices of Torah and mitzvos we have built we must ask ourselves, as we stand on the threshold of our Heavenly judgments, *Mah ani lechayei HaOlam Haba?* What have I made of *myself*? Am I forever bound to the Torah I have learned and the mitzvos I have performed? And how can I know that? The answer is to reflect on a *maaseh*, a curveball Heaven has thrown your way. How do we react when the unexpected comes upon us, when the trivial challenge confronts our conscience? And if we have *chanced upon* such a scenario and tackled those challenges with dignity, honor, and unswerving allegiance to Hashem and His Torah, then and only then do we really know who we are.

Reb Sholom Dov Ber, the Rashab, once remarked, "To tell a story, one needs to be skilled; but what requires even more skill is to know how to listen to one." If I may humbly add, "And what requires the most skill is to know how to respond when you encounter such a story."

Each story that has been chosen for this collection of *Touched by a Story* carries with it a timely — no, a timeless — lesson. The stories are eternal. What happened to the people in these stories might happen to you. How we react and how we respond will determine *Mah ani lechayei HaOlam Haba?*

It was one of the darkest periods of Jewish history. Sixty years ago the Gerrer Rebbe was huddled together with his closest chassidim. Millions had died and millions more would soon perish. Nearly everyone had lost a close family member, neighbor, cousin or friend. But the Rebbe would not diminish his celebration, his *oneg Shabbos*, experiencing the sweet joy of *Kabbalas Shabbos* as he always had. And as the *chazzan* began *Lecha Dodi*, the Rebbe began to sing the traditional, melodious *niggun*. Suddenly the Rebbe's son looked up at his father and cried out in desperation and wonder. "*Tatte, maasei yadai tove'im bayam ve'atem omrim shirah?* Father, G-d's creations are drowning in the sea and you still sing out in joy?" The Rebbe looked deeply into his son's eyes and responded, "*Mein tei'ere zin* — my precious son. *We must always sing shirah. It is up to the Aibeshter if he chooses to listen … But we must always sing.*"

The heroes and heroines in these stories have triumphed. By responding to their challenges with nobility and grace, their *neshamos* have resonated with *shirah* — an indescribable *shirah* that emanates from the deepest and most holy parts of our *neshamah*. And this *shirah* — which is a reflection of how they have reacted to their *"maaseh"* — demands that we humbly salute them. Their quiet dignity and strength causes us to reflect and to declare, as Rav Yosi did, "*Mei'chelkecha yehi chelki* … *umigoralcha yehi gorali* — May my portion be like yours and may my lot be like yours."

We are moved by their spirit, stirred by their courage, inspired by their bravery, and humbled by their achievements. We must now learn from their actions, as they have answered the call of *Klum maaseh ba leyadcha*.

And now we have the privilege to be touched … by their story.

Acknowledgments

AS I UNLOADED MY GROCERIES FROM THE shopping cart into my relatively new Chevy Suburban, I could not help but notice an elderly woman by the curb staring at me. She motioned for me to come over and when I did she asked me if I would give her a ride home. I readily agreed and pulled the SUV up to the curb. The woman appeared to be in her mid-70's. She spoke a broken English at best and told me that she came from Russia. We made small talk as she asked me about my family, my wife and children, their ages and if they were boys or girls. She then shared with me that she had only one child, a daughter, and that unfortunately she did not speak to her much. A soft, misty rain was falling as I listened to my passenger share with me her family life. After seven or eight minutes I pulled up to her run-down apartment building. She once again thanked me and I helped her carry her groceries into the house. As I turned to leave, she asked me if I liked being rich. The question caught me off-guard. It was so up front and direct. With good reason I have never considered myself rich but I naively began to explain to her that I had purchased the Suburban only because the payments were a few dollars more than my previous car payments. She quickly shushed me, motioned with her hand as if to wave off what I was about to say, smiled and remarked, "Your children — I'm talking about your children."

It has been nearly two years since the first **Touched by a Story** was released. Much has changed in our lives. Each day that goes by I am more awed and humbled by the kindness of the *Ribbono Shel Olam. Ein anachnu maspikim lehodos lecha Hashem Elokeinu.*

In Book 2, I wrote a story about a young man who worked very hard and overcame great odds to score a 90 on a Gemara test. The *rebbi* rewarded him with a chocolate cake in the shape of a 90. That young man is my *talmid*. His real name is Menachem. The *rebbi* who rewarded him with the cake is my rebbi as well, **Rabbi Anshel Hellman**. The day after the book came out there was a knock on the door. My *talmid* was standing there; he had just arrived from Cleveland. In his hands he held a tray covered with aluminum foil. It was from Rabbi Hellman. Menachem gave me the tray and when I opened it I was pleasantly surprised. It was a chocolate cake, in the shape of a 2, as a reward for writing my second book! Rabbi Hellman has used all methods imaginable to motivate and inspire hundreds of *talmidim*. To have him as my rebbi is a treasure beyond compare.

I thank the **Mirrer Rosh Yeshivah, Rav Nosson Tzvi Finkel,** for dedicating his life to give me and so many others the badge of honor of having learned in **"The Mir."** Over the past year I have had the honor of speaking on behalf of the Mir on a number of occasions. On one of those occasions, I was *zocheh* to speak in front of the Rosh Yeshivah. I witnessed firsthand his unswerving commitment to the yeshivah and his ability to set aside his own personal challenges for the sake of Torah; it is nothing short of amazing. I am honored to be called a *talmid*. May he continue to have the strength to lead the yeshivah for many years to come.

The **Rosh Mesivta** of the **Talmudical Academy of Baltimore, Rabbi Tzvi Teichman,** continues to encourage me; and my principal, **Rabbi Yaakov Schwartz,** has always been a close friend. **Mrs. Tzipporah Schorr, Rabbi Mordechai Soskil, and Mrs. Amy John** have been extremely supportive and encouraging as I have enjoyed my teaching experiences in **Beth Tfiloh.** You are each special to the children whose lives you reach.

Camp Ma-Na-Vu, under the leadership of **Rabbi Shloime Klein,** has been my family's summer home for the past twelve years. Serving as the head counselor, I have had the privilege to work together with many great *mechanchim* in providing unforgettable summers. With *siyata d'Shmaya* our camp has left an indelible impression of Torah and *Yiddishkeit* on thousands of children from all over the globe. Thank you. **Yisroel Yehuda Klein** has been a wonderful friend. I have benefited greatly from an outstanding *talmid chacham,* **Rabbi Pinchos Wachsman.**

The farsighted vision of the ArtScroll founders, **Rabbi Nosson Scherman** and **Rabbi Meir Zlotowitz,** has benefited the world in an incomparable way. Their unparalleled *harbatzas Torah* has given Jews of all backgrounds access to Torah as never before. May Hashem give them strength to continue in their *avodas hakodesh.* A special debt of gratitude to Rabbi Scherman for reading the manuscript. Thank you.

Rabbi Gedaliah Zlotowitz is always positive, energetic, and encouraging. He has precisely the right words at the right time. He has also given me the audacity to dream. While I envisioned a book, he visualized a series. While I hoped to reach hundreds, he anticipated thousands. His friendship and advice make this entire venture worthwhile. I can never thank you enough.

Avrohom Biderman never likes to be thanked publicly for all the work he does. But suffice it to say that without him this book would not have happened. I would imagine the same may be said for many other projects as well. His good humor and wit turn trying challenges into manageable and even enjoyable situations. *Ashrecha …*

I would like to express my appreciation to the many members of the ArtScroll team who did so much to make sure that this book is accurate, well written and beautifully presented. Among them, **Mendy Herzberg,** who somehow managed to efficiently coordinate the editing and production while always keeping his cheerful demeanor; **Eli Kroen**, whose inspiring covers have become a trademark; **Mrs. Mindy Stern**, who deftly wielded her editor's pen in her quest to assure both factual integrity and literary grace; **Mrs. Faygie Weinbaum**, whose conscientious proofreading and eye for detail are justifiably renowned; **Chaya Perel Teichman**, who typeset the book in record time; and **Sara Rifka Spira** and **Suri Reinhold**, who carefully entered the many revisions of the book. To the rest of the gifted ArtScroll staff — I can only thank you for what I know and there is so much more that I don't. *Yeshalem Hashem kigmulchem hatov.*

My editor, **Mrs. Susan Leibtag**, is the one who pushes me to do my very best. She is always honest and gracious. It is difficult working with a big-headed author. Sometimes I insist on things being done my way. She has the uncanny ability to transform the wording and yet still make me feel as if it has always been my own. This is not only smart editing but also an act of benevolence and kindness. And this describes who she really is. While she gives so much of her life to others and their institutions, she never is the one who takes the credit. As always, it has been an honor.

My parents, **Dr. Abba and Sarah Spero,** are shining examples of how we are to lead our lives — with *simchah,* gratitude, and *bitachon.* I am forever grateful to have them as my parents.

My in-laws, **Rabbi Yehuda and Nussy Lefkovitz,** have helped in every way imaginable. They are extremely loving and wonderful parents and grandparents. Their unobtrusiveness dispels the "in-law" myth. Both my parents and my in-laws have displayed *kibud av ve'eim* in a manner rarely performed. It is a lesson for us all.

Rabbi Moshe "Pappa" Lefkovitz, together with his wife *ybd"l* **Mrs. Gertrude Lefkovitz,** dedicated many years of his life to *chinuch* and teaching. May he continue to be the "prince" that he is.

Rabbi and Mrs. Yerachmiel Berger are loving and supportive. They should only continue to have nachas and *gezunt.*

Rabbi Yehuda and Rebbetzin Chana Leah Moses *ob"m* should continue to count their "flock" from *Shamayim,* with *nachas.*

To the countless individuals who added to this book by sharing their stories with me — Thank you ... **Rabbi Dovid Barkin, Rabbi Yitzchak Pollack, Rabbi Yoni Alon, Rav Moshe Herschel Zoberman, Rabbi Nachman Kahana, Mr. And Mrs. Nissan**

Selah, Rabbi Asher Newman, Rabbi Shraga Hershkowitz, Rabbi Binyomin Hershkowitz, Rabbi Yossi Flamm, Rabbi Sruly Fuchs, Rabbi Aron Basch, Rabbi and Mrs. Doniel Metzger, Rabbi Pinchos Rabinowitz, Dovid and Sorala Lefkowitz, Rabbi Aaron Feldman, Rabbi Ephraim Wachsman, Rabbi Tzvi Falik, Rabbi Avrohom Notis, Rabbi Yanky Shifrin, Rabbi Refoel Mendlowitz, Binyomin Ribiat, Fishel Gross, Rav Chaim Dov Keller, Rabbi Yisrael Asia, The Yankelove Family, Moshe and Yehudis Spero, Rabbi Yehuda Goldfeder, Rabbi Tzvi Feuer, Rabbi Kobi Robinson, Rabbi Yaakov Weber, Avromi Lieberman, Mrs. Vicky Berglass, Rabbi and Mrs. Shalom Hoffman, Rabbi Chaim Zev Levitan, Yanky Lefkovitz, Rav Moshe Menachem Taubenfeld, and Binyomin Barer.

My students at **Yeshivas Chofetz Chaim — Talmudical Academy**, in **Camp Ma-Na-Vu**, and in **Beth Tfiloh** have been such a wonderful audience. My greatest supporters and my greatest critiques. They are the reason I teach.

My siblings, **Chaim and Rebecca Spero, Moshe and Gila Spero, Chesky and Chavi Schneider, Yehuda Spero, Yanky and Shana Lefkovitz, Sroli and Zahava Lefkovitz, Shuku and Chayala Lefkovitz, Ezzy and Esti Feuer, Efraim and Leah Blumenkrantz, and Eliyahu and Sivi Rokowsky** are always encouraging. I am privileged to be part of their family.

My children, **Tzvi Aryeh, Avrohom Yosef, Efraim Shimon, Miriam Brocha, Shmuel Avigdor, and Chana Leah** are the most wonderful children one could ever have. You are our entire life and we are very proud of you. May you continue to be such a source of *nachas*.

And, finally, my wife **Chumi** has once again insisted that she not be included in the "thank-you's." That's the way she is. But suffice it to say, *Sheli veshelachem shelah he* — Everything my children and I have is because of her. Thank you.

Table of Contents

Tefillah

Chesed / Kindness

Rebbeim and Talmidim / Teachers and Students

Teshuvah

Torah

Faith

Mesiras Nefesh / Self-Sacrifice

Kiddush Hashem / Sanctifying Hashem's Name

D'veikus BaShem / Cleaving to Hashem

Gevurah / Courage

Mitzvos

Tefillah

A Shining Star

THEY HAD HEARD ALL ABOUT IT FROM THEIR FRIENDS.
Camp Yedidim was certainly a wonderful camp. Its pic-
turesque grounds and modern facilities made it the ideal
place for a child to spend his summer vacation. A boy could have
a great time running and playing, all the while building lifelong
friendships with kids from all over the world. With a strong emphasis on Torah learning and *middos tovos* it was rightfully referred
to as "Heaven on Earth." But this boy, Shaul, or Sholi as he was
called, was different from the typical Camp Yedidim boy. Sholi was
a special child.

Most special children do not interact with other people. They
are in a world of their own. Somewhat of a medical mystery, this
condition at times is accompanied by a genius-level intelligence.
But one thing was most certainly clear. This special child possessed
a very special *neshamah*. Mark and Julie Blum knew this about their
son, but they also knew that their Sholi was different from most
special children.

From the time he was a very young child, there were long periods of time when Sholi would not talk or even notice other people. In fact, on one occasion Mark left for work while Sholi was staring at the wall in the family room; when Mark returned from work eleven hours later Sholi was in the very same place! But when he turned 4, something miraculous happened: he began to speak.

At first it was slow. But his thirst for interaction with people was insatiable. His progress was astonishing. All his parents could do was thank Hashem and watch in disbelief as events unfolded.

Now it was nine years later, and Sholi was 13 years old. His bar mitzvah had been quite special. With not a dry eye in the shul, he *lained* beautifully and proudly sang his *Haftarah*. His parents were overwhelmed. They now thought that perhaps he was ready for the next hurdle. They wanted to send him to sleep-away camp, a camp for regular children, not one for special children. After some research, they decided on Camp Yedidim. All they needed was for the director, Rabbi Greenbaum, to agree.

At first the camp director was hesitant to take a boy who was a little bit different. After all, how would the other boys react? Would they play with him and include him in their games? And, even more important, would they mock him and make him feel uncomfortable? After some consideration, Rabbi Greenbaum decided to give it a try. He suggested to Sholi's parents that they start with a short trial period, after which they would assess whether this experiment was in fact working. Sholi's parents were ecstatic — and when Sholi heard about it, his smile stretched from ear to ear.

One of the conditions made by Rabbi Greenbaum was that Sholi would have a "shadow" counselor staying with him throughout the day. This counselor would act as an older friend to help ease Sholi into the daily routine. Eli Safran, a caring, kind and gentle 18-year-old yeshivah boy, someone who would understand Sholi's needs, was assigned this task.

Finally the day arrived. After months of anticipation, Sholi arrived at the camp bus. His smile was infectious, and his face absolutely radiant. One was able to sense the *kedushah* inside this pure, special child. He loved to please others and looked for their affection in return.

The boys in the bunk noticed that Sholi was different and they acted in a caring, sensitive manner to him immediately, even as they were unpacking and setting up their bunkhouse. There were so many things that were unique about him. The head counselor, Moshe Kimmel, introduced himself to Sholi and assured him that he would help him in case he needed anything.

The next morning, after the first night in camp, Moshe opened the door to his own bungalow and was shocked to see Sholi standing there fully dressed. At first Moshe was concerned that something was wrong.

"Is everything okay?" he asked, worried that perhaps having this unique child in the camp wasn't such a good idea after all.

Sholi stood straight as an arrow, gave Moshe a big grin, and saluted! He announced to Moshe that he wanted to escort him to the office every morning for the wake-up announcements. He was going to be Moshe's personal bodyguard. Moshe couldn't help but smile. "We're best friends," said Sholi. "Right?" Sholi's brilliant smile and pure, innocent question would become his trademark. He had become a beloved figure in camp almost overnight.

Every day Sholi, the first one in the shul for davening, would point to his *siddur* and motion to his counselor just before *Shemoneh Esrei* as if to ask, "Am I supposed to say *Yaaleh VeYavo*?" Obviously, the answer every day was the same. There was no need to recite *Yaaleh VeYavo,* since it was not Rosh Chodesh or a Yom Tov. And Sholi would proceed to daven with great *kevannah.*

Finally it was Rosh Chodesh Av. Sholi's counselors and junior counselors knew what was going to happen. Today was the day. Sholi stood up to prepare for *Shemoneh Esrei* and all eyes were on him. As was his custom, he pointed to the page where *Yaaleh VeYavo* was found. He then motioned to his friend, Eli, asking if he should recite the special paragraph. Eli smiled and nodded in the affirmative. Suddenly, in victorious fashion, Sholi lifted his hands in the air. One would have thought he had just won a championship game. His excitement at being able to say *Yaaleh VeYavo* was as great an expression of joy as they had ever seen.

∽൭ᏚᎲ

The summer was one to remember. But it finally came to an end. Many hugged good-bye as the buses pulled up. The boys climbed onto the buses with heavy hearts. Moshe Kimmel waved good-bye to his campers. He was sad to see them go, but somewhat relieved that another incredible yet exhausting summer was now about to end. Suddenly the buses stopped and Sholi dashed out of the third bus. He ran directly into Moshe Kimmel's arms and hugged him tightly. Sholi was smiling as always but now tears were forming in his eyes. "I'm going to miss you, Rabbi Kimmel. We're best friends. Right?"

Moshe hugged him. He held onto him and reassured him that they would always be best friends. He told him how much he would miss him, but assured him that they would always keep in touch. He hugged Sholi one last time, at the same time lifting him up off the ground. Sholi in his innocence apologized, "I'm sorry, Rabbi. I can't lift you up. I can't lift you. You're too heavy."

Moshe held tightly onto Sholi as he cried, "It's all right, Sholi. You already have. You've lifted us all up ..."

For You and for Me

THE YOUNG COUPLE HAD GONE THROUGH ANOTHER round of procedures, but the hoped-for results did not materialize. Reuven and Leah Wolberg began to wonder if they would remain childless forever. This depressing thought prevented them from truly enjoying any *simchah*. They could not help but wonder if they would ever be able to celebrate their own son's *bris* or their own daughter's *kiddush*. Would they ever be privileged to walk their own child down to the *chupah*? At every event they attended, the conversation would be the same. People spoke about schools and homework assignments. They joked about how they felt as if they were going through school once again. One mother complained that she wasn't getting enough sleep at night because her baby was keeping her up. It's not that these individuals were cruel. They just didn't know any better. They simply had no idea that the woman sitting next to them would give away everything just to be able to have a baby who woke her up in the middle of the night. But with each unsuccessful sequence of procedures, the probability of having a child was becoming more unlikely. Could it be that they would never know the joy of holding a child of their own?

One day, a friend of Reuven's suggested that he go to a certain Rebbe for a *berachah*. Reuven wasn't the "Rebbe type." Raised in a *litvishe* home, he had never gone to ask for *berachos* from Rebbes. He had had many such opportunities, but just never felt comfortable doing so. But that day had been a particularly depressing one; he had received a bar-mitzvah invitation from one of his friends who had gotten married the same time as he had. Despite the feeling of despair generated by that invitation, he decided to give this Rebbe a chance.

Reuven waited in line along with many others. They had probably come for any number of reasons. This Rebbe was known for his understanding and warmth. And certainly there were no shortage of problems that people wished to discuss, but Reuven was more than a bit skeptical about unloading his troubles on a man he did not know. Nevertheless when his name was called by the *gabbai* Reuven quickly jumped up and made his way inside the room.

The Rebbe was looking down and his eyes were closed; he seemed to be davening or at least deep in thought. After a moment, he opened his eyes and greeted Reuven warmly. Reuven waited until the *gabbai* left the room and then began to tell the Rebbe of the terrible heartache he and his wife were experiencing. He described how they dreaded attending *simchos* for fear that someone might ask them which schools their children attended. Finally Reuven, who had been so skeptical at first, found himself crying and begging the Rebbe for a *berachah*.

The Rebbe looked into Reuven's eyes and waited for him to compose himself. He pulled the young man closer, held out his hand to him, and looked deeply into his eyes. Reuven felt as if the Rebbe could actually see his broken heart. Finally the Rebbe spoke.

"I know exactly how you feel. My son Tzvi Yosef and my daughter-in-law have been married for nearly fifteen years. They describe the way they feel precisely the way you do. They too anxiously hope, wait, and anticipate having a child of their very own. They have cried endlessly and have begged for my *berachah*. But I never had an answer for them … until now. I just thought of a wonderful idea. There is a tradition we have, *Kol hamispallel ba'ad chaveiro hu ne'eneh techilah* — One who prays on behalf of a friend, his prayer is answered first." The Rebbe then looked at Reuven and proposed, "What if you would daven on their behalf and they would daven for you?"

Reuven was numb. He had expected some miracle potion and mystical esoteric blessing. But this was different. It was so touchingly human. The Rebbe also had *tzaros,* but he knew that sometimes the prayer of a simple Jew who overcomes his or her own selfish needs and pleads on someone else's behalf is something that can break down any barrier … even when the gates of heaven are sealed shut.

> *Miraculously, within a year the Rebbe attended two simchos as Reuven and the Rebbe's son each celebrated the birth of a firstborn child!*

The Motza'ei Shabbos Minyan

ONE OF THE MANY FASCINATING ASPECTS OF YERU-shalayim is the preponderance of *minyanim. Minyanim* take place everywhere one turns — in big shuls, in small *batei midrash,* even in private apartments. More noticeable to the outsider than the physical surroundings, though, is the fervency of the davening itself — the kind of *kavannah* one rarely sees these days. But in the Yerushalayim of yesteryear, the davening was of a different genre. And one of the most memorable *minyanim* was the Motza'ei Shabbos *minyan* of Rav Zerach Braverman.

In the early 1900's Reb Zerach would make his way from his home to the *Kosel* after Shabbos to commence the new week with an unusually meaningful *minyan*. There were many other prominent members of the city of Yerushalayim who attended the *minyan* — simple shoemakers and unassuming blacksmiths who were fluent not only in the Talmud but in the mystical writings of the Kabbalistic works as well. Together they would gather, well after most had already concluded the Shabbos, for Reb Zerach's *minyan*.

Watching and listening to Reb Zerach daven was an unforgettable experience. And that is precisely why these people came, to be imbued with *kedushah* and piety, to experience *dveikus*. Among those who came to this weekly *minyan* was none other than a young Shlomo Zalman Auerbach. He too looked forward to beginning his week with Reb Zerach's davening. It was the one *minyan* he would not miss. That is ... until one disappointing Motza'ei Shabbos.

Reb Shlomo Zalman headed toward the *Kosel* as usual and waited as the rest of Reb Zerach's *minyan* gathered. But instead of Reb Zerach leading the Maariv service, another fellow came up in his place. The *mispallelim* were informed that Reb Zerach did not feel well and as such had decided to daven closer to home. To an outsider, there was no way to tell that he was missing. The fervor and intensity were present as always. But for Reb Shlomo Zalman it just wasn't the same. In fact, he never went to that *minyan* again. Curious as to why he stopped, one of his earliest followers questioned him. His answer spoke volumes.

"Every time Reb Zerach davened he would give a *krechtz* at certain points of the *tefillah*. For instance, in the words that directly precede the *Shema*, he would sigh, '*Oy, ve'ahavascha al tasir mimenu le'olamim* — may You not remove Your love from us forever.' That '*oy*' had so much feeling, so much emotion in it. When Reb Zerach was not present the man who took his place gave a *krechtz* too, but something was missing; it lacked Reb Zerach's depth of feeling. I had come to depend on Reb Zerach's *krechtz*, his *emesdi'ke* davening, to start my week. Without it, the *minyan* just wasn't the same."

This incident gives us a glimpse of Reb Shlomo Zalman's incredible sensitivity and his appreciation for the true feelings that need to be expressed during davening. For this he was not willing to compromise.

Anything for a Minyan

T HESE DAYS, IN MANY CITIES, FINDING A *MINYAN*, OR creating one when needed, is not very difficult. One need only make a few phone calls and the required quorum arrives; or one can find a shul with a *minyan* at a convenient time. But there are places where it isn't so easy. In some cities one has to arrange his entire schedule around the availability of a *minyan*. While the effort may be enormous, the reward is no doubt equally great.

There were many who gave their lives to daven with a *minyan*. They have done so in battlefields in the thick of war, in concentration camps while their brethren were being led to their slaughter, and in ghetto basements knowing that getting caught meant certain death.

In 1942, in a concealed room in a ghetto alleyway, a knock was heard on the door, a soft tapping but not the code that had been taught to the insiders. The congregants were worried, but when the door opened and little Zalman, 7 years old, stood there, they were relieved. The little boy's father, however, was angry that Zalman had risked both his life and the lives of their fellow Jews by identifying the doorway which hid the small *minyan*. As the father raised his hand to smack his son, little Zalman held up his own hands to protect himself and cried, "Tatty, haven't I been punished enough by the wicked Nazis. Must I be punished by you also?!" His father stopped short. *My own little son, in the midst of all of this horror, wants, as much as I do, to be part of a minyan for davening. Why am I getting angry at him?*

And so the scenario has played itself out in many cities and towns, in countries all over the world, for centuries. The desire to daven with a *minyan* is embedded in the psyche of a Torah Jew, and helps to shape and define who we are as a people.

One particular incident, which took place over 250 years ago, demands re-telling. It transpired in the city of Aram Soba, where the Sephardic *Mekubal,* Rav Mordechai Leviton, resided. He was already an elderly man, but had always been very careful to attend *minyan* three times daily. As he grew older and was no longer able to brave the elements to go to shul, he had asked the people of the town to join together at his home for a *minyan*, and they readily complied. But one day a terrible storm broke out. Explosive cracks of thunder rumbled through the air while streaks of lightning lit up the sky. The time for Minchah drew near and Rav Mordechai began to wonder whether the people would come together today for the *minyan.* At first only a few people showed up, among them his loyal and devoted student Eliyahu.

He asked his *talmid* to go and gather the rest of the *minyan.* A few moments later a sopping wet Eliyahu appeared with the unfortunate news that the people were just not willing to get drenched. Upon hearing this, Rav Mordechai bent down near his bed and reached underneath it. Eliyahu could not figure out what his rebbi was doing. Rav Mordechai stood up with a small bundle in his hands. He placed it on the table in front of Eliyahu and started to cry.

Eliyahu was startled to see that the package was filled with money. He looked around his rebbi's dilapidated apartment and wondered why he had not used this money to fix up the place and make it look a little bit nicer. "Eliyahu, I had been saving this money for a very important purpose. I planned on using it to pay someone to learn Mishnayos in my memory after I pass on to the next world." He now looked up at Eliyahu with tears in his eyes. "But instead I want you to use it now. Tell those who refused to come for the *minyan* that I will pay them for their efforts. Let them brave the elements and come here to daven."

Eliyahu looked at Rav Mordechai and realized just how important this *minyan* was. Moments later he returned with the last few individuals. Rav Mordechai offered the money but no one dared to touch it. It was just an honor to be there.

Loneliness and Liveliness

THE FIRST DAY OF A NEW SCHOOL YEAR IS CHALLENGing; teachers and rebbeim must prepare themselves for the unexpected. Among other concerns, there is the possibility that the children might try to "test" the new teacher. Many times the teacher's future will be determined by what happens on that first day.

Rabbi Shtuckman, on his first day of teaching in the Netivot elementary school, Yeshivat Shemesh U'maor, walked into his eighth-grade room and was greeted by a group of about twenty boys. They seemed to be a respectable bunch, and as he went up and down the rows he asked each child for his name. Rabbi Shtuckman quickly jotted down the names, forming a seating chart for the classroom. When he got to the last boy he heard the child utter a very strange name — "Yochanan HaSandlar Elbaz."

He waited for the chuckle but none came. Unsure as to whether this innocent-looking boy had an impudent side to him, Rabbi Shtuckman glanced around the room to see if any of the other children in the class were smirking, but surprisingly no one was. Apparently this was really the boy's name. Grateful that he had not questioned the boy about his name, he made it a point to stop at the principal's office immediately after school to find out more about the boy with the interesting name. When he did so, the principal smiled; apparently the question had been asked before. He proceeded to tell Rabbi Shtuckman the boy's story.

The year was 1992 and Yaron Elbaz had been working on a highway road just outside Beit Shemesh. Yaron had chosen this type of physical labor as his profession for a number of reasons. The pay was good, he liked working outside, and he enjoyed the physical challenges of the job. Besides, he had to support only himself and his wife; unfortunately, they still were childless after ten years of marriage and assumed that they would remain so.

Some of his traditionally minded friends had suggested that he go to pray at the holy sites in Israel, but Yaron was highly skeptical of prayer, and besides he just didn't have the time. One day Yaron noticed an unusual amount of traffic heading north. His friend Yoav explained that that day was Lag BaOmer, a day when thousands of Jews from all types of backgrounds head up to the burial place of the Rashbi — Rebbi Shimon bar Yochai — whose *yahrtzeit* is on that day.

Yoav stopped working for a moment, wiped his brow, and suggested to Yaron that he also make his way up to the *kever* of Rebbi Shimon. But Yaron balked at the idea. With all the traffic it would take him forever to get there, and anyway, who is to say that any of those prayers would have an effect. So back they went to working with the hot tar and repairing the cracks in the roads.

The next year, on the same date, the two co-workers happened to be working at a site within an hour's drive to the city of Meiron, where Rebbi Shimon was buried. Yoav, who had a few children of his own, felt that this time he would be able to convince his "non-believing" friend that it was worth his while to make the trip up the road to the hallowed burial site. And though Yaron hesitated at first, he could not help but wonder if he would ever be in the area again. And so, with much skepticism, and with a large dose of disbelief, he headed up the road to pray at the *kever* of Rebbi Shimon. As soon as he neared the city he was greeted by a traffic jam the likes of which he had never seen before. The cars were bumper to bumper as far as the eye could see. Now that he had time to think, the old doubts arose again, and Yaron decided to turn his car around and head back home.

But then he thought of his wife and their quiet life. He looked at the cars next to his filled with children, the families from all sorts of backgrounds — chassidic, Sephardic, some not religious at all. He wanted a child so badly. He thought again of his wife and the pain they bore together; he thought of the many children who lived on their block and decided that he would do his best to reach the *kever*.

Hours passed and the long line inched forward. One by one, car by car, the row of vehicles made its way up the hill. The crowd was so great that everyone had to park about a kilometer away and proceed by foot to the *kever*. As they trudged forward they were approached by a stranger who mentioned that there was a *kever* of another very great man in the area — the revered Tanna, Rav Yochanan HaSandlar. If they wanted to avoid the crowds, they should go there. Yaron looked at Yoav and although at first they didn't take to the idea (after all, their intention had been to pray at Rebbi Shimon's *kever* on his *yahrtzeit*), ultimately they decided that it was worth a try.

They made a small detour to the *kever* of the great Rav Yochanan HaSandlar and when they got there were shocked to discover that the entire area was completely empty. While throngs of people were just a short trip up the road, there was literally nobody here. Not a soul. Yaron approached the *kever* with awe and reverence and then started to pray. The words did not come easy to him. Of course, he had prayed a few times in his life, but at this time he was almost completely removed from religion. However, as his heart opened in prayer, he began to cry bitterly as he spoke: "Rebbi Yochanan HaSandlar! You know how I feel. When I come home every day I see tens of children filling the block with their joyous cries of laughter and delight. And then I walk into my apartment and it is silent. The silence is deafening. And the same is true with you, my dear rebbi. Down the road there are thousands who have come to pay tribute to the great Rashbi, and yet I have come to your *kever* and there is not a soul here. You know the feeling, the hurt and the pain. I beg you to please intercede on my behalf and beseech the Heavenly Throne that we be blessed with a child." Yaron finished his desperate plea and then, exhausted, walked away.

Incredibly, nine months later he and his wife were blessed with a son — a child he named Yochanan HaSandlar in honor of the Rav at whose grave he had prayed. But although he was grateful to this Tanna for his help, he had not made the next leap — to begin appreciating and keeping the laws of the Torah. His precious son Yochanan HaSandlar Elbaz grew up completely devoid of anything even remotely Jewish. He was a boy of 12 who had never heard of Moshe Rabbeinu or Avraham Avinu!

Every week Yochanan HaSandlar would go out with his friends who played in a local soccer league. Although he himself did not play, he liked to watch his friends. One of them had started to learn with a local man about the basic concepts of Judaism. The man would come to the soccer field to speak to the boy and slowly Yochanan HaSandlar began joining in the conversation. The idea of mitzvos started to appeal to him. The mitzvah of *tefillin,* especially, intrigued him, and with his bar mitzvah fast approaching, he asked the man if he would be able to start putting on *tefillin.* All this time he made sure to hide everything from his father, who was not only not religious but antireligious. But the more the boy learned, the thirstier he became for the truth of Torah. Before long he was completely enamored with the mitzvah of *tefillin* and greatly inspired by what he was learning from the man.

One day Yaron came to the soccer field, and when he asked the other boys where his son was, they seemed to be avoiding his question, as if they were keeping a secret. Without saying another word, he decided that he and his son had to have a talk about where he had been and what he had been doing.

Yaron walked through the door and asked his son how the soccer games were going. Did he have fun? When his son replied that he enjoyed his time there, Yaron exploded in a burst of rage, "Why do you lie to me? What are you doing there?" As he grabbed his son's arm he noticed the marks of the *tefillin* straps. His son had been wearing *tefillin* and now he was caught red-handed! Yochanan feared his father's rage. He looked into his father's eyes and waited for the inevitable punishment and beating which would no doubt soon be coming. The silence lasted a long time. And then Yaron walked outside, lifted up his hands to the heavens, and called out, "Yochanan HaSandlar, *nitzachtani* — you have defeated me!"

Rabbi Shtuckman listened to the story and wiped away his tears. He now knew that he had a special boy in his class. And a very special someone looking after him ... Rebbi Yochanan HaSandlar.

Ask for Anything

H E JUST COULD NOT SEEM TO GET IT. NO MATTER how much his rebbi drilled the Gemara into him, Meir Braunfeld was simply unable to grasp the concepts. But this was always the way it had been for the 10th-grade boy. He had struggled his entire life to understand what his teachers were saying. It was actually somewhat surprising that someone who had suffered from so much frustration his entire life would turn out to be such a sweet young man.

But Rabbi Lowenstein noticed that lately things had changed. Afraid to inquire about what had precipitated the change in Meir, the rebbi just pretended it was normal for Meir to ask the complex questions he was now asking daily. At first it was the oncoming question of the Gemara that he was predicting. And then it was a *Tosafos*. The next day Meir asked the same question that the *Ketzos HaChoshen* had raised. Something strange was happening. It was as if someone had kidnaped the old Meir and replaced him with an extremely bright individual. Finally, after a month of Meir's test scores averaging over 100 percent, Rabbi Lowenstein decided that he must find out what had happened to the boy who used to ask such absurd questions that he was known as the "dummy" of the class. The change seemed nearly miraculous!

Rabbi Lowenstein asked Meir, after one of his now typical phenomenal days of learning, if he could stay a few moments after class. The rebbi had something important to discuss with him. Meir waited until the rest of the boys had left and then approached his rebbi, wondering what he could possibly have wanted. Rabbi Lowenstein fumbled for the right words, afraid that he might insult Meir. But Meir figured out what his rebbi wanted to talk about and saved him any further discomfort.

"Rebbi," Meir began, speaking with confidence, nothing like the old Meir who used to stammer every time he opened his mouth. "Do you remember the talk you gave us right before Purim? You taught us that Purim is a unique day, one that is much underappreciated. You explained the special rule of '*Kol mi sheposheit yado nosnin lo* —Anyone who sticks out his hand, we give to him.' You went on to explain that this does not apply only to poor people who are collecting money; rather, it applies to every Jew, no matter what he is asking for. You begged us not to let the day of Purim go to waste. You implored us to dream big and to ask Hashem for anything we wanted. Well, I did that."

By now Meir was sobbing and perhaps he was embarrassed, but the rebbi, too, was crying as he listened in amazement. "I came to the *berachah* of *Atah Chonein* and I started to cry. When I got to the *berachah* of *Shema Koleinu,* I mentioned to Hashem the rule you had taught us about giving the poor what they ask for. And then I said, 'Hashem, I don't need money. But I am poor in other ways. I am poor in my ability to understand and to learn and I desperately want to learn. So I beg You. Please give me *daas* and *binah* — *give me knowledge and understanding.*'

"Rebbi, ever since that day everything has been clear." Meir wiped away the tears that were coursing down his cheeks. Perhaps he was crying over the pain of all those years of shame and suffering. Or perhaps it was for joy, for receiving the precious gift he wanted so badly.

The Last Prayer of the Warsaw Ghetto

*T*HIS POTPOURRI OF JEWS, A HODGEPODGE COLLECTION from as many countries as one could imagine, rummaged through the rubble and destruction of what used to be the Warsaw Ghetto. The Germans had made it a point to bring together individuals who would not be able to easily communicate with one another, thus minimizing the risk of planning an escape. They had been gathered together to clean up what once was the most glorious pulsating Jewish city in all of Europe. And now nothing remained. Warsaw was finally *Judenrein*.

Perhaps, if they had any tears left, they might have cried. The Warsaw Ghetto was completely decimated, demolished to the point where it was no longer recognizable — a pile of shattered glass, wood, cement, and rubble. But most of all — blood. The blood of thousands of slaughtered Jews stained the ground and now this group of men, mere skeletal bodies, were ordered to clean up the debris.

Nothing had made sense since the world had gone mad. Did others know? Did they care? These and other questions had occurred to these prisoners when their names were called and they were loaded onto a bus. Where to? They did not know. But usually when numbers were called, the people bearing these numbers were never heard from again. And on the way here that thought was constantly with them. Would they ever see their fellow inmates again? Their families? Their neighbors and friends? Who knew …?

As they rummaged through the wreckage, one of the older men announced that today was Yom Kippur, the holiest day of the year. And although they were not in their hometown shuls davening in a *kittel* and *tallis,* perhaps they should form a *minyan.* And slowly, the idea took hold, and their lifeless eyes lit up. A spark of hope was kindled inside of them. Yes! That would be the perfect revenge — to commemorate the memories of the loved ones with a davening that would shake the very heavens. And so, in a small courtyard on Genesha Street, a few dozen skeletal survivors gathered together and began to daven. The *chazzan,* Yosef, who had davened for the *amud* for many years in his hometown, ascended to the *amud,* but somehow the words seemed to elude his memory. Try as he might, he was simply unable to recall the prayers which had always come so easily to him.

Yosef, a Salonikan Jew, struggled mightily to recall the meaningful words of Shacharis, Mussaf ... anything! But nothing came to his mind. Not one of the many beautiful, significant, "our lives are hanging in the balance" *tefillos* could be recalled.

As the group waited for Yosef to begin, time was running out. The "free" moments they were stealing away from their work were quickly passing. Finally the flustered Salonikan *chazzan,* surrounded by an exhausted group of prisoners who were completely alone in this world, stood atop the rubble of Genesha Street and uttered a *tefillah* that came from the deepest recesses of his soul. "*Ribbono Shel Olam* ... after everything we have endured through the torture of Auschwitz, trembling we stand before You now ...

"*Hineni he'ani mimaas ... nirash venifchad ...*

"On top of a pile of rubble in a destroyed street of the Warsaw Ghetto ... We desperately turn to You and beg — *Shomer Yisrael* ... Guardian of Israel ... Watch over this last remnant of the Jewish people ... *Ve'al yovad Yisrael* ... Please don't allow this last remnant of Your nation to be destroyed ...

"Because we stand here and proudly declare — *Hashem Hu HaElokim!*"

Safe and Secure

E KNEW IT WOULD NOT BE LONG IN COMING. Immediately after September 11, 2001 Paul Blitz prepared to be dispatched to fight the war against terror. As the next few weeks passed, the announcement came that the United States of America would be going to war against Afghanistan and its Taliban government. President Bush addressed the nation, and families of soldiers braced themselves for the unknown. Anxious and eager young men and women traveled thousands of miles to defend and protect their country from the wicked regimes of Afghanistan and, then, Iraq. Osama Bin Laden and Saddam Hussein had changed the world forever, and now American forces were being sent in to restore order in these countries, to free them from their tormentors, and to eliminate the threat of terror.

Paul Blitz, a staff sergeant in the American Armed Forces, has served his country for nearly twenty years. Well respected and admired by those who know him, he spends his free time, when not on active duty, teaching in Baltimore's Yeshivas Chofetz Chaim, also known to many as Talmudical Academy, or TA. His students enjoy the way he conducts and disciplines the classes, instilling in them his own brand of forthrightness and self-control. They know that the "correct response" is always a "Yes, sir" or a "No, sir." Although non-Jewish, he respects and admires the rabbis and their way of life. Once a year he takes his classes on a field trip to a local army base, where he dresses in his full army uniform. For the boys, as well as for Paul Blitz, it is an enjoyable as well as a meaningful excursion. But when he left to fight the war in Iraq, a feeling of uncertainty permeated the school. The students and faculty wished him well and promised that they would pray for his safety and well-being.

The heat had reached 110 degrees Fahrenheit in the sandy deserts of Iraq. Stationed in the middle of nowhere, Sergeant Blitz was taking a short break in one of the officers' tents. While there, he was approached by two young men, no older than 18 or 19, who seemed eager to talk. He responded to their salute with "At ease, gentlemen," and asked them how he could be of help. The two young men looked at their sergeant and expressed a sentiment that probably most feel but few are willing to admit. "Staff Sergeant Blitz, we're scared."

He looked into the young soldiers' eyes and saw the fright. He could not help but think to himself that these young men are only slightly older than the boys he taught back home. And they were carrying the weight of the world on their shoulders. He searched to find the right words to alleviate their fear and concern. He placed a reassuring hand on the shoulder of one of the soldiers and shared with him a comforting thought. "Private, overseas in Baltimore, we have 800 Jewish children praying for our well-being and safety. Soldier, I guarantee you that G-d is looking after us." The young soldier thanked his commanding officer, reassured that everything would turn out all right.

And on May 5, 2005 Sergeant Blitz returned to Talmudical Academy and was welcomed back by the students and faculty. He stood before them in his army uniform and thanked them. "Gentlemen, 208 men were in our unit, 38 of them directly under my care. And 208 men have returned safe and sound. Thank you."

To Hear With Your Heart

One of the greatest challenges facing a congregation is the temptation to speak in the middle of chazaras hashatz, the chazzan's repetition of Shemoneh Esrei. It is unfortunately viewed by some as somewhat of a "spectator sport," and not given the proper recognition and respect. Often the rabbi of the shul or the gabbai must stop the recitation of the Shemoneh Esrei to restore order and decorum, and then will allow the davening to continue, thus causing unnecessary interruptions in the middle of the davening. But a fresh perspective on what transpires during this auspicious time might allow us to better appreciate what this portion of our prayers is really all about.

I T WAS WELL KNOWN THAT WHEN THE HOLY REBBE OF Rizhin would conduct his Friday-night *tisch,* he would not speak words of Torah. In fact, he almost did not speak at all. And yet, hundreds would flock to bask in the presence of the Rebbe. Although they could not imagine what others saw in this type of gathering, two young cynics set out to see for themselves what everyone was talking about.

They made the journey to Rizhin and prepared themselves for the Rebbe's *tisch* that Friday night. But, unfortunately, when they finally arrived, the *tisch* had already concluded. The only one who remained was a gentile man who apparently had the job of cleaning up after the *tisch* was over. They walked over to the man and inquired as to the nature of the gathering. "What is it exactly that goes on here?" They smiled cynically as if to question the authenticity of the entire assembly.

The simple, well-meaning, non-Jewish janitor stared at the two young men and answered their snide remark with his honest evaluation of the events that had just transpired. "The holy Rabbi sits in the front of these two long rows of tables. He sits there and doesn't say a word. And all of his followers — they sit here and listen to what he doesn't say."

The young men were taken aback by the response. The non-Jew's articulate description, laced with tremendous respect and admiration, took them by surprise. That simple answer touched them, and suddenly they wanted to be at the *tisch* more than ever

— but as participants, not as spectators. They now understood that sometimes it is what a person does *not* say that can penetrate deeply into another's soul. It is the unspoken word that is most powerful. They nodded their heads as if to show their agreement with the man's assessment and walked out of the room convinced that there was indeed something quite special which they had missed out on.

When the *chazzan* repeats the *Shemoneh Esrei*, we, the congregation, are asked to sit quietly. That silence is the congregation's opportunity to "hear," to contemplate the words of the davening, the words of praise. To talk during that time is to miss what davening is all about. One who speaks during this quiet song of praise is disrupting the beautiful melody of silence that is *chazaras hashatz*.

Don't Forget Us

In this story two fascinating concepts merge. One regards the Hadran which is said when one makes a siyum on a masechta. In the Hadran we recite: "Al tisnashi minach," and then, "lo sisnashi minan." The words express the hope that we will not forget what we have learned, and, in turn, that the Torah we have learned will not forget us. The other concept concerns a practice common in some European communities of decades ago, but practically forgotten these days. It is called "Shlog ois di Aron Kodesh." Someone close to an individual in need would enter the town shul when it was empty, walk up to the Aron Kodesh, open it up and cry, beg, plead for a yeshuah — for a sick person's recovery from illness, for shidduchim, for parnassah. In the following story these two concepts come together.

*T*HE TWO CHAVRUSOS HAD LEARNED TOGETHER FOR many years, and had finished nearly one-third of *Shas*. The relationship between Reb Ahron and Reb Nochum, although rooted in Torah, ran much, much deeper. They anticipated each other's questions and worked through each other's logical explanations. And with each Torah thought their bond strengthened.

Because of their intense study sessions, the two middle-aged friends never went home for lunch, instead using every precious moment to learn a little more. Every day one of the younger *bachurim* in the yeshivah would bring these two veterans their lunch, happy to have the privilege of doing so.

One day, Reb Nochum mentioned that of late he had not been feeling well. Reb Ahron responded that over the past two or three weeks he had noticed a certain fatigue in his friend, a lacking of his customary "fire," and encouraged him to take some tests, just to make sure it was nothing serious. But the tests revealed something serious indeed. It was cancer.

The prognosis was not good and Reb Nochum battled the fatigue, nausea, and exhaustion in order to continue his intense schedule. But he was losing the battle. And he knew it. On occasion he would call his *chavrusa* and, in a choked-up voice, apologize for missing learning. Reb Ahron had to control his emotions as he reassured his dearest friend that everything would be fine. But he began to fear otherwise.

Their daily lunches continued to be brought by a dedicated messenger. He would place them on a table in the back of the *beis midrash* and then leave. But one day he was shocked to discover that the gate to the entrance of the *beis midrash* was locked. Undaunted, he climbed the fence, but then he could not open the door to the *beis midrash* itself. He looked around for an open window, very curious as to why the door that was always open was now locked. When he peeked inside he saw an awesome, unforgettable sight. Reb Ahron was doing something which this *bachur* had heard of, something which he knew was a common practice in Europe in previous generations, but which he had never seen with his own eyes. Reb Ahron was pleading before an open *Aron Kodesh,* crying and speaking as if to the Torah itself!

As he listened, the student heard Reb Ahron's words — words reminiscent of the famous *Hadran* which is recited as we complete each *masechta*. In the *Hadran* we "speak" to the *masechta,* promising not to forget it, and asking it never to forget us.

As the young messenger stealthily watched what was happening, he was deeply touched. Reb Ahron spoke in a passionate tone. *"Bava Metzia* — don't you remember Reb Nochum learning through your most difficult *sugyos*? *Bava Kamma* — Reb Nochum *chazered* you over and over. *Yevamos* — Reb Nochum needs your help. PLEASE!!" Reb Ahron cried bitterly, begging, demanding intervention. And then, finally, after his impassioned plea Reb Ahron stood in front of the *Aron* and cried, his shoulders heaving.

The young man watched in awe; it was a scene he would never forget.

A few months later, incredibly, Reb Nochum had a *refuah sheleimah.*

The Cup Runneth Over

LEVI KADINSON WAS WHAT ONE MIGHT CALL AN "AVERage" fellow. He had a good job as an accountant, lived in a nice neighborhood in Monsey, New York, and had an average-size family. But there was one thing about Levi that was not average at all. And that was his davening. While he did not appear to be such an unusually spiritual person, when it came to his davening there was certainly something quite unique about him. He would pray with incredible emotion, swaying back and forth while davening *Shemoneh Esrei, shuckling* with tremendous intensity. Most people in the shul took it for granted. They knew that when it came to davening Levi was quite literally in another world. But once a guest at the synagogue, Avraham Wolf, witnessed Levi's davening and was anxious to find out more about him. When no one was able to give a satisfactory explanation as to why Levi davened with such intensity, Avraham decided to ask Levi himself.

He waited until after Levi had finished davening Maariv. The other congregants had left and it was just the two of them in the building. Avraham approached Levi and said that he couldn't help but notice Levi's davening, and wanted to know what had inspired him to daven with such passion and feeling.

Levi smiled shyly and looked around to see if anyone else was in the shul. "I'll tell you what it is, but it has nothing to do with me. It all comes from my mother. When I was a little boy, no more than 6 or 7 years old, I lived in a house where everything was always spotless. My mother kept an immaculate home. Not a thing was ever out of place. When we came into our home we would take off our shoes; and we never brought food out of the kitchen. But then one day my mother called me into the dining room and told me she needed me for a minute. I walked in and noticed that there was a large pitcher on the table. It was filled to the brim. Any little movement would cause it to spill all over. I looked at my mother and wondered what it was that she wanted. She then instructed me to push the table.

"I looked at her as I wondered what type of trick she was playing on me. She couldn't have possibly wanted me to spill the water over the table and the floor. She had always been so careful and immaculate. But when I hesitated she prodded me to push the table. Finally I pushed it ever so slightly, and when I looked, nothing had spilled.

" 'Give it a shove, come on.' My mother was now speaking in a more forceful tone, and not wanting to upset her, I gave the table a shove. The water began spilling over. 'Harder!' my mother urged, and then I gave one final shove. The water flooded the table, carpet, and chairs. Realizing what I had done, I turned to my mother and started to cry. She smiled and cried as well. 'My dear Levi,' she said, 'Hashem is like this pitcher — He is filled with *rachamim,* to the brim! And He is waiting for us to give a good *shukle*, a sign of our desire to cling to Him; and with that one good shake, Hashem's *rachamim*, His mercy, will pour forth!' "

Avraham thought for a moment, smiled, and walked away sheepishly. He was so happy that he had happened upon this extraordinary individual who had a powerful story to tell — a story with an eternal message.

Chesed / Kindness

A Beautiful Present

THE LAST-MINUTE PACKING WAS HECTIC AS USUAL. Baruch Fried, a fifth-grade rebbi in the Torah School of Greater Washington, was preparing to go to his wife's parents for the second days of Pesach. His wife Aviva was from Paramus, New Jersey, and the ride up there would take between three and four hours, depending on traffic. After loading the last few items into the car, they drove away.

Typically, Sunday is not a great day for traveling. But today traffic would be even heavier than usual because it was Easter Sunday, one of the busiest travel days of the year. Surprisingly, however, the trip was uneventful and they reached Paramus a few hours before Yom Tov. It was then that Aviva suddenly realized that she had forgotten a very important item — her children's medicine.

The two Fried boys suffer from a rare protein deficiency that has caused them to have numerous medical issues and many abnormalities in their development. With only about eighty such cases in the United States, the Frieds knew it would be practically impossible to find the special medicine they needed for their children. Having them skip their medicine was not an option. And so, the Frieds frantically began making calls to find a pharmacy that might possibly have the medication. But all their efforts were falling short. As time moved on they began facing the grim prospect of having to drive back home to retrieve the vital medication.

Finally, after many phone calls and getting some useful information, they decided to call their friend in New Square, Shmuel Zalmanowitz, a kind *chassidishe Yid,* who they knew would have the medication. Shmuel immediately offered to share his extra medication with them and they were delighted. But, unfortunately, they now realized that it was too late to drive to New Square and then back to Paramus. Shmuel assessed the situation and immediately suggested that they meet at a place somewhere between the two locations. Hopefully, each would have enough time to make it home in time for Yom Tov. Hard as it was for the Frieds to inconvenience this kind man and perhaps prevent him from getting home in time for Yom Tov, they knew they had no choice. So they set out to meet him.

When they reached the meeting place — the Pathmark in Monsey — it was less than an hour before Yom Tov. They were pleasantly surprised to see that Shmuel was standing outside his car waiting for them! On the hood of his station wagon was a lot of delicious Pesach chocolate, and a new copy of "Spirit" magazine; and not only did he bring the medication, but he also brought all the supplies (syringes, gauze pads, and alcohol swabs) even though Baruch had told him that he had these items. It was all wrapped up beautifully with a stuffed animal on the side. This was too much to believe! Baruch and his friend Shmuel greeted each other warmly, and Baruch thanked Shmuel profusely for his selflessness and kindness. Baruch then went back to his car and administered the proper dosage to his two boys.

Realizing that he had less than 45 minutes left to Yom Tov, Baruch was about to begin the ride to his in-laws' home when one of Shmuel's boys ran up to the door of his car. In his hands was a yellow toy school bus.

"What's this for?" Baruch asked, completely bewildered.

"It's for your children. I want them to have it." The young boy, dressed in his Yom Tov finest, had the appearance of a little angel.

Although Baruch was very moved by the child's gesture, he felt that he could not accept the present and insisted that the boy keep it for himself. But Shmuel wouldn't hear of it and after much persuasion Baruch finally agreed to keep the present. He had a hunch, though, that the toy had belonged to one of Shmuel's children, and that he had convinced his child to give the toy away to Baruch's children. By now it was really getting dangerously close to sunset and Baruch could no longer argue the point.

As he was about to pull away he noticed the other little boy in Shmuel's car crying. Baruch now realized he was right. *They must have taken the toy away from this child,* he thought. Baruch felt terrible and decided that he would not allow himself or his children to be the cause of another child's unhappiness. He was most certainly not going to keep the toy. His children probably would not even appreciate it.

Very quickly, he walked to Shmuel's car. "Please take it back. I see that your little boy is crying." Shmuel smiled at Baruch and began to explain. "My 4-year-old is not crying because someone took away his present. It's just the opposite. He's crying because he also wants to give your children a present!" Overwhelmed by this display of consideration and generosity, Baruch shook his head, smiled in disbelief, and wiped a tear from his eyes.

"By the way," Shmuel called out, "I just want you to know that these are their very own *afikoman* presents. They just received them and they wanted your children to have them. They knew it would make them a little bit happier."

> Baruch and his wife had been through much hardship and pain. They knew that the road to raising their children would have many roadblocks. But their job was made just a little bit easier by a father and two young children with very big hearts.

The Great Linen Robbery

NO ONE COULD FIGURE IT OUT. WHO WOULD dare think of stealing from the Rebbe of Rudnick, Rabbi Yekusiel Yehudah Halberstam? After all, he was such a gracious, kind, and caring person. Nevertheless, that evening, at around 7 o'clock, the rebbetzin had come running into her husband's study. The unthinkable had happened. Someone had broken into their home and stolen their entire set of linens. The pillows, blankets, and sheets had been taken directly off their beds! Who would dare break into the Rebbe's home and steal his belongings? Didn't these people have shame? And what was most surprising was that the Rebbe's attendants had not noticed anything unusual. The Rebbe reassured his rebbetzin that everything Hashem did was for the best. He suggested that they forget about it. He was afraid that word would spread throughout the town, and the townspeople would overreact. But the mystery of the missing linen remained unsolved. No one seemed to have any answers ...

Earlier that day, a woman had tapped lightly on the door. She knew that the Rebbe was not receiving visitors but she felt that she had no choice. The door opened and the Rebbe greeted the woman as if he had been expecting her. "Rebbe," she cried out. "Mazel Tov. My daughter's a *kallah!*" The Rebbe's initial reaction of joy and blessing was tempered somewhat by the fact that the girl's mother was crying. It seemed so strange. Since her tears did not appear to be tears of joy, the Rebbe asked her why she was crying at a moment of such joy.

At first the woman kept her composure. She explained that although she was quite grateful that her daughter had finally become a *kallah,* she was ashamed that she had nothing to give to her. Normally, a *chasan* was given not only a *nadan,* a wedding dowry, but also dishes, pots, and many more items to help the young couple set up a household. But she was a widow. Not only couldn't she provide the standard *nadan,* but she could not come up with the money for any of the other basic necessities either. She could not afford to buy dishes. She could not supply them with tablecloths. She couldn't decorate their apartment with even the most basic furnishings. The embarrassment and humiliation she felt not only for herself, but more importantly for her daughter, was now too much to bear. And so, she turned to the kindest person she knew — the Rebbe of Rudnick.

The Rebbe listened to her words and understood her plight. Even though she tried to regain her composure, the love she felt for her daughter and her desire to provide for her was so strong that the woman was literally inconsolable. After much thought, the Rebbe decided on a plan of action and told her to come back at 6 o'clock that evening, but to use the side entrance of the house.

Shmuel Greenbaum, one of the Rebbe's close attendants before the Second World War, was walking down the street on his way to the local *shtiebel* when he noticed something strange. Someone, although he had no idea who, had parked a wagon directly outside the side door of the Rebbe's house. And even stranger, it seemed like linen was being stolen from the Rebbe's house. Shmuel quickly ran up to the door to stop the thief, but when he grabbed the man he was shocked to find that it was the Rebbe himself!

"Rebbe, I'm so sorry. I thought …" The Rebbe turned toward Shmuel and spoke to him in a firm manner. "I ask you to please keep what you are seeing now to yourself." Shmuel asked the Rebbe what was happening and whether he could help out. The Rebbe led Shmuel into his room and asked him to help strip the linen from his bed and fold it up so it could be put into the wagon. The Rebbi revealed that it was for a *Yiddishe meidel,* a *kallah.* Shmuel was instructed never to divulge the secret of the missing linens, as long as the Rebbe was alive.

Indeed, until the day the Rebbe left this world, no one ever solved the mystery of the "Great Linen Robbery."

Mikey and Eli

NESTLED AWAY IN THE SCENIC SUBURBS OF Marriotsville, Maryland is a jewel of an institution — the Weinberg Academy. It caters to the needs of young men who have, for whatever reason, not fit in the "normal" school system. These boys come from all over America, as well as other countries, to search for and find what no one else has been able to provide for them — the key to unlock their *neshamos* and their potential.

These young boys often endure mighty struggles; there are many impediments on their paths to finding themselves, to finding their niche in life and their talent. Often, on this road, an individual must take risks, must bare his soul, and open himself to the possibility of defeat and disappointment. It is the hope of these young men — and the dream of their parents and teachers — that they will be able to remove the obstacles which stand in their way so that they can find a path of their very own where they too can taste the beauty of a Torah life and the splendor of Judaism.

Many of these boys have failed before, often more than once. They have been rejected by their peers, classmates, and sometimes quite tragically and perhaps inadvertently by the ones who have loved them most. Some are focused on their failure and constantly live with it; others are trapped by their insecurities, suffocating from their paranoia. It is a tragedy that way too often the majority of those who are fortunate not to have such a child refuse to acknowledge the suffering and plight of these children and their families.

This is a story about two of those young men, two of the most opposite and different personalities that have ever come together in a classroom. One of the boys, Eli, a twelfth grader, was challenged in many different ways. He was not able to function, to do normal activities, like other young men. But it was something special to watch him daven; when he did so, he talked to Hashem as he would talk to his true father. He enunciated each and every word; it was hard to imagine a young man with more *yiras Shamayim*.

Many of those in the school were blessed with an above-average-intelligence level. Some had nothing short of genius I.Q.'s. But Eli was not one of them. He had many learning disabilities. But his desire to learn and to grow, especially in his Torah learning, was humbling even for those who were accomplished Torah scholars. He loved Hashem and he loved His Torah. It was that simple. Minor hurdles like not being able to read well or understand the material being presented in class, while frustrating to many, did not prevent Eli from reaching for the stars.

The others in the twelfth grade were a colorful bunch. Some sat with their headphones on and listened to the music of their choice. Most of them listened to music containing lyrics that were filled with venomous, spiteful, and virulent words. In a sense they related to the music because they saw their lives reflected in the depression and sadness of those empty songs.

Some of the students occupied themselves by playing meaningless games on the computers at their desks, using it as a means to pass the endless hours. Moshe, one of the more miserable of the bunch, passed his time by losing himself in the world of sleep, hoping that when he woke up he might be someone else. But when he would pick his head up he had that same glum, unhappy, "I wish I didn't have to be here" look on his face.

Then there was Mikey. Clearly one of the leaders of his class and the school, Mikey prided himself on his ability to keep a rigorous workout schedule. One hundred push-ups followed by 500 sit-ups, forty curls with 40-pound weights in each hand allowed him to beam with pride as he finished his twice-a-day workouts. But none of that self-discipline and hard work went into his schoolwork. Mikey didn't like to learn and he did not like being religious, or for that matter, doing anything religious. He hated davening and despised all Torah subjects. So he would just sit in the back of the room and fool around while any serious learning was going on.

Rabbi Baruch Rothenfeld came to the Weinberg Academy in the afternoons to try to instill a desire for learning Torah in the students. During the last period of the day he taught them *Maseches Taanis,* with the goal being to complete the *masechta* in its entirety and then celebrate with a large *siyum.* On and off, the boys would pay attention. Some would focus on the learning and others would slip away, with never more than half of them around the table ready and prepared to learn. Only one boy was a constant. Eli.

No matter what was going on around him, he had the desire to sit right next to his rebbi and to concentrate or at least try to concentrate on the subject matter being taught. And as Rabbi Rothenfeld moved through the *masechta,* page by page, Eli was always sitting at his side. Every exclamation of *"Zugt di Gemara"* was followed by Eli's childish repetition of his rebbi's cry, *"Zugt di Gemara."*

One day, the boys came in from their final recess of the day and Rabbi Rothenfeld tried to calm them down and get the class settled. As always, the characters assumed their customary positions and places. And as he encouraged them to open their Gemaras, Eli took his usual seat — right next to his rebbi.

They boys opened their Gemaras and Rabbi Rothenfeld prepared to speak when suddenly he was jolted by a question. "Rebbi, do you think I'm retarded?" The question came from Eli, whose droopy eyes belied his enthusiasm for learning.

Everyone stopped what they were doing and looked at Eli. A thick silence filled the normally bubbly room and the students all looked toward their rebbi. No one moved and no one dared to make a sound. "Why would you think that you're retarded?" Rabbi Rothenfeld, who always seemed to know what to say, was completely dumbfounded, utterly speechless. *What could he possibly say to this innocent young man?*

"Just last night my father told me, 'You know, Eli, ever since you were a little boy the doctor always told us that nothing is ever going to be easy for you …' " The words seemed to just hang there in the air. No one spoke. Because nobody had anything to say.

Finally, the unlikeliest of characters spoke up. "You know what, Eli? Last night my parents told me, 'Mikey, school's not for everyone.' I looked at them and said, 'Are you calling me retarded?!' They of course denied it, but I promise I'm going to prove them wrong. I'm going to make something out of myself!" For the first time the athlete who didn't really care about anything was speaking with passion and fervor. As Mikey spoke, Eli nodded vigorously. And then Mikey directed his comments to Eli, "Eli, don't ever let anyone tell you that you can't do something. It's not about what people think. It's about what's inside of a person ... And Eli, you have a special *neshamah* ..."

Rabbi Rothenfeld could not speak. Neither could anyone else. He had not even known if Mikey knew what the word *neshamah* meant, and now he had just spoken from his heart and from his own *neshamah*. Eli smiled. He seemed to be pleased with the answer. A moment later the classroom slowly returned to its original, zany state. But for one moment in time the insanity had stopped. It had stopped long enough for the vulnerable boys in the Weinberg Academy to perceive the radiance and warmth of a *Yiddishe neshamah*. And now they were that much closer to finding the road to fulfillment.

Chicken Little

ALTHOUGH RAV ISSER ZALMAN MELTZER LIVED A long life, he had never been "a picture of health" and brimming with energy. When he had been in his 20's he had contracted a debilitating disease that left him quite weak for the remainder of his life. Nevertheless, quite amazingly he was able not only to lead the Etz Chaim Yeshivah in Yerushalayim for most of the first half of the 20th century, but he led it with tremendous energy and strength.

As he grew older however, it became increasingly more difficult for him to make the relatively short walk from his home to the yeshivah. Many of his students tried to persuade him to come less often, perhaps giving *shiur* fewer times a week. But Reb Isser Zalman would not hear of it. He loved the yeshivah, loved his *talmidim,* and loved teaching Torah. And he was unwilling to compromise on any of the three. The end result was that he continued to maintain his taxing schedule even when his physical condition made it extremely difficult to do so.

There were various groups of *talmidim* who were privileged to walk him home daily after *shiur.* They made certain to take the shortest route from the yeshivah to his home. However, at certain times of the day Reb Isser Zalman insisted on taking a longer route. Regardless of how much the *talmidim* pressured him to give the reason for this, he refused to provide an explanation — dismissing their inquiries by saying that he simply wanted the exercise. But it just did not make sense. This was a man for whom every second of the day was accountable. Not a moment was wasted. And besides, when he walked he was certainly uncomfortable and most probably in pain every step of the way. Why was he taking the longer route at times? Finally, after his students persisted, he revealed his reason.

"I noticed that at a certain time every day there is a little chicken, one which is easily frightened, that feeds on some bread on that street." He then looked up at his *talmidim* and sighed, "How can I disturb the *menuchah* of that little chicken?"

6,000,001

*F*OUR YEARS AGO, MRS. VICKY BERGLASS CHAPERONED a group of nearly forty senior students from Ramaz High School in New York to Eastern Europe, to learn about Jewish life there before and during the Holocaust.

They visited cities filled with rich legacies, cities that had once pulsated with Jewish life and were now nearly devoid of anything that resembled the past. They had visited Warsaw and were near Lublin when Mrs. Berglass received a phone call from the Rav of Cracow telling her that someone named Shimon Kluger had passed away and asking for a favor.

Shimon was a tragic figure. After the war had ended many years ago, Shimon, emotionally scarred by all he had seen and endured, entered into a mental state where he refused to believe that the war was over. His extreme paranoia completely over-took him, and he holed himself up in a dank, dark apartment, convinced that if he would come out, he would be caught and sent away. He simply would not believe those who told him that the war was over. His Polish neighbors took pity on him, brought him food, and took care of his basic needs. And now he had passed away.

The Rabbi of Cracow wanted to know if Mrs. Berglass and her students would be able to help bury Shimon. In Cracow itself there was no *minyan* of Jews and he felt it would be a spe-cial honor to this man — who had suffered for so long — to be given a proper *Yiddishe* burial. Although they were now near a place named Sandomierz, a village near Lublin, hours away from Cracow, Mrs. Berglass immediately agreed to the request, but on one condition. She wanted Shimon Kluger to be given a proper *taharah,* the ritual bath which purifies the body of the deceased. When the Rabbi informed her that he had never done a *taharah,* she assured him that since she was actively involved in the *Chevrah Kaddisha,* the Jewish Burial Society, she could teach him what to do. And although there were no *tachrichim* (burial shrouds), she instructed him as to how he should per-form the *taharah.*

With Shabbos fast approaching, she prepared her students for the job they were about to perform. But they never could have pre-pared themselves for the sight by which they were greeted.

Standing at the entrance of the old cemetery in Auschwitz were six impeccably dressed men — wearing gray tailcoats with top hats and gloves — carrying what was obviously a very expensive coffin. When she inquired as to what was happening, Mrs. Berglass was told that these respectable non-Jewish people had prepared an elaborate funeral for the man they had come to know. Maybe it was pity, maybe it was guilt, but they had spared no expense to bury Shimon in the manner he deserved.

After expressing her appreciation to these men she informed them that she and her students would now take over the rest of the burial service. The twelfth graders took the places of the well-dressed pallbearers and the ceremony proceeded. They walked until they reached the site, and the procession followed. But to their surprise, no actual grave had been prepared. When Mrs. Berglass inquired, they informed her that a crane would normally do the hard labor of digging the grave. It was then that she looked at her students. The hour was late. But Shimon deserved it. She and the students decided that they would dig the grave themselves. However, there was only one small shovel — certainly not adequate to prepare an opening deep enough for the coffin. And so, slowly, one by one, the students bent down on the ground and began to dig with their hands. They dug with purpose, frantically, perhaps even hearing the *kol demei achicha tzo'akim eilai* — the voices of those whose blood drenched the ground. Or perhaps they sensed the presence of the millions who never had a chance to have their bodies buried, instead being offered as *korbanos olah,* whole, pure, innocent sacrifices, through the chimneys of Auschwitz and Maidanek. Or perhaps they were just doing everything they could for a man whose soul was lost sixty years before and for the first time in so many years no longer had any reason to fear. They finished digging Shimon's grave. And then gently lowered him in.

As their tears blinded their vision, they covered his *aron.* The appropriate *tefillos* were recited and a heartrending *Keil Malei* was delivered.

Shluf gezunt, Shimon ... Sleep well, Shimon.

Hashem yinkom damo ...

The Never-ending Nightmare

WHEN MIKE TRESS RETURNED FROM VISITING THE Displaced Persons (DP) camps after the war, he wanted to share his experiences with the Jews in America. He felt that in order to raise the funds needed to help the survivors of the Holocaust get on with their lives, he had to make the donors aware of what these people had lived through.

Mike, one of the most charismatic leaders of American Jewry, was a leader of the Agudas Yisrael movement, and eventually became the prototype for laymen who knew how to listen to the *gedolim* and then lead with their guidance. A successful businessman, he sacrificed everything for his greatest love — the Jewish people. As a multitalented orator with tireless energy, he was the perfect choice to lead the effort to help the *she'eiris hapleitah* rebuild their shattered lives. But to do this he needed to experience firsthand what he had only heard about. His encounters changed his life forever.

And on the evening of February 10, 1946, at the Hotel Pennsylvania in New York, Mike delivered the speech of a lifetime.

Dressed in his United Nations Relief and Rehabilitation uniform, he spoke with passion about the time he had spent in the DP camps. He described the conditions in Zilesheim, Feldafing, and Fernwald as well as the dire circumstances in St. Otillien, Garmish, and others. But there were two particular incidents that broke his heart as well as the hearts of his audience.

He described how he spent a particular night on a hard floor with nothing more than a straw-filled sack to cushion his body.

After an exhausting day he had managed to finally fall asleep when he was startled by a man who had woken up and lit a candle. Mike was curious as to what the man was doing. And his curiosity grew as the man walked around with his candle, apparently searching for something. Suddenly he cried out in a trembling, haunting voice, *"Zei zenen nisht dah! Gevalt, ich hub zei alein farbrent!* They're not here! I burned them myself!" Horrified at what he had just witnessed and unable to fall back asleep, Mike waited until dawn, when the first rays of the sun broke through and some of the other men began to rise. When they did, he asked the first one he could about the haunting scene he had witnessed the previous night.

The man nodded as if to express that what Mike had witnessed was not a one-time occurrence. It was an event that happened quite often. A few years earlier the wife and six children of the man with the candle had been sent to the gas chambers. And as tragic as that in itself was, it was not so unusual or different from what so many others had gone through. But what was different and apparently the cause of this heartrending practice was the fact that this man was a member of the Sonderkommando, the group of individuals who had been selected for the horrific task of placing the dead bodies into the crematoriums. And he was there when the bodies of his cherished family had arrived for cremation …

"Zei zenen nisht dah! Gevalt, ich hub zei alein farbrent! They're not here! I burned them myself!"

The second episode had also transpired in one of the DP camps, but in a different camp on a different night.

The scenario began pretty much the same. Again it had come after a long, exhausting day of work. And again Mike had nothing more than a straw-filled sack to sleep on. He slept among the *she'eiris hapleitah,* his brethren who had survived. Shortly after he had fallen into a fitful sleep, he was jolted awake by a distressing cry, "Mama! Mama!"

Mike jumped up and quickly searched the dark room. Scanning the skeletal bodies he spotted a young boy, no older than 8, who was screaming for his mother. The scene was as emotionally charged as one could possibly imagine. Mike ran over to the terrified child and held him closely as the incessant cries of "Mama … Mama … " filled the still nighttime air. As he held onto the little orphaned boy ever so tightly, he hugged him and kissed him and made him a promise that he would never forget, "I'm sorry. I don't know where your Mama is and I don't know where your Tatty is. But one thing I can promise you. You will never be alone again."

When Mike Tress finished his unforgettable speech there was dead silence in the hall. The audience was shocked. It would` take them a while to regain their composure. And when they finally did, they erupted in applause. But by then Mike Tress was already gone.

After all, there were so many lives that needed to be saved.

One of Our Very Own

SHMUEL'S FAMILY FELT LIKE THEY WERE TALKING TO A brick wall. No matter what they said, nothing changed. The year was 1896 and Shmuel Hensfeld, who had come from a traditional Vizhnitzer chassidic home, had left the ways of his family. For a child to leave the fold was considered an unusually tragic event. And since it was so unusual, Shmuel's family had no "road map" to help them find a way to reach him.

His friends, teachers, and relatives tried to speak to him. But nothing was working; he was completely disenchanted with the traditions of his past. Shmuel struggled with his own demons, and felt helpless in their grasp. It was as if something other than himself was forcing him to rebel. This rebellion relegated him to the fringes of his peer group, and he felt totally isolated. He was in so much pain. It hurt so badly and he wanted just to tell everyone that he needed warmth and caring and love. But he couldn't. And his anger and resentment grew.

Wherever he walked he was looked at with disdain, contempt, and derision. The problem fed upon itself; the more resentment he felt from his community, the angrier and lonelier he became. Slowly but surely Shmuel became the outcast of Vizhnitz.

And then one day he received a message from the Rebbe of Vizhnitz. When word spread throughout the town that the Rebbe had asked to see Shmuel, most wondered what Shmuel would dare to say to him. And few if any gave the Rebbe any chance of succeeding to transform this lost soul.

Shmuel walked into the Rebbe's room with a cynical attitude and plenty of emotional baggage. The door closed and a few hours later Shmuel emerged with red eyes, a broken heart, and a shy but noticeable smile. Not long after that, Shmuel worked his way back ever so slowly — into his family, his community, and of course his faith.

Shmuel would not disclose what the Rebbe had said to him. All that was known was that from that moment on Shmuel became extremely close to the Rebbe, turning to him for advice, encouragement, and guidance on every matter. But those close to the Rebbe asked him what he had said to change Shmuel's attitude. His answer is both timeless and eternal.

"When one takes a piece of wood and places it into a river, no matter how many times that wood is washed over, it remains a piece of wood. And this is because the wood is a foreign object. The river maintains its identity and so does the wood — with neither willing to compromise in any way. However, if one were to take a big block of ice and place it into a river, it might take a while but eventually that block of ice will blend into the river and ultimately become part of it. And this is because the river and the ice are really the same element. The components are perhaps different, as one has become hard and indifferent due to the cold and frigid atmosphere. But as the block enters the river and water washes over the hard chunk of ice, it loses its rough edges, becomes smoother and smaller, and ultimately returns to its original state."

The Vizhnitzer smiled at his disciples and they understood the message he had given the rebellious boy. While the rest of the community had shunned Shmuel and made him feel unwanted, the Rebbe had convinced him that he was still part of the flowing river. Yes, perhaps hardened because of the cold environment, but scared, anxious, and desperate to be loved and to be accepted once again.

With the tragic amount of children at risk, we know what our job is. We must be able to look past the hardened edges and to love them unconditionally. They are all part of the big beautiful river we call Klal Yisrael.

Gracefully Saved

Many cities have them. They are dedicated, selfless volunteers who spend much of the week working to make the Shabbosos of others better in some way. They cook all sorts of delicious food to give to those who cannot afford or are unable to make their own Shabbos; fish, chicken, salads, wine, challos, and many other extras are prepared. There is one principle to which all involved are totally committed — maintaining at all costs the privacy and dignity of the recipients, so that these individuals can retain their self-respect and pride.

ALL THE PACKAGES ARE PREPARED AND DISTRIBUTED with an incredible amount of sensitivity and understanding. The organizers and volunteers try to maintain a low profile to ensure that those receiving the packages have no idea who brought them. These programs — the "Tomchei Shabbos" or "Matan BeSeiser" or "Ahavas Yisrael" organizations — are often the crowning glory of the cities in which they operate. The following story depicts what these groups and their volunteers are all about.

Eliezer Gruchkind, a successful businessman, had his hands full. Not only did he run a successful, full-time diamond business, but he also ran the local Tomchei Shabbos near his home — which also turned out to be a full-time affair. Balancing the two was quite a grueling task but Eliezer managed to do so with professionalism and integrity. He made sure to attend every meeting of the organization and to be present when the food packages were distributed. Most of the people in need were from families he did not know. On the rare occasion when he found out that someone he knew was coming to pick up his package of food, he made it a point to keep out of sight and allow the individual his privacy.

Once, as Eliezer was entering the shul to help prepare the packages, he noticed out of the corner of his eye that his next-door neighbor was coming to pick up a package. Eliezer was shocked. His neighbor was a successful businessman who couldn't possibly have been in need of handouts — or was he?

Eliezer's immediate need was to somehow prevent his neighbor from seeing him; he wanted to spare the man any embarrassment. And he had only seconds to figure out how to get out of the way.

Eliezer was fumbling with his keys and realized that he was not going to have enough time to hide himself before his neighbor would see him. The regulars at Tomchei Shabbos knew Eliezer's schedule, and knew not to arrive when he was coming to prepare the food, to insure their privacy. But this man was a first-timer, and didn't know the ground rules yet.

Suddenly Eliezer had an idea; he began to bang loudly on the door, demanding that someone inside open up. As people began to arrive to pick up their packages, they noticed him … and so did his neighbor, who quickly walked around the building to avoid running into him. As soon as Eliezer saw his neighbor walk away, he pretended to mutter and rant to himself, acting like someone who had come to pick up his own package.

Anything to save a fellow Jew from embarrassment.

Family Is Family

IT HAPPENED DURING ONE OF THE MANY SKIRMISHES IN the city of Yerushalayim prior to 1948, and shooting erupted in many places. The furious gunfire ignited the streets and alleyways, and merely walking into one of the volatile zones meant risking one's life. Yet, inexplicably, Rav Isser Zalman Meltzer was seen trudging hastily through the streets toward the home of one of his brothers-in-law.

Well advanced in age and quite weak, Rav Isser Zalman was obviously having difficulty walking. Finally, one of his disciples inquired as to what could possibly have been so important that he was risking his life for it.

At first Rav Isser Zalman avoided the question, instead encouraging the fellow himself to find a safe place for the time being. After both men found somewhere to wait out the worst of the battle, the aging Rosh Yeshivah spoke with incredible sensitivity and compassion.

"I have just sent a volume of *Even HaAzel* to the printer for publishing. But as I was leafing through the manuscript one last time, I realized that I had inserted a thought from all of my brothers-in-law except for one. I tried to imagine what he would feel like if he was the only one not included in the *sefer*. Perhaps he would feel slighted. So I quickly went to his home to ask him for his insight on a perplexing passage of the *Rambam*. This way I would be able to immediately include what he told me to explain the problematic *Rambam*."

Even amidst the perils of war, there was only one thing that mattered to Rav Isser Zalman — the feelings of a fellow Jew, including his brother-in-law.

A Morning Stroll

ARRIVING ON AN EARLY MORNING TRAIN, CHAIM Lichter was completely exhausted from his three-day business trip to Belgium. It had been something of a whirlwind visit, but he had met with much success, buying a good supply of diamonds — enough for a month's worth of sales. As he walked up to his two-story home in Lucerne, Switzerland, he stopped suddenly as he noticed Rav Moshe Soloveitchik walking with his wife. It was 4 o'clock in the morning! He wondered why the Rav and Rebbetzin were walking around at such an unreasonable hour.

The next morning Chaim woke up for the 7 o'clock *minyan* as always. Although he was utterly exhausted, davening with a *minyan* was a priority in his life. Quite curious about what he had seen just hours before, after Shacharis Chaim went into the *beis midrash* where Rav Moshe always davened and greeted his rebbi warmly, telling him that he had just returned from a business trip out of the country. He halted a moment, then hesitatingly asked Rav Moshe if everything was all right. The rebbi didn't seem to understand the import of the question, so Chaim explained he had seen the Rav and his wife walking in the street at 4 a.m.

Rav Moshe then related that a young father had called him at around 3 a.m., having been in the city so that his child could undergo a serious heart operation. Tragically, the operation was unsuccessful and his 2-year-old daughter had just passed away. The heartbroken stranger had called to ask the Rav about various laws of *aveilus*. He had been here only for the operation and did not know whom else to call. Rav Moshe continued, "I answered his questions and told him how sorry I was about the tragedy, but then I hung up without even getting his name. I had no idea who he was and I knew that he must need a shoulder to cry on. With no further information to go on and without having any idea which hospital he was in, my rebbetzin and I decided that we would go from one hospital to the next searching for this broken young father."

Rav Moshe looked up, his eyes filled with tears. "What a shame that I was careless and did not ask him for his name. I wasted so much time just looking for the grief-stricken father. Who can imagine his loneliness and pain."

> At the end of Rav Moshe's life, when he was extremely weak, he could not daven himself, but allowed someone else to say the words and he would try to repeat them. However, when he reached the blessing of Refa'einu, he somehow found the strength to pronounce the names of the ill individuals for whom he prayed daily — 73 names! Even while his own body had failed him, his neshamah would not — and could not — stop thinking of others.

An Orphan's Guardian

HE WALKED INTO THE SHUL, SHY AND UNASSUMING, looking around, clearly uncomfortable in his surroundings. The young man, Binyamin Hollander, was a 13-year-old boy who lived in the Meah Shearim neighborhood in

Yerushalayim. After a prolonged illness his father had just passed away. Binyamin, the oldest of the seven children, had taken most of the responsibilities upon himself during his father's illness, and now he had even more on his frail shoulders.

During the week of *shivah,* Binyamin had not had the opportunity to reflect much on the tragedy that had struck his family. He had loved his father so much, but in the past few months had had precious little opportunity to speak with him, to ask him for help and advice. Now Binyamin felt that he was the head of the family, and was more frightened and insecure than ever. He had grown up way too fast. Whenever he had problems in the past, the first person he would go to was his father … and now he felt very alone.

For the first time since *shivah* had ended, he was going to need to daven for the *amud.* The thought of walking into shul and having unfamiliar people look at him as a *"rachmanus* case" was one thing he dreaded. He had come to shul with plenty of time to spare so he would be able to secure the right to lead the congregation in the davening.

As the regulars were filing in Binyamin started to worry. He was concerned about having to be the one who was going to daven aloud in front of everybody. He was anxious about people who would surely whisper about him. But most of all he was simply afraid that someone else was going to grab the *amud* away from him. What would he say when some other adult who had also lost a parent would just assume that he was going to lead the congregation? And now it was just a few minutes until the davening was about to begin and Binyamin felt that he wanted to cry. But he steeled himself, promising himself that he wouldn't cry in front of these men, as he didn't want to appear weak and immature. As the men were preparing to daven, no one took much notice of the young boy hanging around the *amud* — except for one kind man.

Reb Moshe Shimon Diskind had noticed the boy as soon as he walked into shul. Although he did not know the boy, he was aware that a man had passed away in the neighborhood, and therefore had made it a point to come by. Suddenly he grabbed a *tallis* and stood by the *amud.* No one would dare challenge Reb Moshe Shimon for the *amud.* Although there were some others in shul who were also *chiyuvim* — obligated to say *Kaddish* for a deceased relative — they figured that Reb Moshe Shimon must have *yahrtzeit*. Binyamin noticed that Reb Moshe Shimon had grabbed the *tallis* and he too was saddened that he would not be able to daven for the *amud* the very first time he needed to. And then, just as davening was about to begin, Reb Moshe Shimon called Binyamin over and handed him the *tallis*.

Binyamin was shocked. But Reb Moshe Shimon continued this practice for the next week, ensuring that Binyamin always had the *amud*. Slowly, the relationship continued to build between these two — an orphan who needed guidance and a caring, elderly man. Amazingly Reb Moshe Shimon spent the next year securing the *amud* for this boy. He had made it his mission to look after this *yasom* and continued to do so for many years. When Binyamin married and had children, Reb Moshe Shimon was their *zeidy*. Binyamin had found his guardian and was forever thankful that a man had reached out when he needed it most.

When Binyamin grew older, one day in shul he spotted a lonely looking boy hanging around the *amud*. Binyamin smiled and shed a tear as he walked toward the *amud*, grabbed the *tallis*, and handed it to the young man. "Thank you," the boy responded. "Do I know you from somewhere?"

"Well, I used to know a young man just like you."

Diaries and Diets

Recently, the eating disorders that are so prevalent in society at large have crept into our own culture. Bulimia, anorexia, and numerous other disorders affect many of

our youth, often resulting in a tragic situation and bring-
ing in their wake suffering to the individual involved and
to his or her entire family. While there is no specific treat-
ment or cure for these disorders, the reassurance, confi-
dence, love, and support that one gives to the victims and
their families is absolutely priceless. This is a story about
one of those families.

*L*EAH AND HER PARENTS ARRIVED IN ISRAEL FROM America and headed immediately to the home of Rav Leizer Shach. They had already tried everything. The experts had given their professional advice and some of Leah's friends in whom she had confided had given their encouragement and love, but so far nothing had worked. She just would not eat. Her diagnosis was anorexia, although the medical term was really unimportant to her. For her entire life her parents had showered her with nothing but love; they were positive, upbeat, and always complimentary, but somewhere along the way she had become very concerned about her appearance and felt she was not thin enough. And that is when it had started.

Now, three years later, she was pencil-thin and clinging to life. While many of her friends were now married, she was in no condition to even go out. As a last-gasp effort Leah's parents had begged her to go see Rav Shach. She walked into the Rosh Yeshivah's room and sat demurely in the chair which he had offered her. She avoided eye contact and tried her best not to contribute to the conversation unless absolutely necessary. But the Rav spoke to her, and he promised her that if she would eat in a healthier manner she would find a wonderful *shidduch* and be blessed with beautiful children. As the conversation progressed, she seemed to open up to what the Rosh Yeshivah was telling her. Her gray, lifeless eyes glimmered for the first time in months and she began to relate her feelings to Rav Shach. She could hardly believe that one of the most important people on the planet was finding the time to speak to her. He motioned for a plate of food to be brought to the table and he placed a small portion in front of her. He smiled at her and encouraged her to eat while they spoke. Slowly she nibbled from the plate, at first taking small bites and then bigger ones. Bite by bite he encouraged her, raising her spirits. As she ate she noticed the smile on the Rosh Yeshivah's face growing wider. She became completely oblivious to the presence of her parents in the background. To Leah, it appeared as if there were only two people in the world — the Rosh Yeshivah and herself. And she could not believe that he was giving so much of his precious time to her — a young woman in need.

When she finished her portion and prepared to leave this Torah giant's presence, her parents wondered how this momentous meeting would end. As Leah was about to leave, Rav Shach asked her for a favor. "Could you please keep a diary of what you eat every day and send it to me? I'm worried about you."

The thought that Rav Shach had taken such an interest in her — an ongoing interest — was music to her ears. Slowly Leah's eating habits improved. Every day she would record her food intake and every week she would send her diary to Rav Shach. The weeks and months went by and her eating improved daily. It was not an easy road — but after much effort, Leah won the battle. She had done it! A year later she began to go out with a young man who eventually became her *chasan*. They got married and were blessed with a beautiful family.

When we think of the thousands of people who turned to Rav Shach with the pressing problems of our generation, it is amazing that he took so much time to deal with this one young woman. But for Rav Shach this wasn't just an anonymous young woman, it was a *Yiddishe tuchter,* and every Jewish girl was his daughter. And because of that caring concern, this young woman won the greatest battle of her life.

A Worthy Friend

*Many of Rav Tzvi Hersh Meisels' heroic deeds through-
out the war saved and gave hope to thousands, both
young and old. The Veitzener, as he was known, recounts
some of these episodes in his sefer "Mekadshei Hashem."
Among them is a heartrending story of an encounter that
he had with a young man. This narrative causes us to
look at our relationships with others as well as ourselves.
Who are we? Are we willing to sacrifice for others? In an
agonizing situation, one young man rose above all others;
his mesiras nefesh will live on forever.*

I T WAS EREV ROSH HASHANAH AND 1,400 YOUTHS IN
Auschwitz, many of them young children, were herded up
like cattle, gathered together to await their final destiny. While
the younger ones were perhaps too naive to understand what was
about to happen, the older ones knew it, all too well.

When the distressing news began to spread throughout the
camp, an unimaginable sadness prevailed. These unfortunate Jews
had seen and experienced every imaginable death, but this time
seemed worse than ever because there was such a large number
of children in the group to be killed ... it was too painful to bear!
Overcome with helplessness, 15-year-old Akiva Mann came running over to Rav Meisels. "Rebbe, vus vet zein mit Moishele? What's
going to be with Moishele?" As Akiva spoke, torrential tears poured
down his sunken cheeks. "We can't just let him die!"

The Veitzener knew that Akiva was referring to Moshe Rosenberg,
a 20-year-old boy who appeared to be much younger. He was
beloved by all the students in the yeshivah they had once attended,
and was respected as a brilliant *talmid chacham*. The Rebbe thought
of the words of *Tachanun* which have haunted us throughout the

ages: *Nechshavnu katzon ... latevach yuval ...laharog ule'abed ... lemakah ule'cherpah."*

He tried his best to calm Akiva but the boy was inconsolable. And then, through his sobs, Akiva came forth with a proposal that might well have shaken the Heavenly Throne. "Rebbe, I have a large sum of money which I can use to bribe the guards to allow me to change places with Moshe."

The Veitzener stared in disbelief. Here was an angelic 15-year-old who wished to give his life to save another boy — a young *talmid chacham*. It pained Akiva that he was going to live when others were dying. *What had he done to continue living?* But the Veitzener could not allow his emotions to influence his ruling. It was clearly forbidden for Akiva to sacrifice himself for the young man he so respected. When Akiva heard the Rebbe's decision his head dropped in disappointment, and he continued to cry as he slowly walked away.

But then a moment later a clearly distraught Akiva reappeared in front of the Rebbe. "I'm sorry, Rebbe, I just cannot accept your ruling regarding Moshe and myself." At this point Akiva was frantic. "Why should someone as insignificant as myself live when a future Torah giant like Moshe dies in the gas chambers?! He will add so much to this world! I'm sorry, Rebbe, but I am going to go and switch places right now. Just tell me that it will not be considered as if I have committed suicide. Please, Rebbe — Please — "

Rav Meisels held onto the broken young man and commended him for his heroism but explained that what he was trying to do was clearly forbidden. And as Akiva sobbed on his Rebbe's shoulder, the Veitzener looked toward the heavens and wondered how much greater a sacrifice could a human being be willing to make ...

And as the sun set and night settled in on that fateful Rosh Hashanah, Moshe Rosenberg, along with 1,400 other *korbanos,* ascended to Heaven through the chimneys of Auschwitz.

An Unexpected Guest?

REUVEN KARLSBURG LOOKED AT THE AIRPORT MONItor and threw his arms up in despair. There was no way he was going to make the flight back to Eretz Yisrael in time for Shabbos. He had had a feeling when he left America on this stopover flight through France that he would not make it back in time. And now the unexpected delay proved him right. So instead of spending Shabbos with his family he would be spending his Shabbos in Strasbourg.

But the problem was that he did not know anybody in Strasbourg. So he simply waited until a few hours before Shabbos and then asked to be driven to one of the synagogues. Although Reuven had been here once before and was vaguely familiar with his surroundings, he was not comfortable enough to ask someone to stay and eat in their home for Shabbos. But Reuven underestimated the community, and especially one individual, Meir Talisky. Meir was one of the movers and shakers of the small community, and he was the one who usually hosted needy people who showed up in the synagogue. Immediately after the *Kabbalas Shabbos* prayers and Maariv, Reuven waited around, hoping that someone, anyone would invite him for a meal. His wish came true.

Meir gave Reuven a warm "Shalom Aleichem" and escorted his guest home. They walked into the tastefully decorated house, which was a short walk from the shul. When everyone was given a seat at the table, Reuven was surprised to see that a place setting had already been set for him. Obviously one of Meir's children had run ahead to inform his mother that a guest would be coming and she had set the table accordingly.

The meal was delicious, entertaining, and highly uplifting. Meir sang with his children and shared some inspiring Torah thoughts with his family and his special guest. After the meal Meir and Reuven sat down to talk, and Meir was surprised to learn that he had eaten at the home of Reuven's parents in Eretz Yisrael when he was a young man learning in yeshivah. Small world, isn't it? Their conversation lasted well into the night, and after the meal Reuven was shown to his room. The rest of Shabbos was uneventful and after Havdalah Reuven expressed his thanks and admiration and the two parted ways.

Two years later similar circumstances brought Reuven to Strasbourg, but this time he knew to which address to go. He walked into Meir's home on Friday night and the two embraced as if they were long-lost friends. As Reuven looked around the table, he noticed that there was already an extra place setting for him. Puzzled, he looked up and asked Meir whom he had been expecting. Meir smiled but shied away from answering. After the meal Reuven made it a point to ask Meir's oldest son for an explanation. He proudly agreed.

"Reuven, it is not often that we are privileged to have guests in our area for Shabbos, but we desperately want to have them. So Friday night we always set an extra place setting and before we go to shul my father davens in the corner and pleads with Hashem to please send us a guest." He then looked up at Reuven, "And every once in a while we are lucky enough to have one."

Just a Friend

MRS. SHANI ROSENTHAL LOOKED AT HER clock. It was 6:30 a.m. and her children would be waking up soon. Her husband had left almost an hour ago to attend the morning Daf Yomi *shiur.* She checked the children's bedrooms and saw that they were sleeping peacefully. She then gave one last check in her son Yaakov's room. Yaakov, a 12-year-old boy, had been born with Down syndrome. He was a pleasant young man and attended a special school for children with this sort of disability. Normally, he would wake up earlier than the rest of the children, but he had learned to go downstairs and play quietly while the rest of the family slept.

Perhaps that is why Mrs. Rosenthal wasn't the least bit alarmed when his bed was empty. No doubt he had once again woken up early. She descended the stairs and quietly called out his name. "Yaakov — are you all right?"

Moving from room to room, she checked all the places where he normally played and became increasingly worried, as he was not in any of them. Living in a large house, she figured that Yaakov probably couldn't hear her calling him. After checking the basement Shani started to get nervous. He wasn't in the room where the Legos and building blocks were kept, and he was not playing on the computer, an activity he had recently started to enjoy. Finally she decided she would check one more place before alarming her husband. She walked toward the front of the house and turned on the light in the living room — and nearly fainted. Yaakov was sitting in a chair listening intently as a strange old man was telling him a story. She looked closer and was shocked to see that the man was none other than Reb Aaron Soloveitchik, the Rosh Yeshivah of a yeshivah in the area. She cleared her throat and Reb Aaron turned around, apologizing profusely. But it was she who felt the need to apologize. "I'm sorry. Why is the Rosh Yeshivah here at this hour of the morning?"

Reb Aaron excused himself and explained, "I was on my way to Shacharis and I noticed Yaakov roaming outside about three blocks from here. I asked him if he was lost and he told me he was ... but he knew his name and address. I decided to bring him home but since it was so early in the morning I figured that instead of alarming anyone it would be smarter just to tell him a story quietly while everyone else was sleeping." Reb Aaron finished his explanation and Mrs. Rosenthal, though slightly embarrassed, thanked the Rosh Yeshivah profusely for his help.

As he got up to leave he politely refused her offer of a cup of coffee. He was on his way to Shacharis. She walked him to the door and Reb Aaron turned once more to say good-bye to Yaakov. Yaakov waved and as Reb Aaron walked out the door, he turned to his mother, hugged her and whispered, "Mommy — he — my — friend."

Torn and Tattered

In Petach Tikvah there lived a man named David Baran. An elderly Jew, he now enjoyed much Yiddishe nachas from his children and many grandchildren. But he had not always thought it would be this way. If you were to have asked him, when he was a young man, if he was going to be living a Torah life he most probably would have laughed. At that time, Torah and mitzvos were the farthest thing from his mind. But one Yom Kippur everything changed.

*I*N THE TOWN OF LOMZA HUNDREDS OF OUTSIDERS CAME to participate in the meaningful and heartfelt Yom Kippur davening for which the yeshivah was famous. At the time, David, who was a young man, was uninterested and uninvolved in religious life. One Erev Yom Kippur David happened to be walking down the street and encountered hundreds of people hurrying toward the yeshivah. They were already wearing their Yom Kippur shoes as it was nearly time for *Kol Nidrei* and they were going to the yeshivah early to prepare themselves by reciting the special private prayer, *Tefillah Zakah*.

This was the last place David wanted to be. He had serious questions and doubts about religion and G-d and had made up his mind to stay far away from the yeshivah that Yom Kippur. But something inexplicable, inside of him, pulled him in that direction. He felt an intense internal struggle.

As he stood a short distance away from the yeshivah he noticed a very bizarre sight. Walking in and out of some small public bathrooms was an angelic-looking figure. Dressed in his white *kittel* the man was walking into each of the outdoor bathrooms for a few moments and then emerging. Puzzled, David approached the man and was shocked to see that it was Rav Eliyahu Dushnitzer, the *mashgiach* of the yeshivah. "I'm sorry to be so nosy, but why are you walking in and out of the bathrooms?"

Rav Eliyahu looked at the young man and explained quite simply, "For the next twenty-six hours there will be an overflow of people here for the Yom Kippur davening. I want to make sure that the facilities are adequate and that there will be enough paper." And with that he slipped into the next stall to continue with his pre-Yom Kippur ritual.

David was deeply affected by this simple act of a great man. He smiled to himself, feeling that he had received an answer to the questions that had been tormenting him. Instead of walking away from the yeshivah, he walked toward it. Fifty years later David marvels, "What had Rav Eliyahu done? Checked on the condition of the bathrooms? And yet he had done much more. He had pierced my heart and helped me find my way back home."

One Little Letter

It is most gratifying to receive phone calls regarding stories in the book. Often people call to compliment, sometimes to lend constructive criticism, and sometimes they

*call to share an incident of which they were reminded
when they read a particular story. Many stories in the
"Touched by a Story" series are filled with emotion, but
when Meir Talker called me about one of them (Gold
Watches and Golden Years — Volume 2) and told me that
it brought him to tears, I was surprised. While this story
is certainly moving, it is not one that would evoke such
strong emotion. It is a story about Rav Moshe Lefkovitz
who was called up to the Torah in the presence of his
rebbi, Rav Ruderman. When the gabbai called Rav Moshe
up to the Torah as "Reb Moshe," Rav Ruderman immediately protested, insisting that he be referred to as "Harav"
Moshe. When Moshe explained that the title didn't matter
to him, his rebbi told him, "If you are identified as Rav,
then you will act like a Rav!"*

*Now while the story is certainly beautiful it is hard to
understand why it would bring someone to tears. But
Meir explained why the story had moved him so.*

*I*T WAS A WEEK AFTER MEIR TALKER HAD LOST HIS FATHER
and he, along with the rest of his family, was still reeling from
the blow. They had loved their father dearly and sorely missed
his paternal presence. *Shivah* was difficult and when it was over
Meir felt somewhat uncomfortable going back into shul. When
Shabbos arrived Meir knew that he was supposed to receive an *aliyah.* And so, when the *gabbai* of the Beis Yitzchak shul approached
him, he clearly stated his full name, Meir ben Harav Shlomo. The
gabbai nodded but when he called out Meir's name, he omitted the
title "Harav," instead referring to Meir's father as "Reb" Shlomo.
This omission troubled Meir and he approached the *bimah* and
corrected the *gabbai* on his "innocent" mistake. But when it was
time to state his name again for the *mi shebeirach,* the *gabbai* once
more omitted his father's title. Meir was shocked. What was the big
deal? Why had the *gabbai* not referred to Meir's father by the title

he had earned? He recalled his father proudly sharing with him the fact that he had received *semichah* — and had become "Harav" — when he was merely 21 years old. And now, when the pain of his father's death was still so fresh in his heart, Meir felt as if someone had poured salt on an open wound.

Meir walked around the *bimah* back to his seat but could not let go of his pain. And so, after davening he approached the *gabbai* and asked him why he had not given his father the proper title. The *gabbai* shrugged off Meir's query by dismissing it as shul policy. "In our shul, only the Rav is called Harav."

Shul Policy?! Meir had never heard anything of the sort. The ache in his heart grew and although he wanted to just forget the whole matter he couldn't, so he approached the Rav to find out why the shul had such a policy. The Rav, a warm and caring individual, listened to Meir's question and was shocked. "We have no such policy in our shul." Meir was astounded. The coldhearted, insensitive *gabbai* could have prevented all this if he had just added the letter *hei* to "Reb" and turned it into "Harav." He could have saved a fresh mourner so much pain and heartache. But he didn't. And he wouldn't.

It is now four years later. And as Meir shared his emotional story with me he passionately added, "Couldn't he have seen the unshaven stubble on my face? He knew I was an *aveil*, and he was aware that my father's title meant so much to me, but he didn't care. I want you to know that I still feel the pain of the disrespect he displayed to my father." And so he told me that when he read the story of Rav Ruderman demanding that Moshe Lefkovitz proudly carry the title of "Harav," it once again reminded him of the painful memory of that Shabbos morning.

Unnecessary pain caused by a *gabbai* who refused to utter one little letter.

Yiddishe Kepelach

WITH MANY ORPHANS EXPECTED TO ARRIVE, THE Ponovezher Rav was desperate to gather pillows and blankets to accommodate their needs in his orphanage, known as "Batei Avos." This was not only a matter of *tzedakah,* providing for the needy; this was also a matter of ensuring that these children remained true to their heritage. They were a particularly unique group of orphans, the *"Yaldei Tehran."* Their story was complex. The bulk of these *yesomim,* stemming from Torah-observant homes in Poland and Soviet Russia, had been plucked from war-torn Europe and sent to Teheran. From there they had been brought to Palestine and placed in the Atlit absorption camp, on the outskirts of Haifa, which was run by secular Israelis. The managers of the facility did everything within their power to rid these children of their heritage. They resorted to mental and even physical abuse. Now, after much pressure by religious groups, some of these children were being brought to the Batei Avos orphanage, in the hope that their *neshamos* could be saved.

It was Friday and the children were expected on Sunday, so the Rav knew that he had to act quickly; he called for an emergency *asifah*, a gathering of the "who's who" of Bnei Brak on Shabbos afternoon to speak on what he called *"Inyanei DeYoma."* The crowd gathered from all over the city, and included laymen as well as *talmidei chachamim.* Men, women, and even children came out in droves to hear what the Rav had to say. Before long the largest shul in Bnei Brak was packed to the rafters, and the Rav slowly made his way to the front of the room.

He looked around at the anxious crowd and began, "The Gemara tells us that if one has a servant he must treat him with the utmost dignity and respect. It's as if 'he has acquired a master for himself.' In fact, *Chazal* tell us that if the person owns only one pillow, he is required to hand it over to his servant. But how, may I ask, does this coincide with the rule of *'chayecha kodmin'* — that one's own life takes precedence over someone else's? The answer is that *Chazal* knew that a Jew cannot possibly sleep when he knows that his servant is not being provided for. Hence the law is that you must hand over your pillow for precisely that reason — because *chayecha kodmin*, and the only way you will be able to sleep is if you give it to him."

And then, with tears streaming down his face, the Rav burst out in a heartfelt plea, "*Rabbosai*, we have a large group of *yesomim* — with *Yiddishe kepelach* — who will be coming to our city tomorrow and we don't have pillows and blankets for them. I beg you please, for your own sake, *chayecha kodmin*. How will you sleep knowing that these children don't have something on which to rest their heads in comfort?"

In seconds the crowd began to stir. Immediately after *Havdalah* they went home and within an hour the Rav had a line of hundreds of men, women, and even children, standing in front of his home with pillows and blankets. And much like Moshe Rabbeinu when funds were being collected for the Mishkan, the Rav had to plead with them to please stop bringing — the orphanage was overflowing! Those present will never forget the sight of one woman standing at the Rav's door begging him to at least take one more pillow. And who could blame her?

All she wanted was a good night's rest.

Rebbeim and Talmidim / Teachers and Students

All for the Sake of One Child

THE TWO BROTHERS BURST THROUGH THE FRONT door and tossed their knapsacks onto the floor. "Guess what, Mommy. Tatty is going to be speaking at the *Haschalas Mishnayos* assembly!" Moishe and Yehoshua Leib Levine were ecstatic and could hardly control their excitement. They knew they were supposed to have a special guest speaker on the day they received their Mishnayos, and when the principal Rabbi Kurtzman made the announcement they were overjoyed.

The night before the assembly Yehoshua Leib, the more excitable of the two boys, could hardly sleep. Many of the other boys' fathers had spoken at different assemblies, and now it was finally going to be his father's turn. He twisted and turned from one side to another but simply could not get the excitement out of him. And who could blame him? Not only was his father going to be speaking, but Yehoshua Leib was going to receive his very own Mishnayos.

All morning Yehoshua Leib jumped around in his seat. The assembly was scheduled for later in the day, but as he looked around at all of his classmates wearing their special white shirts, his excitement was building. Finally, after lunch was over, the countdown began. Now all they had to do was await Rabbi Kurtzman's special announcement for the boys to gather for the assembly.

Rabbi Kurtzman opened the assembly by speaking to the students about the importance of learning Torah. The boys eagerly waited for the chance to receive their very own Mishnayos. But first they would have the opportunity to listen to Rabbi Levine, Moishe and Yehoshua Leib's father. Rabbi Levine spoke about how privileged we Jews are to be the only nation chosen to learn Hashem's Torah. The boys listened to his every word as he told story after story about different Torah giants. And then, after 15 minutes, he thanked the boys for their wonderful behavior and wished them well.

As soon as Rabbi Levine finished speaking he glanced around the room one more time. He had seen Moishe sitting together with his classmates, but where was Yehoshua Leib? Again he scanned the room, this time looking more carefully. But again there was no Yehoshua Leib! As Rabbi Levine left the auditorium he hoped that his son had just gone out to the rest room, but when he walked toward the boy's classroom, he was filled with apprehension. And then he saw him. Sitting further down the hall was Yehoshua Leib, studying with an older student who often helped him practice his reading. Rabbi Levine was distraught — his own son had missed this special moment! Yehoshua Leib had probably been called out of class moments before the students were taken down to the assembly. When the boy saw his father walking down the hall, his little face showed the sudden recognition of this terrible mistake, and he started crying inconsolably.

Rabbi Levine took his son to the office to call his mother but she couldn't calm him down either. She decided to come to the school to console her heartbroken son.

She made the short trip to Yeshivas Ohr Emes and was greeted by a very sad little boy; hard as she tried, however, the child simply would not stop crying. Finally she went to Rabbi Kurtzman's office. Her attempts to stay calm and composed failed her, and she cried out, "Rabbi Kurtzman, how could you have done this? How could you have forgotten my son?"

She was waiting for Rabbi Kurtzman to say, "Mrs. Levine, you have to understand …" But he didn't.

He looked at Yehoshua Leib's red eyes and tear-stained cheeks. "You're 100 percent correct. I made a mistake. And you know what? We're going to do the whole thing over again."

Mrs. Levine wasn't sure she had heard correctly. "You mean his class is going to go down and have the assembly all over again?" Mrs. Levine asked incredulously.

"No. I mean that that all three classes are going to have the assembly all over again." So incredibly, instead of going to learn their first Mishnah, all three classes went back down for another assembly.

Rabbi Levine sat in the front, this time right near his little Yehoshua Leib, whose smile stretched from ear to ear. Rabbi Kurtzman began to speak and explained to the boys that the most important thing about learning is *chazarah,* reviewing what one has learned. And thus it was befitting to begin their career of learning Mishnayos by reviewing what Rabbi Levine had said.

But when Rabbi Levine got up to speak and looked at his son Yehoshua Leib's beaming smile, he conveyed a completely different sentiment. He too felt it was important to extract from this incident an unforgettable lesson. "It's true that it is very important to review everything one learns. But there is one message Rabbi Kurtzman has taught us that is even more fundamental to our learning. And that is that every single Jewish child is precious. And it was worthwhile to delay starting to learn the first Mishnah for the sake of one child's feelings."

Yehoshua Leib Levine could not have agreed more.

Broken ... and the Best

*I*T WAS ALL SO VERY FRUSTRATING. EVERY TIME SHMULI Gurlitz tried to understand the Gemara the class was learning, he felt like he was facing a brick wall. Nothing made sense. He simply could not follow the steps and the thought process of even the simplest portion of Gemara. Unfortunately it had always been that way for Shmuli. Ever since he had started learning Gemara he had found it very difficult.

Growing up in Bnei Brak, Shmuli had no lack of role models from whom to choose. He was often found wandering around the *beis midrash* looking for someone who would learn with him and help him out. All the older boys liked him and did the best they could to help him understand the material. But as the years went by and the rest of the boys in his class were growing and developing in their learning, Shmuli was still struggling, always trapped, he felt, in a dense web of confusion. Every time his rebbi would explain the concepts Shmuli would find himself perplexed about the subject matter; and what hurt most was how easily most of the other boys understood everything. The frustration grew and the depression haunted him day after day. He so badly wanted to become something, somebody, a great *talmid chacham*. On that rare occasion when something finally penetrated his mind, the feeling was so rewarding! But it happened so rarely, and he just needed to feel it more often.

Years went by and his wish of becoming a *talmid chacham* was as strong as ever. Shmuli was now 16, and although his desire to grow in learning had not waned, his inability to comprehend had not changed either. The combination of these two factors was making life unbearable. Something had to give.

Shmuli's rebbi, Rabbi Yosef Bittersfeld, was quite aware of the young man's frustrations and of the fact that the tutoring and mentoring did little to increase his comprehension of the learning. Finally, one day Shmuli told his rebbi, "Rebbi, I need to speak with you — privately." Reb Yosef could tell that Shmuli was at the breaking point. He invited Shmuli into his study and closed the door. As soon as Shmuli sat down he burst out crying. "Rebbi, I can't go on like this! I can't take it anymore!"

The panic in Shmuli's voice was different than anything Reb Yosef had heard in his twenty-five years of teaching. He sensed that this 11th-grade boy was in real trouble. He looked into the young man's tortured face and listened as Shmuli poured out his heart and bared his soul. "Rebbi," he cried, "I don't want to live anymore. I just want to end the pain ..."

Reb Yosef held onto Shmuli as the boy sobbed uncontrollably. "It's okay, Shmuli. I'm here for you ..."

Reb Yosef knew what he had to do. He gently guided Shmuli outside, and the two of them walked down the streets of Bnei Brak to the only address Reb Yosef would trust, to the home of Rabbi Yaakov Yisrael Kanievsky, the "Steipler Gaon." The Steipler spoke to Reb Yosef for a few moments and then asked to speak to Shmuli privately. He held onto Shmuli's hands and with his piercing eyes gazed directly at the boy. "Listen to me. I want you to know something. I never use this expression, but I want you to know how much I mean what I am going to say. I promise you with a *shevuah d'Oraisa* — an oath by the Torah — that when you struggle to comprehend the Gemara you are learning, the A-mighty says to His Heavenly Court, 'At this moment in time I want everyone else's learning — that of the Steipler, Rav Shach, and the Brisker Rav — to move aside so that I can listen to this young man learning.' "

Shmuli stared at the Steipler in disbelief. The familiar feelings of frustration and panic fought with new feelings of hope and relief. He thought to himself, *Could it really be that my clumsy learning is so special in the eyes of Hashem?* And so he further questioned the Steipler, "How do you know that? Please tell me ... I must know."

The Steipler quoted the Midrash in *Vayikra* that states that the vessels the A-mighty uses are *keilim shevurim,* broken vessels. *Broken vessels,* thought Shmuli — *that's me! I am broken, but I am still special and Hashem still wants to hear my learning!*

Shmuli shook his head in disbelief. He sat still for a moment, then slowly raised his eyes to meet those of the Steipler.

He thanked the great Rav for his encouragement, knowing that this *gadol* had changed his life forever. He walked to his rebbi and gave him a warm, thankful hug. Shmuli knew now that he would continue to try and would never give up — and that no matter how successful or unsuccessful he was in understanding the learning, it was his effort, his love of learning, that mattered. He wiped the tears from his eyes and walked out the door with his rebbi, no longer a broken, dispirited teenager, but now a hopeful, encouraged young man ready for the challenges that lay ahead.

Shmuli persevered and continued to work hard. And soon he began to feel accomplishment and growth in his learning. Inexplicably, it would seem, he started to catch on. Before long he became a budding young Torah scholar. Because he now knew that *he* was worth the effort …

Sh! Sh! … He's Sleeping

The first time I met him I was able to tell that he was a warm, caring individual. He was visiting from Eretz Yisrael to receive treatments for the cancer from which he was suffering. His beard had almost completely fallen out from the chemotherapy and radiation. A far cry from what he must have looked like not long ago, his smile still radiated from his face, his "chein" was still clearly evident. His name was Muttel Gewirtzman and he had been a melamed in a Boyaner cheder for the last thirty-five years. I couldn't resist and I asked him for his best story. He told me he didn't really have any, that every day, with every child, there was always another story in the classroom. But then he shared with me a little episode that struck a chord …

The young boy appeared to be feeling ill. His face was flushed and he seemed to be somewhat nauseous. His rebbi, Rabbi Gewirtzman, asked him if he wanted to take a walk just to get some fresh air. And then the rebbi offered him a snack and a drink. Finally he instructed the boy to put his head down on the desk for a few moments. "A few moments on the *shtender* is as good as a few hours in bed," he would often tell them. He cared for the *talmidim* and they knew it. He loved them and took care of all their needs. His class of first graders was a lively bunch and they needed someone who would look after them and worry about their needs.

He was the type of rebbi who allowed the boys the freedom to roam about the room during davening, as long as they davened with exuberance and enthusiasm, as long as they davened with *"geshmak."* He also had the same philosophy about learning in the classroom. If a boy was a bit more lively and spirited, the rebbi permitted him to move about the room. The boys all knew that their rebbi was special and they loved him for it. On the rare day that school was called off because of a snowfall, instead of using the time as a vacation day to get away from the kids, he utilized this opportunity to call each boy and ask him how he was enjoying his day off. The next day he would immediately see the results from the children who felt the love and caring of their rebbi. The learning would be that much better, that much livelier.

But one day Reb Muttel woke up feeling very weak. He knew something just wasn't right. In the classroom, the children saw that he was missing some of his cheerfulness and asked him if he was feeling all right. Reb Muttel knew he had to go to the doctor. A series of tests was run, and a day later Reb Muttel discovered that his life was going to change drastically. He had cancer.

The treatments were draining. He was always tired and exhausted, struggling to perform even the most menial tasks. But he tried his best not to let his condition affect his performance in class. Try as he might, the children noticed that he was not his usual, upbeat self. He lost most of the hair on his face and some of the boys were scared of him because of his ailing appearance. Instead of walking around the classroom in his usual lively manner, he now had to sit most of the time and rest. The principal encouraged him to take some time off but Rabbi Gewirtzman insisted on doing his best to maintain the only sense of normalcy that remained in his life.

One day, the principal walked by Rabbi Gewirtzman's room and noticed that something was wrong. Instead of the usual boisterous clamor, there was an uneasy silence. Hoping that the class just went out for some extra recess — but dreading the worst — he opened the door a crack and peeked inside. What he saw he will never forget.

The entire class was sitting there — still and silent. They motioned to their *menahel* with their fingers on their mouths that he shouldn't make any noise. The *menahel,* Rabbi Goldfarb, looked around and could not figure out what was happening until they pointed to the front of the room. Sitting down by his desk was their rebbi, his head down and his spirits defeated. He had done all he could. He had literally given every bit of his strength — but he needed to rest for a moment. When the boys saw that the rebbi they loved so much was not feeling well they told him that he should put his head down for a minute. They promised they would be quiet. They promised to behave.

The stunned *menahel* nodded and quietly closed the door. The boys would be quiet. Their beloved rebbi needed to rest.

Just a Phone Call

*I*T WAS A TIME OF GREAT JOY IN THE SHMULEVITZ HOME. Their youngest son was getting married and the *chasunah* was to take place that evening. Most of the preparations for the wedding had been taken care of without the need to disturb the *chasan's* father, Reb Chaim, who was a busy Rosh Yeshivah. His time was precious and lately he had been ill. Finally, a taxi was called to take the family for the short drive to the wedding hall.

The Rosh Yeshivah was a brilliant *talmid chacham*. And his brilliance was matched by his deep sensitivity and concern for each and every *talmid*. A *talmid* was not just someone whom Reb Chaim taught; rather he felt it imperative to try to personally meet the needs of each of the students. Although occupied with his learning every moment of the day, when he sensed a *talmid* in need, he addressed the matter immediately.

The taxi waited outside. The driver was getting a bit impatient, having already waited 10 minutes for Reb Chaim to leave the house. He honked the horn a few times and waited as the meter continued to run. He dragged on his cigarette as he waited, his impatience growing. This was supposed to be a quick trip, only a three-minute drive to the local wedding hall. What was the wait for? The driver turned to the other members of the family but they simply shrugged their shoulders as if to say, "Our father knows that there is a taxi waiting. He heard the horn. If he is still inside it must be for a good reason."

Finally, Reb Chaim's son walked back into their home, located on the main floor of the Mirrer Yeshivah building. He saw his father talking on the phone. He seemed to be reassuring someone on the other end. *Who could it be?* his son wondered. *Who could possibly have called to bother the Rosh Yeshivah on the evening of his own son's wedding? Didn't he realize that this was not the time to be speaking to his father?*

Reb Chaim's son waited for another few moments and after hearing what his father was saying, he realized what had happened. On the other end of the conversation was Moshe Blechman, the oldest unmarried *bachur* in the yeshivah. And incredibly — though not surprisingly — Reb Chaim had called him to say that at this moment of *simchah* and joy in his own life he wanted his *talmid* to know that he was thinking of *him*! And until Reb Chaim was convinced that Moshe Blechman had been reassured that he had not been forgotten, Reb Chaim would not — could not — go to his own son's wedding!

Shame and Sheimos

About 100 years ago, one of the great halachic decisors was the Chelkas Yoav, whose many responsa cover a wide range of halachic issues. The clarity in this collection of she'eilos u'teshuvos is remarkable. But the story that lies behind the unpublished work of this great individual is perhaps an even greater testament to how great he really was.

*E*VERY WEEK THE STUDENTS OF THE CHELKAS YOAV would meet at the venerated sage's home to discuss the various letters and questions that had been submitted to him on a wide variety of topics. Some concerned monetary matters while others discussed marital issues. On occasion a question regarding *kashrus* would become the topic of conversation. But no matter what the subject matter, the wise sage would display dazzling clarity in answering each and every *she'eilah*. The visit to their teacher's home was a highlight for these future *poskim*. They hoped that they, too, one day would be able to deliver a *p'sak* on even the most perplexing halachic inquiries.

Kalman, one of the weaker students in the group, seemed unusually interested in the writings of his teacher. Hours after the rest of the group had left, he would remain behind seeking more information, wanting to clarify the most intricate nuances and the finest distinctions of every possible circumstance. The Chelkas Yoav appreciated and admired the young man's diligence and encouraged him in his pursuit of the unadulterated truth.

One day, immediately after the weekly get-together, Kalman pulled out a pamphlet of his own *chidushim,* his own original thoughts regarding various halachic matters. The other students in the group glanced over the pages and were shocked to discover that these were the exact thoughts and sometimes even the exact words of their rebbi, the Chelkas Yoav. What impudence! How dare Kalman steal the ideas and concepts of his rebbi and present them as his own. The other students immediately challenged him and warned him not to publish these *chidushim* as if they were his original thoughts.

The Chelkas Yoav, who had been absorbed in learning, was startled to hear the commotion outside his room. When he entered the adjacent room he sensed the thick tension and asked what was going on. Meir, one of the more outspoken of the group, apprised him of what had happened and of the outrageous audacity that their fellow student had displayed.

Sensing a disaster in the making, the Chelkas Yoav sent the entire group on their way. But Meir, who had remained behind to speak to the rebbi, peeked into the backyard and noticed that his rebbi had a shovel in his hand and was digging a hole in the ground. He was curious as to why his rebbi was digging; he certainly was not a gardener and his time was too valuable to waste on mundane things like yard work. After some thought Meir concluded that his rebbi must be burying some *sheimos,* some tattered *sefarim* that were no longer usable. Entering the yard, Meir observed his rebbi reach into an envelope, remove some sheets of paper, kiss them lovingly, and then throw them into the ground.

"Rebbi, can I help you in any way?"

The Chelkas Yoav was startled, and almost seemed to be trying to hide what he was holding. But when Meir grabbed the pages to assist in their burial, he was shocked to see that these were his rebbi's own original Torah thoughts, the very same ones that Kalman had plagiarized.

"Rebbi, why are you throwing out your own *chidushim*?"

The answer that Meir heard from the Chelkas Yoav revealed the rebbi's almost unbelievable greatness of character. "These are my *chidushim.* And indeed they are very precious to me. However, I know that if anyone ever finds out that I was the originator of the thoughts which Kalman put into his booklet, Kalman would be devastated. His reputation would be destroyed forever, and it would cause him irreversible damage and pain. That is something I cannot do."

There are few things as precious in life as one's own original Torah thoughts. They come from the deepest recesses of one's neshamah. And to the Chelkas Yoav there wasn't anything as precious as the chidushim that he had written ...
Nothing except a talmid's feelings ...
A dishonest, deceitful talmid's feelings.

Knowing Who You Are

H E WAS JUST NOT INTERESTED. AT LEAST NOT NOW. Simchah Perlman, living in the DP camps after World War II, watched as others put their lives back together again. Many were religious Jews for whom belief in G-d defined who they were. As for him ... he had been through too much to care anymore. He had lost everything, including his relationship with G-d. He knew that it sounded terrible but he had to be honest with himself ... and that was just the way he felt.

A few of his acquaintances had tried to convince him otherwise, but he had told them that he needed more time. And with everything Simchah had gone through, who would dare to argue? In fact, after watching his wife and children die before his very eyes, he would have preferred not to continue living at all. But that is not what happened.

And now Simchah had holed up inside of himself. He had become introverted and withdrawn. He kept his distance from everyone in the camp and tried his best to forget what had happened. His eyes were now gray and lifeless. His soul and spirit had almost completely vanished, hidden deep inside of him, veiled behind the protection of indifference.

And then one day as Simchah was walking through the camp he spotted a small crowd of people heading toward him. As they came closer, he realized it was Rav Yekusiel Yehudah Halberstam, the Klausenburger Rebbe, surrounded by some of his followers. The Rebbe motioned for his disciples to move ahead while he stopped in an attempt to speak to Simchah. But Simchah, who sensed what was about to happen, did not want to speak to anyone — and certainly not the Rebbe. He did not want to be told how important it was to believe. All he wanted right now was to be left alone. He tried to quicken his pace but the Rebbe called out to him, and now he had no choice but to turn around and respond.

"Rebbe, I'm sorry, but I really don't want to talk right now. Is it something that can wait?"

The Rebbe reassured him that it would only take a minute of his time. "Simchah, I know you don't want to talk to anyone right now. And I could never blame you. I just want you to remember one thing." The Rebbe, with his warm, radiant eyes, looked at Simchah and told him only one thing — the only thing he could have told him — "Always remember who you are."

> Years later, Simchah looks at his family of wonderful Torah-abiding Jews and reflects on the uncanny ability of the Klausenburger Rebbe to say the only thing that would have made any impact on him. A discourse about Hashem and Torah and mitzvos would not have accomplished anything. The only thing Simchah needed to hear was that he was somebody, a Jew — descended from noble, illustrious people — and he carried within him the G-d-given ability to rise up from the ashes and to carry on the sacred traditions of his nation.

Leibele the Simpleton

*I*N THE EYES OF THE TOWNSPEOPLE OF YANDERCHOIF, Leibele was nothing more than a fool, someone whose clothes were too big for him so he was constantly tripping over the hems of his pants. On occasion he was embarrassed by the mocking of the townspeople, so he would change into his other clothes, with pants that were three inches too short. But many in the town knew that Leibele was well meaning and sincere. He came to shul three times a week — on Mondays, Thursdays, and Shabbos — and stood in the corner davening, away from most of the congregants. His prayers were quite unique. Leibele was not an articulate individual and most of the words he spoke were mispronounced, incoherent or both. But there was no questioning his genuine sincerity. Leibele meant well.

The scoffers in the town, however, reveled in the opportunity to mock him. They made fun of his walk, his speech, and his clothing. But more than anything, they resented his fervent davening, feeling that he should not daven this way, considering his station in life.

The town was expecting a special visitor, the famed Rav Shlomo of Kashnov. Everyone, including Leibele, was anxious to meet this great man. When the Rav arrived, many waited to see him. Finally, it was Leibele's turn. The moment he walked into the room where Rav Shlomo sat, their eyes locked and, try as he might, Leibele was unable to avoid the piercing glance of Rav Shlomo. Leibele tried to hide behind some of the more important members of the community but was unable to screen himself completely. Finally, after a few moments, Rav Shlomo motioned that he should come closer. Many in the room expected Leibele to make a fool of himself before the great Rav. They actually waited expectantly, hoping this would happen. No doubt the Rebbe would once and for all chide him for his silly behavior. But Rav Shlomo did anything but.

Instead he brought Leibele close and took his hand, shaking it warmly. He looked into Leibele's frightened eyes and reassured him that he had nothing to fear. "Where are you from, *Reb Yid*? Where do you live?" Leibele answered that he lived on the outskirts of town. "*Rabbosai*, why doesn't anyone take care of this *Yid*?" And then in a feverish pitch Rav Shlomo continued, "Don't you know that the entire town of Yanderchoif exists only in the merit of this man?"

All those gathered there watched in amazement as Leibele was truly being exposed, but certainly not in the manner in which they had thought. "Tell me some Torah thoughts, Reb Leibele." And as the two of them huddled, the townspeople waited to hear Leibele, wondering if under his appearance as a fool, he held great Torah wisdom. "Rebbe, I am a complete ignoramus. But I do know that when the Philistines were wicked to the *Yidden,* Hashem sent Shimshon HaGibor to protect them … Hashem did a big mitzvah … right?"

Rav Shlomo nodded and the community watched in disbelief. The incredible straightforwardness of what Leibele was saying only confirmed that he was indeed a simpleton. "But we have an even stronger hero we can look up to. Avraham Avinu together with four other kings defeated the five kings in a big war. Right, Rebbe?" The crowd tried their best to suppress their laughter. This was utterly ridiculous. Leibele was clearly an utter and complete fool. But the Rebbe shook his head as he stared deeply into Leibele's eyes. "Tell me more of your wonderful Torah thoughts. They're so beautiful. Please, tell me more, Leibele. Tell me more."

And there they sat. The two of them. One a Torah giant and the other the simplest of all men. Those who had gathered that night watched in amazement. The scoffers were silenced and the townspeople stunned. Rav Shlomo had *pretended to be thrilled with a simpleton's words.*

> *Or was he a simpleton?*
> *I guess we will never know.*

A Very Important Meeting

URING THE EARLY DAYS OF THE FAMED PONOVEZH Yeshivah, Rav Yehoshua Zelig Diskind, the Rav of Pardes Chana, received an urgent message from the Ponovezher Rav, Rav Kahaneman, that he needed to borrow a significant sum of money for a few days. The money was to be brought to the yeshivah and placed inside his office. However, he explained to Rav Diskind, he would be unavailable for the day as he was going to Yerushalayim to attend a very important meeting with some of the *gedolei Yisrael*. Among those in attendance would be the Brisker Rav.

Rav Diskind quickly secured the necessary funds and brought the money to the Rav's office. Aware that the Rav was in Yerushalayim, Rav Diskind opened the door to the office and was about to put the money in a drawer when, to his surprise, he saw that the Rav was there — sitting in his chair and holding onto a young boy who was crying bitterly.

"I'm sorry — " Rav Diskind stammered, caught completely off guard. He was shocked that the Rav was there. Why hadn't he gone to the meeting in Yerushalayim?

The Ponovezher Rav immediately noticed Rav Diskind's reaction and explained. "Whenever I leave Bnei Brak I make it a point to stop at the Batei Avos Orphanage on the outskirts of the city. And this time, when I walked in, I noticed a young boy crying bitterly in the corner. When I asked one of the counselors why the child was so broken he told me that this boy, who had lost both his parents in the war, had just been informed that his best friend, too, had been killed in Auschwitz."

The Rav's eyes were red and swollen, as he had obviously been crying along with the boy for some time now. He spoke with deep emotion and obvious pain. "I approached this young boy and asked him what was wrong but he could not stop crying. His words were slurred and he sobbed through the story, which was completely incoherent. And he has not stopped crying since."

The Ponovezher Rav then turned to Rav Yehoshua Zelig and declared, "The *gedolim* will have to wait. This child needs me now. I cannot leave."

Rav Diskind watched in awe as the Rav once again held the broken child close to him and they continued to cry together.

Al eileh ani bochiyah...

Teshuvah /
Repentance

Everything Will Be All Right

*I*T HAPPENED SO QUICKLY. A MERE THREE MONTHS EARLIER Berish and Goldie Greenfeld had walked into the doctor's office thinking that she had been suffering from some lingering side effects of the flu. But as time passed and tests were taken, various possibilities were eliminated. The dreaded results came in. She was given three months to live — four if they were lucky.

There comes a time in one's life when the only thing left to do is to make arrangements for the inevitable. Yes, there was always the chance for a miracle. But it was also important to make sure that when the time came, the children — all ten of them — along with her husband would know that there was still going to be a home to come back to.

Three months sounds a lot longer than it actually is. There was so much to do. Appointments. Hospital visits. And, of course, the managing of the everyday chores of the house. So when the tragic moment arrived Berish was really no better equipped than he had been three months before. He could be a father. Perhaps he could have managed to be a mother. But to do both, alone, single-handedly, was overwhelming, distressing and — most of the time — almost impossible.

Nearly a thousand people attended the funeral. The crowd watched as the Greenfeld children — the oldest, a 17-year-old boy, and the youngest, a 4-year-old girl — walked behind the *aron* of their mother. It was a heartrending scene. Of course, many offered to help in any way they could. Some offered to take the younger children for a while. Berish graciously thanked them for their offers but refused to split up the family in any way, even temporarily.

Shivah ended and the family tried to go back to a normal routine. This of course meant that Berish had to double up on his duties. From the time the children woke in the morning until he tucked in the last child at night, Berish spent the bulk of his day tending to their every need. Perhaps if he had had a moment to think about it he would have broken down crying, grasping the enormity and horror of his loss. But who had time to stop and think?

Finally, three months after the tragedy, Berish's mother called to inform him that she was coming for a visit. She just wanted to make sure that he was coping. Even though Berish insisted that everything was fine, she insisted on coming. A mother is after all a mother. She promised not to interfere. She just wanted to visit.

The day she arrived, Berish was already in full swing. Shaindy, his 7-year-old, needed some help with her homework, and Moishele, his 10-year-old, was having a test the next day on the Gemara he had learned in school. Blimi, his 12-year-old, needed someone to pick up some eggs, as she was preparing supper; and 6-year-old Yanky had just come in crying that his leg was bleeding. Berish tended to each issue and one by one the problems were solved.

His mother helped where she could, but marveled at how well they — and more specifically he — were coping. Supper was served, the children were bathed, bedtime stories were read, and then finally the children were put to bed. It was now 10 o'clock and Berish walked slowly into the kitchen, pulled out a chair and plopped down, thoroughly exhausted. His mother, who had prepared a glass of tea for him, watched carefully as Berish put his hands over his face and rubbed his eyes. *Nebach*, she thought to herself, *he must be so exhausted.*

And then suddenly, without warning, it came. At first it was soft, quiet weeping, but then it came in stronger, more violent sobs, and finally a torrential bawling the likes of which she had never seen before. Berish's mother moved closer to her son, who was now crying like a little boy. "Mama, Mama — it's so hard. I can't take it anymore." Until now, he had not had a moment to reflect on the loss — the months of pain, of losing his wife — but now that his mother had come to visit, all his emotions came to the surface. He was confronted by his weakness and frailty, by who he was now and what he had gone through. And his mother held onto *her child* — a full-grown father of ten and now a helpless widower — thinking, praying, *It will all be all right — It will be all right.*

And she hoped that somehow, some way, it would.

In a very moving essay, Rav Tzvi Meir Silverberg applies this heartrending story to our very own lives. On Yom Kippur we were as close and united with the A-mighty as we will ever be. But then somehow, somewhere along the way we lost our relationship with Him, by abandoning the commitments we made. Tragically we don't even realize or acknowledge what we've lost. But then in the middle of winter there arrives a special period of six weeks, the weeks of Shovevim, when the "Heilige Mama" — the Shechinah HaKedoshah, the Divine Presence — comes to visit. And then we stop for just a moment, step back from the hectic, frantic, and frenzied pace of our lives and we bury our faces and cry for what we have lost. But there is only one difference. If we are willing to change and to reaffirm our commitments then our Mother can and will reach out Her hand to help us recover what we have lost.

Candlelights

Writing a book affords one the privilege of meeting many special individuals. One such person is Rabbi Moshe Menachem Taubenfeld. Reb Moshe Menachem's wife, Rebbetzin Shaindel Golda, and their infant son, Shmuel Eliyahu, were on their way back from the Kosel when the unthinkable happened. Their lives were snuffed out by a senseless act of violence — a terrorist bomb. A short while later Reb Moshe Menachem authored a magnificent sefer entitled "Bifkudecha Asicha." Through this book he conveys the indescribable emunah that has carried him and his family through their most challenging times. This particular story illustrates that no matter how lost one may feel, there is always hope — there is always someone who cares.

MOST OF THE ELDERLY PEOPLE IN THE SAN Francisco Bay area are retired. They have either lived there for a long time or have moved there to live out the rest of their lives in a pleasant and relaxed environment. The last thing they are looking for is a major transformation in their lifestyle. But the silver-haired gentleman in his mid-70's had done just that. He had *just* become a *baal teshuvah*.

❧

His story began in 1938. It was two days before Yom Kippur, the day that the Thirteen Attributes of Hashem are read aloud in a distinct paragraph during *Selichos* and invoked in a special prayer. This solemn occasion is viewed as somewhat of a prelude to Yom

Kippur. On this significant day, it was customary for the Belzer Rebbe and his rebbetzin to prepare special candles for various members of the community. The preparation of these candles was regarded as a sacred, hallowed custom, as the ceremony of lighting the candles symbolized that the *ohr haganuz,* the veiled radiance inside one's *neshamah,* was similarly illuminated.

Only a few privileged individuals were allowed into the Rebbe's private chamber when these candles were completed. One of those was Meir the *shochet.* He had come to the Rebbe with Baruch, his 6-year-old son, hoping to at least be able to come within close proximity of the Rebbe. And now, as they entered the Rebbe's inner sanctum, Baruch in his innocence began to ask for whom each candle was meant. The Rebbe answered patiently although those who were gathered around were shocked at the impudence of this youngster. But when one of the Rebbe's attendants attempted to quiet the young boy, the Rebbe cautioned him to be patient.

"And who is this candle meant for?" Baruch pointed to one specific candle.

This time the Rebbe held onto the young boy's finger and he smiled warmly at the inquisitive child. "There is a city in America that you have never heard of. It is called San Francisco. This candle is predestined even for a *Yid* in a faraway place like San Francisco who might be lost and looking to find himself, searching to find his *neshamah.* This candle is for him."

The vicious Nazi war machine destroyed all that Baruch held dear. He survived the war, a young man without a family; a body without a soul. He eventually made his way to the shores of America, where he met a young woman. And although she was not Jewish, it no longer mattered to him. He married her. And for fifty years, Judaism did not exist in his life.

One evening, Baruch, now a distinguished silver-haired gentleman in his mid-70's, was walking down the streets of San Francisco when he found himself standing in front of a synagogue. Something pushed him toward the building. He tried to fight the urge to go inside but he felt strangely compelled to inch closer until finally, cautiously, he walked into the building. He peeked inside and saw a sea of white.

He remembered … though the memories were dim with age. The sounds of men praying came rushing through his memory in a flash. His head began to ache and his eyes filled with tears. His soul was touched. It yearned and thirsted for what once was. And his heart began to pound wildly. He heard a cynical voice inside his head urging him to ignore the feelings and thoughts which now threatened his dormant soul. But he couldn't stop what was happening. He needed to come closer, to feel the long locked-away emotions once again. And then he opened a book, a *siddur* — and he cried and cried and cried.

He did not know if he would ever be welcome again. He had, after all, long ago abandoned Judaism and married a non-Jew. He was as lost as a Jew had ever been. He was sure it was too late. Maybe twenty or thirty years ago he could have started over, but not now. Not when he was past 70.

He was about to walk out, about to turn his back on all this forever. And then he saw lit candles in glass cups — and he remembered the candle from so many years ago. *There is a candle for me too. I remember the Rebbe's words. He was talking about me!* He picked up the *siddur* once again. The words called out to him from the distant past. It was late, the sun was setting, and it was time for the *Nei'lah* service to begin. It was now time for those who had waited to do *teshuvah*. It was late — but there was still time.

Countdown

When one writes a book or two, he or she enjoys the pleasure of people calling to relate stories of their own. Those who call are usually people who enjoy reading and hear-

*ing stories. But the fellow who communicated this partic-
ular stirring episode is, in his own words, "the last person
who would ever call with a story." However, the sequence
of events that transpired on this Erev Rosh Hashanah
made such an indelible impression on his life that he felt
compelled to share his saga. The names and places have
been changed to protect the identity of the characters in
the story, but the facts are true — and very painfully so.*

WITH A LITTLE MORE THAN AN HOUR LEFT UNTIL
Rosh Hashanah, Yanky Soloff headed out to the
supermarket for a few last-minute items. He had
tried to have everything prepared and ready so there would be no
need to run out before Yom Tov, but fate dictated otherwise. He
walked into the large supermarket and quickly gathered a few bot-
tles of soda, a bag of lettuce, and some tissues. Luckily the checkout
line was empty and Yanky was pleased that he would be home in
plenty of time for Yom Tov.

He paid for his items and headed out the door. But as he walked
toward his car he noticed a woman standing nearby with her son, a
boy who appeared to be about 8 years old. As a slight drizzle began
to fall, he decided to ask her if she needed any help; after all, it was
Erev Rosh Hashanah. And Yanky reasoned that he definitely could
use another good deed before the High Holy Days. The woman,
who upon closer look seemed to be completely disheveled,
thanked him for his concern and asked him if she could borrow his
cell phone. He readily handed her the phone as the rain started to
pick up. She made a quick call and as she handed back the phone
Yanky felt that it would be nice if he would offer the woman and
her son a ride home.

"Thank you," she replied, "but I just have to make three stops."

It was now approximately 45 minutes before Yom Tov and
Yanky wondered if he would have been better off just minding his
own business and driving straight home. But he happily agreed.
The woman and her son entered the back seat of his fairly new

minivan and she directed him to the first stop. He drove for five minutes and pulled up in front of a house. She asked him to wait for a few moments and went in. When she came out with a few large aluminum trays and several containers filled with food, he began putting two and two together. This woman and her family do not have any food for Yom Tov!

Yanky could not believe it. This Yom Tov was of the three-day variety and with a half-hour left to the beginning of the New Year she did not have any food of her own. Incredible! She placed the food down in the back of the van and a strong aroma soon filled the air. He tried not to look at the woman and her son but was filled with pity for them. She started to speak about her husband, who seemed to have endured some sort of a nervous breakdown, and minute by minute the story was getting worse.

It was 25 minutes before Yom Tov and by now it was pouring outside. She told Yanky that the next stop was a place where the local food establishments graciously drop off the prepared food they hadn't sold, to be taken by those who needed it. He offered to help her but she refused, instead going in and emerging a few moments later with more trays of food.

She looked at her watch and realized that 15 minutes remained to Yom Tov. As they drove down the long, narrow road which would in turn lead them to her house, Yanky looked through his rearview mirror and glanced at the young boy. He too had a boy that age and the thought of his son having to endure this embarrassment and shame brought him to the brink of tears. The rain was now coming down in a torrential downpour and the clock was ticking away. Suddenly, the pathetic woman looked out the side window of the car. "I'm sorry, could you please stop the car?" Yanky did his best to quickly pull over in the middle of nowhere. What had she seen? What could she possibly want?

He noticed that she ran across the street and seemed to be rummaging through the garbage! A moment later she returned with a few torn, soaked stuffed animals. Yanky gasped but tried not to show his disdain for the woman. "Mister, you really should go get some stuffed animals for your children. They'll love the presents."

By now the tears brimming in Yanky's eyes started to overflow. He wiped them away and quickly explained to his passenger that he did not like *spoiling* his children with so many presents. The boy shook his head in disapproval as his mother crammed the drenched, stuffed animals into the car. The car was now permeated with a wet, clammy odor. It was getting dangerously close to Yom Tov. Fifteen minutes and counting.

They made the short drive to the poor family's home and Yanky insisted on helping the woman bring her packages into the house. He walked up the steps and opened the door. The repugnant smell made him want to drop the packages and run. Run away from the horrible condition in which this family lived. And if he could, to take that sweet 8-year-old boy with him. He had nothing in his life. And Yanky desperately wanted to give this boy something. He wanted to show him happiness — for this boy had none. Or did he?

Yanky watched as some older girls hid their faces in shame as they scurried away into the other rooms. The mother thanked him and incredibly offered him some food. But he thanked her and declined her offer as he looked at his watch. It was 10 minutes to Yom Tov. He was in a rush if there ever was one. But as he was about to leave the home the young boy called out. "Mister, one minute, please."

Turning toward the boy he was shocked to see that the child was holding in his hands an Aleph-Beis matching game. It was brand new. "Could you please give it to your son? I promise he'll like it. He'll love getting a present for Yom Tov." Yanky stood there frozen. He was afraid to speak, fearing that the tears that had welled up in his eyes would come pouring out. Instead he accepted it and then, on second thought, asked the boy to take it back. He didn't want the child to think that he did not want his presents and that his things were not good enough. So he assured him that he would buy something for his son, but he did not want this boy to lose his own gift. And he thanked the boy for his astonishing kindness.

He walked out of the wretched house and quickly got into his car. And then as he started to pull away, he began to cry. He cried and cried and cried. He cried as he never had before. With his tears blinding his vision, he thought of the child — who had so little but felt so blessed. And he thought of himself and his family and the countless blessings which Hashem had bestowed upon them.

He drove up to his own home. The rain had stopped. He wiped his tears, wished his wife a Gut Yom Tov, picked up his *shtender*, and placed it inside his car. It was time to daven. Rosh Hashanah was here. And now he was ready.

The Wake-Up Call

*T*HE LARGE ENTOURAGE WHICH PERPETUALLY FOL-LOWED the famed Rebbe of Ger, Rav Yehudah Aryeh Leib, the Sfas Emes, hung onto his every word. Those who have learned his *sefarim* know that it is his ability to find the prevailing, overarching messages in the eternal words of Torah that attracts followers to his *shiurim*. Thousands worldwide felt inspired, ignited, by this chassidic Master, who was known for his erudition in Talmud as well as for the profundity of his thoughts.

Toward the end of his life, Rav Yehudah Aryeh Leib became deaf. While most elderly individuals would be devastated by the loss of this most necessary sense, the Sfas Emes continued to lead with the same fervor and emotion. In fact, he continued to deliver his in-depth *shiurim* to his disciples. Yet he worried: *How was his deafness affecting those around him?* One day, as he delivered a Talmudic discourse, he found out.

While he was speaking, he noticed that many of his students were suddenly mumbling to themselves. The Rebbe stopped what he was saying and asked those nearest to him for the cause of the disturbance. When no one volunteered an answer, the Rebbe demanded a response. Finally, one brave chassid explained to the Rebbe that they were merely reciting the *berachah* on the sound of thunder — *Shekocho u'gevuraso malei olam*. Suddenly, the Rebbe burst out crying. Wondering what was wrong, the chassidim watched as their exalted leader wept softly to himself. After a few moments he regained his composure and explained, "When I was able to hear thunder, I used the opportunity to think about how much there is to fear and how great the A-mighty is. This would help wake me up from my slumber. But now — what will wake me up? How will I be inspired to do *teshuvah*?"

> *Imagine the impact of this moment on those in the room; saying a simple berachah on what seemed like a routine event had become transformed into an opportunity to listen to Hashem's call for self-reflection and change! One can only imagine that — thanks to the Rebbe's insight — no one, after that day, ever heard thunder the same way again.*

Opening Doors

The atmosphere in the Torah community of Yerushalayim in the early years of the 20th century was sometimes filled with considerable tension. The camp of Rav Yosef Chaim Sonnenfeld was committed to the traditions of old, opposing the outreach to the new nonreligious groups, and feeling that Rav Avraham Yitzchak HaKohen Kook was compromising on certain issues by reaching out to the new "Yishuv." While there were certainly strong dif-

ferences both in hashkafah and halachah between the greatly venerated leaders of the generation, there was also a tremendous respect between the two.

RAV KOOK EXPRESSED THIS RESPECT ONCE WHEN Rav Sonnenfeld's grandson had the occasion to enter Rav Kook's home. The young man was understandably nervous to enter what he perceived as "the lions' den." But when he entered Rav Kook's home, Rav Kook himself greeted the young man with unusual warmth and kindness and then pulled him aside. "I want you to know that if your grandfather was stranded on the other side of the Sambatyon River and rocks were being hurled at him, I would do whatever it would take to save him. That is how much I love him." The young man was at once shocked and pleased. The story that follows further depicts the relationship between these two Torah giants.

Once, these two great men were invited to take part in the celebration of a *bris*. Rav Yosef Chaim was a noted *mohel* and Rav Kook was to be given the honor of *sandek*. As it happens, both great men found themselves approaching the place where the *bris* was to take place at precisely the same moment. While greeting each other they glanced at the double doors in front of them. One was bolted shut while the other was open, providing a narrow passageway wide enough for only one of them to enter. The question was: Which one would go first? Rav Yosef Chaim insisted on Rav Kook walking through first, as he was the Rav of the city. Rav Kook maintained that Rav Yosef Chaim should walk through first as he was the bigger *talmid chacham*. But Rav Yosef Chaim responded that Rav Kook was a Kohen. And so they went on, back and forth, each one trying to convince the other that he should go first. Finally Rav Kook smiled.

He reached out his hand to the bolt of the closed door, unbolted it, and turned to Rav Yosef Chaim, "You see, the reason we can't walk through is because the door is bolted shut. But if we open the door then the two of us can walk through together." Once he unlocked the door, the two leaders walked through the now much wider passageway hand in hand, together.

> *Quite often we fail to see eye to eye with others with whom we disagree, but if we are willing to open the "passageway" a little wider, then we will be able to walk together as one.*

Which One's Worse?

YAAKOV ALWAYS ENJOYED STAYING WITH THE GOLD-enfelds Now that he was looking for a *shidduch* and most of his prospects were in the New York area, he often made the long trip from Chicago, and was happy to have a comfortable, warm, and inviting home in which to stay during his journeys. And that was the Goldenfeld home.

He loved the fact that they cared about him. It wasn't just that they provided him with room and board, but they knew instinctively when he needed to talk, and when he needed peace and quiet. Yosef Goldenfeld's upbeat and cheerful personality coupled with his wife Leah's wise, motherly advice provided the perfect combination. But one day Yaakov awoke to a completely different type of mood. He walked into the living room to discover a very somber and solemn Yosef. "Is everything all right?" he asked.

In a very sad tone, Yaakov was informed that his host's father had passed away during the night. Yaakov was aware that Yosef's father had been sick for some time, and he was very sad to hear that the elderly man had passed away. Yosef was not crying, but Yaakov sensed how broken he was. Although they had been aware that the end was near, it did not make the reality of it any easier. Yaakov remembered the elderly man always smiling and shared that sentiment with Yosef. Thanking him for his words of comfort, Yosef mentioned that he had to go now and inform his mother of the tragic news. Yaakov offered to help in any way he could and mentioned that he was just running to Shacharis and would return soon.

An hour later Yaakov walked back into his home and was shocked to see his host sobbing bitterly, holding his head in his hands and crying uncontrollably. What surprised Yaakov most was the fact that when he had left Yosef seemed to be under control. What had happened? What could possibly have been worse than the news of his own father's death?

A few moments later, Yosef regained his composure. His eyes were swollen and red; he wiped his face with a tissue and then noticed Yaakov standing nearby. "Yaakov, you are probably wondering why I broke down now and not earlier. Well, I went to tell my mother that her husband had died. And all she could say was, 'Oh.' You see, my mother suffers from Alzheimer's and she doesn't even know who I am talking about." Again he started to weep. "And I don't know what's worse — that my father died or that my mother couldn't care less."

> Yaakov internalized this lesson. And when Tishah B'Av arrived later that year the thought struck home. We have lost our most prized and cherished possession — the Beis HaMikdash. But as we sit on Tishah B'Av and ponder this huge loss, and search for the meaning in it for ourselves and for all Jews, we see many people going about their lives without stopping even for a moment to think about the horrifying loss we have incurred. Yosef Goldenfeld's words ring in our ears: "And I don't know what's worse — that my father died or that my mother couldn't care less." Which is worse? That we have no Beis HaMikdash or that so many of our fellow Jews are totally indifferent to this?

An Early Riser

I N THE WEE HOURS OF THE MORNING, *DER RUSISHER melamed*, Rav Mordechai Leib HaKohen Kaminetzki, could be seen walking the streets of the Shaarei Chesed neighborhood of Yerushalayim. It was the early part of the 20th century and Rav Mordechai Leib was a familiar sight in the area. With his lantern in his hand, he would light up the dark streets of the neighborhood as he went along his way. Often, as early as 2 a.m. in the morning, he would already be in the *beis midrash* learning. Perhaps what was most amazing about this elderly *talmid chacham* was that even as he grew older, he maintained this challenging schedule. No matter what the weather brought, no matter if there was violence in the neighborhood, which was not uncommon in those years, he continued with his early morning routine.

This went on even after Rav Mordechai Leib celebrated his 96th birthday! Some foolishly suspected that — like many old people — he was no longer able to sleep and therefore, having nothing else to do, would go to learn in the *beis midrash*. But nothing could have been farther from the truth. The *"Eltere Kohen"* would readily admit that he would have loved to snuggle back under his covers for some more sleep. But he couldn't.

Rav Shalom Schwadron once asked him about his customary early-morning ritual and Rav Mordechai Leib answered with a sobering thought. "Every night I go to sleep, but the first time my sleep is interrupted, instead of going back to sleep I get out of bed and go to learn in the *beis midrash*.

"You see, it is quite simple. Think for a moment about the *dor hamidbar*, our ancestors, during their forty-year sojourn in the desert. *Chazal* describe the practice of the night of the Ninth of Av. Every year the men between the ages of 20 and 60 would dig their own graves and lie down in them. And every year many of them would not get up. They would die in their sleep. And what do you think was the reaction of those who woke up the next morning? Do you think they rolled over and went back to sleep?

"When I was a young man I came down with a life-threatening illness. My condition was so bad that the doctors gave up hope. They were just about ready to declare me dead when, miraculously, I started to improve. Eventually I recovered completely. But I think to myself that really I should have died. For reasons I will never know the decree was put on hold.

"And now," with a small smile forming on his lips he concluded, "when I wake up in the wee hours of the morning I am thrilled to have the opportunity to live another day. Do you think that I can just go back to sleep? I am thankful that I can get out of bed. And it is this thought that motivates me every morning, no matter what, to go as early as I can to the *beis midrash*."

Torah

Unnecessary Apologies

*T*HE BOYS IN MY CLASS HEARD THE NEWS AND LET OUT a loud groan. "*Chazarah*? Another Rashi?" It is difficult for young boys to appreciate the nuance of a wording in a Rashi or a Tosafos. "If the point has come across, is it really necessary to learn it even more in depth?" they ask. I try to convey to them the importance of every word and, depending on a thousand variables, they either listen or they don't. But on one particular day, I shared with them a remarkable story, and they listened and learned as they never had before ...

There was a volume of Gemara which was found after World War II. Most of the pages were worn and some of them were ripped. Apparently, it had been owned by a person named "Yosef Hatzair" — Yosef the young one. At least that is how the young man described himself. Who this heroic figure was, where he lived, and what he did will never be known. But one fact remains unmistakable. This Yosef Hatzair loved Hashem and loved learning Torah.

The tractate that had been discovered was *Maseches Nazir*. The final page ends with the well-known statement, "*Talmidei chachamim marbim shalom ba'olam* — Torah scholars increase peace in the world." The words which follow echo the desire to "return to" or visit the *masechta* once more. "*Hadran alach Hakusim Ein Lahem Nezirus* — We will return to you, *Perek HaKusim*." It was dated Lag BaOmer 1942.

We can only begin to imagine what type of *siyum* Yosef Hatzair made for himself on Lag BaOmer 1942. Did he munch on a cracker, hiding in an abandoned apartment in the ghetto? Was he alone? Did he have anyone with whom to share his joy? He had completed an entire *masechta*! Was he already incarcerated for the crime of being a Jew? We will never know. All we have left from Yosef Hatzair is a memo, a short note he jotted down in the blank space on the top of the page next to the *Hadran*. It is his legacy, the legacy of the entire Jewish nation.

He writes as follows: "I am eternally grateful to Hashem that I have been privileged to complete *Maseches Nazir* for the second time. But *avakeish selichah mei'Ribbon Olamim* — I beg forgiveness from the Master of the World, *shelo lamadti masechta zu be'iyun kemo she'ar masechtos* — that I did not learn this *masechta* in depth as I have learned other *masechtos*. I'm sorry that I couldn't concentrate so well and delve into the words. The treacherous conditions did not allow me to do so."

> *I read this to the boys and then showed them a photocopy of the priceless volume. Suddenly, they did not need an extra break. They wanted to hear the additional insight into Rashi. They wanted to learn just a little bit more "be'iyun." They yearned to be, even if it would be only for today, a little bit better. They owed it to Yosef Hatzair.*
> *We all do.*
> *Hashem yinkom damo.*

I Believe ...

*F*ROM THE EARLIEST STAGES OF THE CHASSIDIC movement, the mantle of leadership has been passed from a Rebbe to his successor. Each new Rebbe has added his contribution to the movement. The Baal Shem Tov's original approach was expanded by that of the Mezeritcher Maggid which in turn developed into many different avenues of serving Hashem — through *dveikus*, fervor and joy. This approach enabled the simple folk to overcome the barriers that in the past had hindered them in their strivings to reach Hashem.

Among those who espoused the Baal Shem's teaching in following generations was Reb Simchah Bunim of P'shis'cha. He too had many illustrious disciples; the two most prominent were Reb Yitzchak Meir of Ger, known as the Chidushei HaRim, and Reb Menachem Mendel of Kotzk. It is impossible to place them alongside one another to rank which one was superior. Nevertheless, with the passing of Reb Simchah Bunim, the Chidushei HaRim and his colleagues accepted the Kotzker as their new Rebbe.

Of the many masterpieces which the Chidushei HaRim authored, the one which might be identified as his magnum opus, was a *"Mishnah Berurah"* of sorts that he compiled on *Choshen Mishpat,* the laws of monetary matters. He had spent many years sifting through the principles, rulings, and bylaws pertaining to this topic. Nearly 100 years prior to the Chofetz Chaim's historic compilation of and commentary on the laws of *Orach Chaim,* everyday living, the Chidushei HaRim had assembled his lifetime achievement. There was only one thing that he needed, or rather, that he wanted. And that was to receive a *haskamah,* an approbation, from his Rebbe, his contemporary — the Kotzker.

It was admirable that he had accepted a peer as a Rebbe, that he had not broken away to form a new sect. It was both selfless and altruistic. Now he journeyed to Kotzk to present his compilation to his new Rebbe. Upon arriving in Kotzk, he proceeded directly to his Rebbe's home. The Kotzker greeted him warmly and was pleased that he had come to ask for his blessing. He reviewed the manuscript for a few hours. When the Kotzker finally emerged from his room, the Chidushei HaRim was waiting, anxious to hear the response.

The Rebbe shook his head. "Reb Yitzchak Meir, this is a wonderful achievement. Its clarity is incredible. I am extremely impressed by this one-of-a-kind commentary." The Chidushei HaRim beamed with pride. He was so pleased that his new Rebbe had found the work to his liking.

"However, I don't think you should print it." Reb Yitzchak Meir was shocked by these words. They pierced him like a dagger.

"The erudition is outstanding. Nevertheless, if people start to use your explanation, they will cease to use the earlier, more classic commentaries on the *Shulchan Aruch*. So I don't think it should ever come to print."

Without a moment's hesitation, the Chidushei HaRim gathered his precious manuscript and made his way to a shul next door. He walked over to the furnace and lovingly kissed each page as he bid farewell to his masterpiece. *"Brich Rachmana, asher kideshanu … ve'tzivanu lishmoa divrei chachamim* — Blessed are You, Hashem, Who commanded us to listen to the words of our sages."

With tears coursing down his cheeks, he placed each page in the furnace. His Rebbe had spoken. His words were the words of the A-mighty. It mattered not what Reb Yitzchak Meir thought. The only words that mattered were the words of his Rebbe, the Kotzker. The *mesorah*, the unbreakable chain from Sinai, had to continue.

And, indeed, it continues until this very day.

Remembering the Ring

*I*T WAS A MOMENTOUS OCCASION FOR RAV GIFTER AND HIS wife as they, together with their youngest son Yisroel and their grandson Tzvi Feuer, headed off toward Leonard's of Great Neck for Yisroel's wedding. They had been staying in the Park House Hotel in Brooklyn, New York. And now, a half-hour into their two-hour trip, Sruly, as their youngest son was called, remembered that he had forgotten to take along a very important item — he had forgotten the wedding ring.

Somewhat frustrated that he had left the ring back in the hotel, Sruly took the first exit and headed back toward the Park House Hotel. On the way back they experienced little traffic and before long they were in front of the hotel, right where they had started an hour before. There was no reason to panic, as they would still have more than enough time to get to the wedding hall in time for the pictures and the *kabbalas panim*.

But as Sruly and his mother rushed to get the ring from the hotel room, Tzvi, who was sitting in the back of the car, noticed that his grandfather was crying. In fact, he was sobbing uncontrollably. Tzvi leaned forward and tried to calm his beloved grandfather, all the while asking him what was wrong. Finally the Rosh Yeshivah composed himself enough to speak.

"Tzvikele, does it really make a difference if one gives his wife a ring or something else that is worth a *perutah* (penny)? Sure, it is preferable to give the ring, but by Torah law both are valid as a method of effecting a Jewish marriage. So it's not so bad to forget the ring. But just now I tried to recall a *Tosafos* —" At this point, once again, Rav Gifter began to cry and in a trembling, panicky voice cried out, "Tzvikele, *gevalt, ich hab fargessen di Tosafos* — I forgot the *Tosafos*! A *Tosafos* can never be replaced!"

Despite his anguish, however, the Rosh Yeshivah forever remained the great man: As soon as he saw his wife and son coming out of the hotel, he composed himself fully and greeted them with a smile. His personal distress would never spoil the *simchah* for others.

This memorable episode remained embedded in Tzvi's *neshamah*. It had affected him in a very profound manner, so much so that he was unable to repeat the story until moved by intense emotion. When the Rosh Yeshivah ascended to his rightful place in the Yeshivah Shel Ma'alah, his grandson Tzvi was asked to deliver a *hesped* on the steps of the Mirrer Yeshivah in Yerushalayim. Broken beyond description, Tzvi began to speak and this telling memory of his *zeidy* came forth.

Yehi zichro baruch.

This story is an excellent example of the Rosh Yeshivah's legacy. He was the embodiment of learning Torah — learning with a relentless, perpetual, unfailing consistency, allowing nothing to impede his growth. He believed in the ability of young men, even in our generation — no, especially in our generation — to maximize their limitless potential and channel it toward becoming as great as they can be. That is what he believed in most, and that is the legacy he left to the world.

When I related this story to Rav Gifter's daughter, Rebbetzin Shlomis Eisenberg, she shared with me an incident that occurred during the *shivah* for her grandfather, the Rosh Yeshivah's father. One of her father's thousands of *talmidim* came to be *menachem aveil*. He asked the Rosh Yeshivah how he was able to remember everything he learned. Rav Gifter responded that it was not because he had such a phenomenal memory (although he did). Rather, it was because of a fear he had. When he learned a *Tosafos* he feared that this might be the last thing he would learn on this world. And he knew that when he appeared before the *Ribbono Shel Olam,* the Master of the World would ask him what he was learning. He was afraid he would not remember. This overriding concern motivated him to learn and to know and to remember every piece of Torah he ever studied.

Hence, when he forgot the *Tosafos,* he simply could not stop crying.

> *It is no wonder that when the Rosh Yeshivah would recite his special pasuk at the end of Shemoneh Esrei — "Mah ahavti sorasecha kol hayom hi sichasi" — he would do so with heartfelt tears.*

It's Not the Grade That Counts

SHUEY BALSAM TRIED HARD. VERY HARD. BUT AS A 10th grader in Yeshivas Ohr Avraham, he was able to maintain only an 85 average. The *shiur,* although difficult, was understandable. With much effort Shuey was capable of knowing it well. His rebbi, Rabbi Newirth, was very proud of Shuey's tireless efforts to grow in his learning. Shuey was a pleasant young man who made the most of his abilities. A few months into the semester Rabbi Newirth announced that he would be giving a test on the first three *blatt* of the *masechta* they were learning. The test would be comprehensive — covering the Gemara, *Rashi, Tosafos,* and countless *mefarshim.* Studying for the test was a difficult task for a bright boy and a monumental one for Shuey. Still, his rebbi felt it was possible for him to score an 85, maybe even a 90. But it would take a good deal of work, a tremendous effort, and — most of all — a great *chavrusa*.

Generally, Rabbi Newirth did not involve himself with the way in which the boys decided to choose *chavrusos*. Unless there was a problem, he allowed them to navigate their way, on their own, through the process of finding a suitable *chavrusa*. But much to his rebbi's chagrin, Shuey chose to learn with the absolute weakest boy in the *shiur*. Had he chosen one of the better boys he would have had a much better chance of achieving success; by selecting this particular young man to learn with he was in a sense settling for a 70 or so.

One day went by and although the two young men seemed to be learning seriously, they were focusing only on the Gemara and *Rashi*. A second day came and went and the scenario was very much the same. The two of them learned in earnest but scarcely covered enough of the material they would need to know in order to do even reasonably well. Finally Rabbi Newirth decided that he would call Shuey and find out why he had settled for mediocrity. That night Shuey was surprised that his rebbi was calling and anxiously went to pick up the phone. Rabbi Newirth made it a point to compliment him on his learning but then, after his initial praise, he revealed to Shuey that he was troubled as to why Shuey had chosen to learn with this particular boy. Rabbi Newirth felt that Shuey was cheating himself and selling himself short. Shuey was able to sense the sincerity and concern that motivated his rebbi's phone call.

"Rebbi, I want you to know that although now I am certainly no genius, I am much better in learning than I was a mere two years ago. Back then when I was in eighth grade, I was extremely weak in Gemara — perhaps the weakest boy in the class. My classmates were relentless in their criticism. They teased me and cracked mean jokes about how dumb I was. You can't imagine how much pain I was in. And then one day before a test, one of the best boys in the class offered to learn with me. I was shocked. We were not good friends and he definitely did not need my help to do well. I was nothing more than extra baggage for him. In my insecurity I questioned him as to why he would want to learn with a dummy like me. But he insisted. I never felt so good. And although I did not do great by any stretch of the imagination, I did not fail. But more importantly — I felt so good about myself. After years of failure I had finally tasted a little bit of success."

At this point Rabbi Newirth was beginning to understand where the young man was heading. "Rebbi, at that point in time, I accepted upon myself the following promise — that if ever there was a boy in the class who was weaker than I was, whom I would be able to help in learning, then I would do everything I could to help him, no matter what the cost. And Rebbi, a good grade on a test is a very small price to pay."

Rabbi Newirth could not believe what he had just heard. This incredibly sensitive young man had used his own suffering as a means of helping another person. His pain was transformed into someone else's happiness. He could have performed well on the test. But he didn't feel that that was the best way to channel his abilities. Instead he determined that he would rather sacrifice his own grade on a test for a friend's benefit.

> When Rabbi Newirth shared this story with me he could not stop the tears from filling his eyes. I foolishly asked him what grade Shuey got on the test. He looked at me surprisingly, "Does it make a difference?"
> I guess not.

One for Me

I T HAD BEEN QUITE AN EVENTFUL DAY FOR ELI LEVY. THE three-and-a-half-hour trip from Baltimore to Madison Square Garden had taken much longer than it should have, but Eli was excited to be one of the few boys in his class lucky enough to attend the Siyum HaShas. The wait at the door and the checking by the security guards only increased his excitement. But now he had finally made it to his seat in the upper deck and was more than happy just to sit back and read the Siyum HaShas magazine that had been given out at the entrance.

While many of those in attendance came to celebrate their own *siyum* and their own accomplishments, Eli's father felt it was important to come just for the experience. Although the Daf Yomi wasn't necessarily for him — he didn't have the time and felt he would not be able to keep up — he still wanted to join in the *simchah* of so many others. And he was happy to have brought Eli along.

Eli sat in his seat and started to take it all in. He looked around and could hardly believe that this was the "Sports Mecca of the World." And now it was being used to host the largest Torah gathering ever. But just as Eli was enjoying the few minutes of relaxation his father asked him if he would like to go down onto the main floor to receive a *berachah* from some of the *gedolim* who were seated there.

Eli's father was that type. He wanted his son to enjoy every experience as much as possible, and now that he was at a "once in a lifetime" event he wanted his son to meet some very special individuals whom he would probably never have a chance to meet again. But Eli was tired. He just wanted to stay where he was. He had traveled long enough and now wanted to relax. He knew that heading down to the floor and getting back up was going to be a whole ordeal and would take at least 15 minutes. But his father prodded him and finally, when he offered him a prize, Eli's eyes lit up.

Normally, when his father offered prizes, Eli knew the selection was limited. But this time he was told he could get anything he wanted. *Anything? Anything! Should he get a basketball or a Gameboy? A Palm Pilot or a new baseball glove? The options were limitless!* It must have meant a lot to his father to offer "anything," and when Eli said that he was going to choose something very good, his father didn't back off. He assured Eli that if he would go down to the floor and get *berachos* from the *gedolim,* then he would buy him whatever he wanted.

So down they went. They received *berachos* from the Novominsker Rebbe as well as Reb Dovid and Reb Reuven Feinstein. Some of the Rebbes who were present also gave Eli a *berachah,* and then Eli's father had the opportunity to meet some of his old friends and acquaintances. Finally, as the building filled up, Eli and his father made their way back up to their seats. It had taken longer than expected, but Eli seemed to be fine with it. He had smiled throughout and was now ready for the *siyum* to begin.

Eli listened in awe as one speaker after another spoke inspiringly about the monumental event. And then, immediately after Rav Chaim Stein made the *siyum,* beautiful singing and dancing erupted. Eli danced with his father and with others he did not know. He was tired but the smile would not leave his face. The evening lasted a few more hours and then it was time for Eli and his father to head home. It would be a long drive but it was worth it.

It took a while for them to get to their car and a few more minutes till they left the parking lot. But Eli's smile would not leave his face. It was nearly midnight and Eli was about to fall asleep when he called out to his father one last time, "Daddy, thanks for taking me." Eli's father was thrilled that the event was all he had hoped it would be. He also wondered what Eli was going to choose for his present. He wondered how much it would cost him. But he didn't mind. It was well worth it.

As sleepy as he was, Eli wanted to tell his father something important. "Daddy, I decided what I want you to get me. Remember? You promised." Eli's father knew that his son wasn't going to let him forget.

"Daddy, I want you to promise me that by the next *siyum* you're going to be one of those making a *siyum* too."

Eli's father was shocked. He didn't say a word. He just thought about what his son had said — and he decided he would do it. It was about time he made the commitment. And then, about five minutes later, he responded, "Okay, I promise."

But it was too late. Eli was already sleeping. He was dreaming of a father who had made a promise he was going to keep. A promise to give his son anything he wanted.

A Night in Shining Armor

A S REFOEL AND CHANI MENDLOWITZ WERE FLY-
ING over Connecticut on their return trip from Eretz
Yisrael, they sensed that something was terribly
wrong. The stewardesses were whispering and running to the front
of the cabin. What the passengers didn't know was that most of the
Northeastern United States was in the same panic; a huge blackout
had struck many states, and most citizens were sure that this was
another terrorist attack. The passengers' frantic attempts to contact
relatives proved futile as cell phones were rendered utterly useless.
The initial fear lasted only a short while, until they received word
of what had happened and were assured that most likely terrorism
was not involved. The more immediate problem was landing the
plane without any guidance from on-ground lighting.

At first, airport traffic control intended to divert their El Al flight
to Washington D.C., and while that was certainly closer to where
the Mendlowitzes lived — Silver Spring — it still did not help them
because their car was in New York at a relative's home, awaiting their
return. In the end, the passengers were told that theirs would be the
last plane allowed to land at Kennedy Airport. Once they landed, they
were informed that airport security would not allow them to disem-
bark for at least an hour. Hot, anxious, and very thirsty, they were
finally released into a darkened airport, where finding their luggage
was quite an adventure. Tired and exhausted, they finally exited the
terminal and attempted to get a cab. And then the full impact of what
had happened hit them. It was an eerie, discomforting sight: All of New
York was pitch black. No street lights. No building lights. Nothing!

The taxi line stretched for blocks, and since all traffic in the area
was slowed due to the lack of traffic lights, they realized that they
would be waiting for a cab for hours. While they were pondering
their next move, a shuttle bus pulled up, offering to take them where
they needed to go for $18, a bargain compared to the $100 the taxis
had been charging. They were completely exhausted as they settled

in for the short drive. When they reached their relative's home they paid the kind driver and thanked him for his assistance. But when Refoel tried the key he realized it did not fit; either he had been give the wrong key or had misplaced the right one. Now what would they do? It was midnight of this never-ending day, and they were at their wits' end. It was then that they noticed a car parked down the street, with people in it. *Maybe these people live on this street and will let me in so that I can make a few phone calls,* he thought.

Refoel cautiously approached the car. The sight that he beheld brought tears to his eyes. Inside were two men — a father and his son — learning together. They had a set time for their learning, and were determined not to let the blackout change their plans. They had decided that learning in a car, however dimly lit it was, was better than canceling. As for Refoel, these men were a sight for sore eyes; and of course they were more than happy to help the desperate couple.

For a long time afterward Refoel could not get the sight of this father and son out of his mind. *Imagine,* he thought to himself, *in a world of utter darkness, a tiny light shines through like a beacon — the light of Torah.*

Ki ner mitzvah veTorah ohr.

You Get What You Deserve

When Rav Shabsi Frankel proudly showed the Steipler Gaon his monumental revised edition of the Rambam, the Steipler smiled broadly and glowingly declared, "The Rambam and his commentators will wait to greet you in Gan Eden!" Reb Shabsi used his means to assemble the various manuscripts that would help to improve the accuracy and quality of the Rambam. A team of tens of scholars worked diligently for many years on the project. But perhaps what is most amazing about this monumental undertaking is the fact that during all those years Reb Shabsi never held himself higher than the rest of his colleagues and employees. He always made them feel important and integral to the success of the project. The following episode illustrates his refinement and humility.

STORED INSIDE HIS HOME WERE MANY MANUSCRIPTS worth millions of dollars. It had been almost impossible to obtain some of these one of a kind manuscripts. Purchasing them was not only a matter of money but required knowing the right people in the right places. Acquiring these documents from universities and collectors was a process that took many years. And when he finally was able to get his hands on them, the team of scholars was ready to work.

Once, Reb Shabsi was sitting at his table working with another respected *talmid chacham* on a recently purchased manuscript. For hours on end they labored, analyzing the nuances in the scripts and comparing them to one another. This intense process required endless patience and a skilled eye. Noticing the need for some refreshments, his wife brought two cups of coffee, one for her husband and the other for a guest he had brought to observe and help out with the new manuscript. Although Reb Shabsi saw the coffee being brought in, his guest did not, and when it was placed down on the table he inadvertently turned around and to his horror knocked it over onto the priceless manuscript. Not only would it cause a loss of thousands of dollars, but now the documents were rendered completely useless!

Reb Shabsi jumped out of his seat and ran into the kitchen. He most certainly was distressed that his valuable manuscript was ruined, but he did not want to cause his colleague any shame or embarrassment. And so two minutes later he emerged from the kitchen with a fresh cup of coffee. "I figured since the first one spilled, you would probably want another one."

The man smiled. He knew that what had happened had probably caused Reb Shabsi to be disappointed and upset. But he also knew that Reb Shabsi understood it was an accident, an accident anyone could have caused. The Steipler's comment about the Rambam and his entourage greeting Reb Shabsi had never rung truer. *"The Rambam and his commentators will wait to greet you in Gan Eden!"* But maybe not because of the reason we had thought.

A Kallah Meidel

*I*T WAS THE 6TH DAY OF ADAR 5764 AND THE LOUD MEGAphone perched atop the car blared the announcement clearly through the Geulah, Meah Shearim, and Zichron Moshe neighborhoods, "The *levayah* for the *meis mitzvah,* Margalit Gamliel bat Avraham, will leave from Beit HaLevayot at 10:30 tonight on its way to Har HaMenuchot." Who was this woman? Why was she considered a *meis mitzvah*?

Upon arriving in Eretz Yisrael many years before, Margalit had held in her hands a precious heirloom — a Sefer Torah which she had brought with her from her home in Yemen. The Torah had been written hundreds of years before and Margalit was determined to bring it with her to the Holy Land. However, when she disembarked she was greeted by a nightmarish course of events. First, the callous officials took away her most prized possession and informed her that it would be kept for "safekeeping." They then herded her through a door to undergo a medical examination which was required before entrance to the country. During the examination, she was mistakenly diagnosed as having leprosy and was sent to a secluded area. She pleaded with the authorities to reverse their erroneous evaluation but they would not listen to her claims and banished her to the Talbieh neighborhood in Yerushalayim, to the Hansen Hospital that treated lepers. She begged them to let her leave but to no avail. Soon after arriving there, she actually contracted the dreaded, and highly contagious, disease.

Almost no one dared to venture into the hospital. But Rav Aryeh Levin, the famed *tzaddik* of Yerushalayim, made it a point to visit often with absolutely no regard for his own health. His overwhelming love for every Jew made it impossible for him to stay away from these pitiful souls. In fact, long after Rav Aryeh passed away, his son Rav Refael visited the hospital with Reb Efraim Holtzberg, and the patients were brought to tears just by seeing the son of the man who had loved them so much.

Margalit remained unmarried her entire life, but incredibly she did not lament the fact that she would never have a child to call her own. Instead she cried over the fact that her most treasured possession had been snatched away from her so many years before, and she feared she would never see it again. So she contacted the officials at Bituach Leumi. She kept track of how much money she had been allotted over the years and began to dream about the possibility of hiring someone to write a Sefer Torah for her.

Day and night that was all she could think about. She just wanted to recapture the lost magic of the Sefer Torah she had once held in her hands. She finally accumulated the necessary funds and hired a Yemenite *sofer* to write the Sefer Torah. Months went by and she was periodically updated on how the project was coming along; finally, she received the good news. It was finished! The day arrived when she was once again reunited with the holiest of all possessions, and with tears streaming from her eyes she had the *zechus* to hold a Sefer Torah once more. It was as if she were holding a child she had waited so long to have.

After the Torah was dedicated and sent to one of the local Yemenite shuls, Margalit returned to the hospital. She appeared to float around as she sang and danced in celebration of the Torah to which she had "given birth." But her run of incomprehensible suffering continued. One day, as she was sitting in one of the outdoor rooms enjoying the sun and breeze, she was given tragic news. There was a terrible fire in the shul which housed her Sefer Torah — nothing remained.

Margalit was devastated. Her precious Torah had once again been snatched away from her. What would she do? How would she survive? Her life had reached an all-time low. But her indomitable spirit remained strong. She found within herself the will to continue. Ignoring all her afflictions, hardships, and pain, Margalit dipped into her unshakable reservoir of strength and love for Hashem and His Torah — and approached the officials of Bituach Leumi once again with a proposal. She wanted to write yet another Sefer Torah!

When the officials and bureaucrats scoffed at her, she begged them to draw on her future checks, even if it meant that she would never have another *shekel* to spend on herself. She wanted this more than anything. As she put it so perfectly to one of her nurses who pointed at Margalit's ragged clothing, "I was not able to have a child in my lifetime. So I want to leave this over as my legacy. Would I rather come to Heaven with a fresh pair of socks or the most treasured possession of the Jewish people?" And then she tearfully cried out, "*This* is my child!"

Once again she employed a trusted Yemenite *sofer* to write another Sefer Torah. When Rav Elyashiv heard about Margalit's mind-boggling commitment to "her" Torah, he aptly described her, "Sometimes a man is worthy to be described as a '*Chasan Torah*.' This woman has earned the right to be crowned a '*Kallah Torah*.'"

Tehi zichrah beruchah.

Holy Ground in the Holy Land

*T*HE CHEVRON MASSACRE OF 1929 IS ONE OF THE DARK-
est chapters in the Holy Land's recent history. The lives of
many families were altered forever. The Rosh Yeshivah of
the Chevron Yeshivah, Rav Moshe Mordechai Epstein, never fully
recovered from the devastating tragedy and died a broken man five
short years later. But concealed in the spilled blood lies a heroic
story of courage, commitment to Torah, and unyielding faith. It
is the story of the first victim of the massacre, Shmuel HaLevi
Rosenholtz, and his father.

Shmuel was loved by all. While his friends admired and
respected his unusual *hasmadah* and friendship, his rebbeim loved
him for that and much more. His brilliance and desire for greatness
made him the apple of their eye. He was quite literally the dream
talmid. Having traveled from America to soak in the sanctity of Eretz
Yisrael, he had one overriding desire — to learn Torah. Nothing else
mattered to Shmuel and nothing would stand in his way.

When some of the others in the yeshivah would leave the *beis
midrash* early on Erev Shabbos to get ready for Shabbos and to perhaps catch some fresh air, Shmuel just wanted to get dressed and
hurry back for what his soul thirsted for most — Torah. However,
with ominous rumors circulating and the threat of danger in the
air, the *beis midrash* was closed on that fateful day, and the *talmidim* were encouraged to remain in a safe place. Although no one
could have even imagined the terrible events that would soon take
place, the boys were warned to be on guard, to be cautious.

Shmuel approached the building but was disappointed to find
it locked. Actually one man was inside, the *shammas*, but he had
not answered the door. So Shmuel found an accessible window and
climbed into the building for what he hoped would be a pleasant

afternoon of quiet learning. But tragically it would not. Hovering over his Gemara, completely oblivious to the mob which had gathered outside, Shmuel learned, repeating the holy words of the Gemara in a singsong tune — the familiar "song" of the Gemara. Suddenly a sea of stones was hurled into the building, shattering windows and spraying shards of glass in all directions, with one of the rocks hitting Shmuel squarely in the forehead. The frightened *shammas* ran for cover — hiding in a water well — and peeked out to see what would happen. Shmuel, his Gemara now covered in blood and with a trail of blood following him, ran to the entrance of the building and opened the door in an attempt to escape. It was a tragic mistake.

The crazed mob of sword-wielding Arabs screamed fanatically and attacked the helpless young man. Within seconds Shmuel was dead. The barbaric mob proceeded to kill tens of others on that fateful day, one of the saddest in our history. Shmuel's lifeless body remained in a pool of blood on the threshold of the yeshivah building. A few days later, when the area was finally secured, Shmuel Rosenholtz, the outstanding and dedicated *talmid* of the yeshivah, was laid to rest along with the other *kedoshim*.

A few months later, Shmuel's heartbroken father, Avraham Yaakov Rosenholtz, arrived from America and asked to be allowed to enter the abandoned building. The yeshivah had since moved to a safer location but no one would deny Reb Avraham Yaakov his request. And so a group escorted the bereaved father to the place where his son's life had been so brutally cut short. He walked toward the building, stepped inside onto the threshold, and began to sob bitter tears. His declaration is unforgettable. "Avraham Yaakov, *shal ne'alecha me'al raglecha* — Remove your shoes from your feet ... *ki hamakom asher atah omeid alav admas kodesh hu* — for the place on which you are standing is holy." And then Shmuel's father continued his heartrending words: "This threshold is a *mizbe'ach*. It is the place on which my son was brought as a *korban.*" He proceeded to walk toward the exact spot where his son had been learning. The bloodstained Gemara was still open on the *shtender*. The mournful father walked over to the *shtender* and in a choked-up voice began, *"Yisgadel VeYiskadesh Shemei Rabbah ..."*

Hashem yinkom damo!

Kametz and Continuity

*A*S THE ELDERLY RAV ISSER ZALMAN MELTZER danced around the Etz Chaim Yeshivah, his many *talmidim* clapped and sang as they watched him. They knew that their revered rebbi was weak and had limited strength to celebrate Simchas Torah, and were awed at his performance. Rav Isser Zalman had been frail since he was a young man, and continued to be frail and sickly his entire life. But every Simchas Torah he found a reservoir of strength that was unbelievable. He would dance and sing with unusual energy and passion, propelling his *talmidim* to do the same.

As each *hakafah* began to wind down, a *talmid* would bring a chair so that Rav Isser Zalman could rest. As the additional *piyutim* were recited, he saved his strength for the next *hakafah*. Although some suggested that he sit out one or two *hakafos*, Rav Isser Zalman wouldn't hear of it.

As the next *hakafah* began, the crowd watched to see what had inspired their Rav to regain his energy. Rav Isser Zalman walked right toward a little boy of about 4 and held the child's hand. Another little boy gravitated toward them, and joined, holding the Rav's other hand. And then a third and fourth. Before long a circle had formed consisting of an 80-year-old Rav and eight 4-year-old boys.

Eyes closed in concentration, with eight little sets of eyes watching him intently, Rav Isser Zalman began humming a *niggun* to himself. The tune sounded oddly familiar, though no one could identify it. But the circle of children slowly picked up on it and before long they were all humming. Suddenly, and with great energy, Rav Isser Zalman burst out into song. *"Kametz aleph — ah!"* And the thrilled children repeated the refrain after him. *"Kametz beis — bah!"* And again they repeated the magical words. *"Kametz gimel — gah!"* Once more the energized young boys burst forth with their response.

As the beat of the song pierced their souls, everyone present could not help but smile. The Rav, together with the children, danced and sang for the next 20 minutes. Eight innocent souls with a man who, after eighty years, had retained that same purity inside his very own soul. Their hands locked, they merged together in a tidal wave of spirit and emotion. But not another soul joined. They wouldn't dare. Standing outside the circle, the entire adult assemblage watched in awe as the purity evinced by a group of singing children touched the essence of their souls. And perhaps as never before, in the famed Etz Chaim Yeshivah in Yerushalayim, the words of the next hakafah echoed in the hallowed hall: "*Moshe emes vesoraso emes.*"

Faith

Hold on, We're Coming

As a 17-year-old boy, I was privileged to spend Simchas
Torah in Boro Park. The most memorable experience of
the visit was the hakafos on Simchas Torah. I watched
in awe as the Bobover Rebbe, Rav Shlomo Halberstam,
danced in the middle of a throng of chassidim. He
clutched closely a small precious Sefer Torah that he held
so dear. And as he danced around he seemed to be limping, as one leg appeared to drag behind the other. I stood
and watched, mesmerized by the dveikus which was
apparent on the Rebbe's face. I turned to the man standing next to me and asked him why the Rebbe was limp-

ing as he danced. He responded that in his estimation the Rebbe was emulating the Sanzer Rebbe.

*E*VER SINCE THE SANZER REBBE WAS A LITTLE BOY HE had walked with a severe limp. Although he tried his best not to let this affect him, the pain as well as the actual weakness in his leg and foot crippled him physically. As a result, when the Sanzer Rebbe grew older he was no longer able to escort those who came to him for a blessing. When an individual would come to the Rebbe for a *berachah,* instead of accompanying the person to the door, a simple handshake and warm gesture would have to suffice. In fact, even if a prestigious guest would arrive at the Rebbe's door, the best he could muster was to struggle up from his seat and hobble toward the door, but never further.

One time, a chassid of the Rebbe's, a simple man, arrived at his door. He explained that he had come to request a special blessing from the Rebbe because he was embarking on a journey. He was planning to travel to Eretz Yisrael directly after taking leave of the Rebbe. The Sanzer smiled warmly and wished the man well. The Rebbe stressed over and over how fortunate the man was to be able to travel to Eretz Yisrael. As the chassid turned to leave, he noticed that the Sanzer was struggling to get to his feet. He motioned that it was unnecessary for the Rebbe to escort him to the door but the Rebbe insisted. He staggered to the door and followed his chassid outside. Although his foot throbbed in pain, he continued to walk, to limp, to hobble — out the door, down the road, escorting the man even to the outskirts of the village. Each step was excruciatingly painful. And finally, when the Rebbe could walk no more, he called out to the chassid:

"*Shik a grus* — send regards!
Tzu yeder boim — to every tree,
Tzu yeder shtein — to every rock,
Tzu yeder Yid — to every Jew,
Tzu unzere Tatta — to our Father Himself.

Un zug zei — Tell them all: We're hurting. We're limping. We're suffering! It's so difficult. It hurts so much, but we promise — We are on our way. We're coming soon.

Open Eyes

IN THE 1950'S, TRAVELING FROM NEW YORK TO PITTSBURGH was no short excursion. This was especially true for a young widow and her 6-year-old son. Rochel was determined, though. She desperately wanted to take her little Shloimele to visit the town where her cousin's husband served as the Rav. Rochel and Shloime did not have much in this world; her husband had died in a tragic accident a few years earlier and she was struggling to make sense and order out of her life.

Her cousin's husband, Rabbi Yehudah Moses, was a gentle man whose warmth did not compromise his stateliness. His distinguished demeanor made him appear to be much taller than his five-foot-eight frame. Rochel had always been terribly fond of him. And now — she needed many things. She needed a purpose, but more importantly she needed happiness. She wanted to be able to resume her life once again. She had lost so much in her lifetime. As a young woman, just a few years earlier, she had suffered the loss of almost her entire family in the Holocaust. She had begun her life anew and was just getting started when her husband died accidentally. It was terribly devastating, so now she was determined to travel to her beloved cousin to try and find encouragement and hope.

As she entered the Moses' home she was greeted with warmth. Her little boy Shloimele was thrilled to be able to meet these relatives, even an older cousin like Reb Yehudah. Shloimele had no family to speak of, no cousins to play with; his mother had been brutally robbed of her family by a wicked person, a man his mother dared not speak of. So he eagerly waited by the kitchen table as Reb Yehudah and his wife served some cake and tea and began to talk.

There was so much to say, so much Rochel wanted to share. It was so difficult living alone, she told them. She suffered from the loneliness, and was plagued by the constant worry of what the next day would bring. And perhaps most painful of all was having no one with whom to share the concerns. As they spoke, she began to unburden herself. She felt the weight of her fears, doubts, and worries begin to lift a little. She watched as her Shloimele finished his cake and milk and ran into the next room to play. And then it all came out. She poured out her heart. No longer able to contain her emotions, she sobbed uncontrollably. How could she continue? How would she raise her little *yasom*? How would they be able to go on? Finally, she burst out in desperation, "Reb Yiddel, every time I close my eyes all I see is my husband!"

Reb Yehudah watched as Rochel cried bitterly. She tried to regain her composure and as she did he spoke very softly. "Rochel, Rochel. I know exactly how you feel. Every time I close my eyes I too can see only one thing. I see my wife and our two beautiful children who were killed in the *milchamah*.

"And that's why I never close my eyes."

> *Reb Yehudah Moses had also had an entire family, an entire life, before Hitler ym"sh slaughtered his wife and children. But with unfathomable faith he had begun his life anew. He married an orphaned young woman named Chanah Leah, who had also lost everything but her unyielding faith. And Hashem blessed them with a new family. And my dear Bubby and Zeidy could only perceive Hashem's berachos because, indeed, they refused to close their eyes.*

> *And as for Rochel's little Shloimele, he grew up and became an outstanding talmid chacham and a guide to literally thousands of talmidim.*

It's Not Your House

IT WAS JUST BEFORE WORLD WAR II, AND AVRAHAM HAD come to the home of the famous Chofetz Chaim for a blessing. He had traveled a long distance, and was a bit nervous about what the sage would ask him and what he would answer. There was really no way to prepare for the conversation. Whatever happened would happen.

Although he had never before seen the Chofetz Chaim, he had of course heard about his saintliness and piety. As Avraham waited, he thought for a moment or two about which areas of his life needed improvement. Could he daven a bit better? Could he devote more time to his learning? Would he be able to find a little more time in his hectic schedule to help others?

Suddenly the door opened and Avraham was ushered in. He sat down and stared at the giant of a human being in a tiny frame. The Chofetz Chaim asked where he came from and what he did for a living. And Avraham answered each question as carefully as he could. Finally the Chofetz Chaim asked him if he owned his house. Avraham thought for a moment and was bewildered as to why the Chofetz Chaim had asked such a strange question. But he answered truthfully that he did indeed own his home, a comfortable one at that.

"Are you sure you own your home?" The question was unusual, if not pointless. But since it came from a man who measured his words more carefully than anyone else, Avraham just chose to answer it. "Yes. I'm positive that I own my home. I bought it outright." He could not help but wonder what the Chofetz Chaim was driving at. He tried to recall how he had gotten the money for the house and was satisfied that the money used to purchase the home was obtained through honest measures.

A thick silence filled the room as the Chofetz Chaim looked intently at Avraham. Finally he spoke in a soft but firm voice. "Reb Avraham, we don't own anything in this world. Today we might be fortunate to use the house. But we never know what tomorrow might bring. Do you understand what I am saying?"

Although Avraham was quite clear about what the Chofetz Chaim had said, he was certain he did not comprehend the deeper implications. But sadly it would not be long until those prophetic words became crystal clear.

✐✿❧

Town after town, village by village, the extermination was the same. The only difference was the methodology that the Germans used to annihilate the men, women, and children. Would they be forced to torturously await their fatal conclusion? Or would they mercifully be shot and killed immediately? But the outcome was never in doubt. The only question was how it would happen.

When they came to Avraham's village, it was not as if their arrival was a complete surprise, yet most of the villagers had not tried to flee. Although rumors had surfaced regarding the fate of nearby towns, often optimistic news was mixed in, which lulled the residents into a false sense of security and prevented them from fleeing. For many of the Jews in the village, there was simply nowhere to go. So they remained where they were, hoping their fate would never be realized. But tragically that was not to be.

Street after street, the Nazi monsters forced their way into houses, destroying anything and anyone that stood in their way. The pattern repeated itself over and over. The sounds of loud dogs barking and maniacal shouting would be heard as the man of the house was brutally escorted out, with his wife and children crying hysterically. A few loud gunshots and the picture would go silent. The husbands and fathers would be led to the outskirts of the village. There they would be lined up, given shovels, and instructed to dig a large pit, a grave — their own grave.

Avraham was among those who had been separated from his family. When the Nazis broke down his door they threw him to the ground and commanded that he leave immediately. Avraham, a proud individual, tried to protect his family and shouted at his attackers to get out of his house. Just then a sinister SS guard grabbed him by the throat, "It's not your house, Jewish swine. It doesn't belong to you anymore." He threw Avraham to the ground and laughed mockingly as Avraham's head crashed against a chair and began to bleed.

And now, Avraham, shovel in hand, stuck his spade into the dirt, mechanically digging, trying not to think of the family he had lost and of the impending doom he was about to experience. As for those around him, some cried softly, others remained oddly quiet, as if they had already died along with their families and they were just lifeless bodies about to join their soulmates in a much better place. Before long the group of Jews had dug a hole large enough to contain them all.

The men were directed to undress and await their fate. They stood in the cold and waited for what seemed like an eternity. Many cried and whispered words of *Tehillim*. And then the commanding officer ordered his men to fire. The deafening blast of rifle shots splitting the silent air was followed by an eerie, deadly silence. The German soldiers put down their guns and walked away, lighting up their cigarettes in a blatant display of their indifference to the brutality in which they had just taken part.

At first Avraham wasn't sure where he was. Was he alive or dead? Finally, he felt blood dripping down his forehead. He was alive! Miraculously, he had just been grazed by a bullet while falling back a split second before all the others. He waited there for a few hours, unsure if anyone had remained behind. And then slowly, cautiously, he got up, pushed the bodies off him and rose from the dead, literally.

He broke down and cried as he had never or ever would again.

And now, as he reflected upon the prophetic words of the Chofetz Chaim, he began to understand. *"Reb Avraham, we don't own anything in this world. Today we might be fortunate to use the house. But we never know what tomorrow might bring."*

"It's not my house — It never was."

Winning the Lottery

HE SHAPIROS WERE THRILLED WHEN THEY DISCOVERed that Rabbi Koppal would be their Efraim's fourth-grade rebbi. The man's sterling reputation, his *yiras Shamayim,* and his warmth and caring were legend in the community.

Day after day, Efraim came home bubbling with excitement. He hardly had time to put down his book bag before he would launch into his retelling of the day's events, "Rebbi said this, Rebbi said that." His love for learning — and for Rabbi Koppal — was tangible. Reviewing Efraim's notes at home was a thrill for both the child and his parents. Especially unique was the heartfelt manner in which Rabbi Koppal was able to transmit the fundamentals of faith to his fourth graders.

Each day would begin with more than twenty boys exuberantly reciting *Tehillim.* The boys would repeat *pasuk* after *pasuk,* concluding with a *mi shebeirach* for all the ailing individuals for whom they had davened. One day Rabbi Koppal showed up with a bigger smile than usual. His daughter had just given birth to a beautiful little baby boy. The boys sang "Mazel Tov" and danced with their rebbi as he beamed with joy.

The next day a big "Mazel Tov, Rabbi Koppal" sign was pasted on the front door of Yeshivah Emes LeYaakov; as Rabbi Koppal walked through the hallway he was greeted by the warmest wishes of "Mazel Tov!" The entire school was overjoyed for Rabbi Koppal. After all, a first grandchild is certainly cause for celebration. But soon word spread that all was not well with the newborn child.

Apparently the baby had developed an infection and now his precious little life was in danger. Day after day the children in Rabbi Koppal's fourth-grade class cried out their *Tehillim* with a sense of urgency. And incredibly their rebbi was able to not only control his emotions but also continue to teach almost as if nothing were wrong. The situation deteriorated and soon the inevitable happened. The beautiful little child — just six days old — passed away.

The principal of the yeshivah, Rabbi Flegler, heard the tragic news and immediately removed the Mazel Tov sign that had been hanging on the front door. He knew that no matter how strong and wonderful Rabbi Koppal was, this had to be a devastating blow. He called him to tell him how sorry he was, but Rabbi Koppal assured him that he and his family had accepted the decree from Hashem. He planned on coming in that day to teach and would speak to Rabbi Flegler further later in the day.

When he arrived at the school, Rabbi Koppal thanked Rabbi Flegler for his kind words but questioned him about one thing. Why had he removed the Mazel Tov sign? Rabbi Flegler, somewhat at a loss of words, whispered softly that he had removed the sign when he had heard the tragic news of the baby's *petirah*.

Rabbi Koppal looked at his *menahel* while Rabbi Flegler tried as hard as he could to avoid eye contact. "Rabbi Flegler, we were *zocheh* to have a little *malach* for six days. Isn't that cause for a Mazel Tov?" Rabbi Flegler looked at his fourth-grade rebbi and realized now what he had known all along; there was no one he would rather have teaching these boys.

When Efraim's parents heard the heartbreaking news of the passing of Rabbi Koppal's grandson, they were curious as to how the rebbi would react. Would he share it with his class, and if he did, how would they react? After all, they had been davening for the baby for the past few days and knew how sick he was.

But when their Efraim burst through the door with his usual bright smile, they figured that his rebbi must have chosen not to address the situation at all. To their surprise, however, Efraim mentioned that his rebbi's grandson had passed away, and, oddly, he still had a huge smile on his face. "Why are you smiling?" his parents asked, curious about his jovial behavior.

"Our rebbi told us that his grandson was *niftar*. But then he quickly told us that we shouldn't be sad. Don't you see, Rebbi told us that his grandson won the lottery. He gets to go straight up to *Shamayim*." And just like that Efraim ran off to play. His parents looked at each other. They always thought that their son's rebbi was special and unique. Now they knew it for sure.

Waiting for You, Abba

"**P**lease, Abba — Please let me go."

Little Shimshon stood in the doorway and begged his father to allow him to learn in shul like the older boys. It was Shavuos night and Shimshon longed to be like everyone else. He too wanted to stay up all night and learn. But the problem was that his father felt he was too young. After all, he was only 6 years old.

Shimshon cried but his father refused to listen. Six-year-olds could not stay up all night. His father was willing to let him stay up late and learn at home, but he could not stay up all night. The day of Shavuos itself was also an important day for learning, one that was generally ignored because so many people were exhausted from the previous night's learning. If Shimshon wanted to, he could learn all day on the first day of Yom Tov. But tonight was out of the question.

With a heavy heart Shimshon stared out the window as his father headed off to shul. And truth be told, his father did not leave without some sense of guilt. Little Shimshon had been so terribly sad to be left out of this big event that the older boys had been talking about for weeks. His tear-filled eyes broke his father's heart. But then he thought to himself, *Right now, Shimshon thinks the day will never come when he will be allowed to stay up, but soon enough he will be old enough.* Yet, Shimshon's father wavered back and forth on the difficult decision he had made. Finally he arrived in the shul and sat down to what he hoped would be a very special night of learning.

But he just could not stop thinking of Shimshon. He knew how badly his son wanted to come. That image of Shimshon at the window just kept reappearing. Finally he gave up trying to fight his heart — he put on his hat and jacket and headed back home. If by any chance the young boy was still up, he would bring him to learn. It would take about 10 minutes to walk back home and he was almost certain that Shimshon would already be sleeping. But when he opened the door he was shocked.

Standing there at the doorway, all prim and proper, was little Shimshon. It was almost as if he had been expecting his father to return. When his father opened the door Shimshon smiled in delight and held onto his father's hand. "Shimshon, I'm surprised to find you standing here. It's almost as if you knew I was coming back."

"Oh, I knew you would come back, Abba. I just knew it." Shimshon spoke with happiness and joy as he skipped on toward the shul.

"How could you have known? I myself just decided to come back."

"I knew because I davened for it. I davened really hard that Hashem would send you back for me. And I knew He would listen."

And as Shimshon skipped forward, his father stood there, stunned. He was amazed and awed by this child's simplistic faith. *If a child calls out to His Father, he will be answered.* His very young son understood this and utilized it to ask his Father for what he wanted.

It was a lesson Shimshon's father would not soon forget.
In fact, little Shimshon never forgot this lesson either,
and grew up to become the great Rav Shimshon Pincus,
a tzaddik whose whole way of life was a reflection of
this one basic tenet of belief — If a child calls out to his
Father, he will be answered.

Titanic Proportions

AS THE AFFLUENT GENTLEMAN SAT IN THE HOME of the Chofetz Chaim, he looked around the humble abode and could not help but wonder why the legendary sage lived such a simple life with only meager provisions and furnishings. He asked smugly, "Why does the Rosh Yeshivah choose to live such a simple life? Where is your furniture and other belongings? Is this all you own?"

The Chofetz Chaim smiled and realized that he had been presented with an opportunity to teach this prosperous individual a lesson in the meaning of life. "And where is *your* furniture, if I may ask?" The overconfident guest smiled, wondering why the Chofetz Chaim would have asked such a ludicrous question. "My fancy furniture is in my home, of course. Wouldn't it be absurd for me to carry it around? After all, I'm not going to be here forever. I'm here only temporarily." He then looked at the Chofetz Chaim, who was gazing at him with care and affection. Slowly, the rich man understood what he had just said, and was overcome with a sense of shame and foolishness. He had stepped into his own trap. The Chofetz Chaim had chosen not to weigh himself down with unnecessary, burdensome materialistic belongings. Of course he hadn't! The man's own words suddenly reverberated with altogether new meaning: *"My fancy furniture is in my home, of course. Wouldn't it be absurd for me to carry it around? After all, I'm not going to be here forever. I'm here only temporarily."*

The wealthy prospective donor then asked if he would be able to view the yeshivah. The Chofetz Chaim readily agreed and directed him to the relatively humble *beis midrash,* which was bustling with activity. The room was, as usual, packed with young men speaking animatedly to one another, arguing various points and "talking in learning," exemplifying the *Kol Torah* as it was meant to be. But the wealthy layman, instead of expressing his delight and satisfaction, communicated a sense of disapproval and annoyance. "Why are these young men dressed in such plain, simple clothing; and why is it so noisy in here? Can't they speak to each other more softly?"

Once again the Chofetz Chaim sensed that it was an appropriate time to convey the eternal message and credo of Torah.

"There was once an extremely wealthy man who fostered a life-long dream. He dreamt of building a ship of titanic proportions, one in which no expense would be spared. And as he wished, so it was. The builders spent years constructing the magnificent ship and finally it was completed. The wealthy man was invited to view the ornate spectacle and the tour began on the top deck.

"The crystal chandeliers and marble flooring were rivaled only by the golden dishes and silverware. Each design was more original than the next. The ballrooms were exquisite and tastefully done. And so it was with each level he viewed; he was more and more impressed with the splendor and magnificence. Finally, after observing the top three decks of the ship, he eagerly anticipated the opportunity to inspect the lower deck, but those in charge explained that there was no reason for him to see it. The lower deck contained the steam engines. Why would he want to see them? But the man insisted; and when he viewed the dirty caverns holding the steam engines and surveyed the sweating, toiling workers, he wondered aloud why this level could not be converted into luxurious staterooms like the ones he had seen on the upper decks. When he suggested this, they stared at him in disbelief. What a ludicrous thought! How can one think of ridding the ship of the very engines that run it?"

The Chofetz Chaim concluded his story and looked at the mortified benefactor. He now understood it all. Or at least he was beginning to. The world carries on with its material needs and desires that are taken care of in various ways. But what propels it all is the learning that takes place in the Torah study halls across the world, where the budding scholars are working hard, day in and day out, to keep the "engine" running.

The Numbers on Their Arms

More than sixty years ago, the Jewish people experienced incredible suffering — herded like cattle, treated like livestock, and ultimately slaughtered like sheep. The words which we recite each Monday and Thursday in the prayer "V'Hu Rachum" — "Nechshavnu katzon latevach yuval" — had never rung truer.

Nearly all the concentration camp inmates had been branded — like livestock — with an identification number, which served to dehumanize them in the eyes of the Nazi murderers. In the following two stories, we read about survivors who utilized these numbers not as a mark of humiliation but as a badge of honor and distinction — thus bringing about unusual triumph and the ultimate revenge.

THE FIRST STORY IS BASED UPON A LETTER SENT TO RAV Yitzchak Zilberstein. The letter describes a moshav which was comprised mostly of *Shomer Shabbos* families. All workers in the moshav knew that they had to stop their work before Shabbos. Working on Shabbos in this moshav was simply not an option. One Friday evening, however, one of the members of the moshav ran into the shul in a frenzy. Right outside the limits of the moshav a team of construction workers repairing the road were still working as Shabbos approached, and appeared to be in no rush to leave. This member of the moshav had pleaded with the crew to wrap up now and return on Sunday morning but they would hear nothing of it. The bulldozers, dump trucks, and other miscellaneous vehicles rumbled along, and a crowd of protesters quickly gathered. Something had to give, as the two sides were on a collision course.

Finally, the confrontation came to a head as a man in his late 50's, heavily tanned and sporting a healthy build, stepped forward. As foreman on the site he declared that he would be more than willing to continue the job on Sunday as long as he received orders from the "Big Boss." And as of yet he had not. Hearing this, the uproar increased, with no apparent resolution in sight.

Suddenly, a diminutive man stepped forward. Everyone knew Moshe, but he was a quiet person who rarely drew attention to himself. Moshe made his way to the front of the crowd and addressed the foreman, "You're waiting for a notification? Is that what you're waiting for?"

Moshe rolled up his sleeves and it appeared that he was preparing for a fight —although he was the least likely person to revert to physical assault. By now Moshe was standing front and center, staring at the foreman, passion in his voice and fire in his eyes. "Do you need a certificate that we are all Jews and that the Torah commands us to keep the Holy Shabbos?" Bracing for the inevitable, the group prepared themselves for the battle of words to escalate into a full-blown fistfight. But suddenly Moshe thrust his arm forward, "Here it is! Branded into my arm! It is my membership number. It was burned into my arm in Auschwitz so that I would never forget that I am a Jew! No matter what, no matter when!" Pointing to his arm, Moshe screamed, "This is where it is written. Here it is! Is this not enough of a command from Our Supervisor that we can never work on His Shabbos?!" Moshe, his eyes filled with tears, stopped; his heavy breathing could be heard by all. His pain and pride had joined together in one unforgettable moment. Then, slowly, Moshe rolled down his sleeve, turned, and walked away.

Suddenly the foreman ran after him and grabbed him, "I know! I also know!" He too rolled up his sleeve and bared the numbers tattooed on his arm. They stared together at their numbers, and then cried on each other's shoulders. The entire assemblage watched the awesome sight of these two survivors sharing an eternal, unspoken bond. Members of the same "club," the emotional foreman hugged his new friend and promised that not only would he stop working now, but he would never work on Shabbos again!

After all, the "Big Boss" had given the order.

The second story is found in Reb Menashe HaKatan's Haggadah, *Maggid Mishneh*. On the night of Pesach one is encouraged to recount one's own personal redemptions, so Reb Menashe created a section in the back of his Haggadah in which he conveys the personal miracles and tragedies his family experienced.

He arrived in Birkenau on the first day of Shavuos. Although not yet aware of the certain doom awaiting them, a feeling of dread overcame young Menashe. He felt as if he had entered through the gateway to *Gehinnom*. He, his parents, and his sister and her six children were greeted by bellowing shouts of *"Shnell, Shnell!"* and the announcement that they should leave their belongings where they were. Quickly two long lines were formed and before them stood the Angel of Death, Dr. Joseph Mengele, shouting *"Rechts!"* and *"Links!"* — motioning with his finger who shall live and who shall die.

Within a short while Menashe was separated from his family forever. As he was being led away to forced labor he turned and watched as his family was led in another direction. With the gray billows of smoke from the crematorium and the nauseating stench of death permeating the air of Birkenau, a very poignant — but uplifting — thought filled Menashe's mind. *The day of Shavuos is when the Jewish people received a precious gift from Hashem; and today Hashem has received a precious gift in return. On this, the first day of Shavuos, my family did not merit to have a Jewish burial. Much like Nadav and Avihu they ascended in a cloud of smoke straight up to You, Hashem, in Heaven.*

Bikrovai ekadeish …

A short while later Menashe was officially indoctrinated into Auschwitz, but he was no longer Menashe ben Eliezer Zev. He was *A 8274*. When he was transferred later to Buchenwald he received another number. He was also *121926*. In an incomprehensible display of *emunah* in *hashgachah pratis*, Menashe searched for meaning in the two numbers and discovered that if one were to add up each set he would find that each one equaled 21 — the numerical value of the word *"ehekeh."*

Hashem revealed the name *"Ehekeh Asher Ehekeh"* to Moshe — "I will be that which I will be." In other words, "When I am bestowing goodness on My people and when I am seemingly withholding goodness from My people, I am always the same loving G-d." This was the message Menashe carried with him throughout the war, and as he continued to rebuild his life he would always remember it. Even when Hashem's Presence is shrouded in a veil, He is always watching over His beloved people.

A Place You Dream Of

OPENING THE LETTER, THE CHOFETZ CHAIM BEGAN TO read it, and after just a few lines he realized that the writer of those lines was highly distressed. An enlisted soldier, a young man in his 20's, portrayed his life on a remote army base, hundreds of kilometers from the nearest Jew. He complained about his existence, which was barren of all opportunity to come close to Hashem. He had no shul, no *siddur,* no Shabbos, no kashrus, no Torah learning; he feared that he was dangerously close to falling out of touch with *Yiddishkeit* altogether. "Rebbi," his words were filled with desperation, "how can I survive as a *Yid* in this spiritual wilderness?"

Realizing the isolated soldier's precarious frame of mind, the Chofetz Chaim replied with encouragement, warmth, and a lifesaving, timeless proposal. "My dear friend, if you find that it is truly impossible to perform even one mitzvah, if you find yourself starving for the smallest bit of *kedushah,* then there is one thing you must always remember to do. Whenever you have a free moment, face eastward and speak to Hashem. When you face eastward you will be channeling your thoughts to Yerushalayim, thus uniting with your people and your Father. When you face Yerushalayim and direct your thoughts there, you are *in* Yerushalayim! And no matter how far a *Yid* is removed from Yerushalayim, Yerushalayim is *never* removed from him!"

An Ode to Odelia

In "Touched by a Story 2," we related the heartrending story of Odelia Selah, a 5-year-old girl. It was Erev Yom Kippur and Odelia's mother, Mrs. Gita Selah, spoke to some thirty nonreligious Israelis. She showed them a moving video of Rav Amnon Yitzchak pleading with a large audience of irreligious Israelis to accept upon themselves Torah and mitzvos for the sake of a sick young child. They at once came forward in droves and eagerly committed themselves for the sake of a young boy; and a few months later he miraculously recovered. Mrs. Selah begged her audience to do the same for her daughter and after her emotional plea, a little girl who had obviously undergone much treatment hobbled in with her walker. Her big, beautiful eyes glowing, she stood in front of them — and one by one they stepped forward and committed themselves for Odelia.

I FIRST REALIZED THAT SOMETHING WAS WRONG WHEN I spoke to Nissan, Odelia's father, and asked him if I could come get a haircut. "Of course," he replied. However when I showed up for the haircut no one answered the door. I called a number of times but no one answered the phone. Finally, Nissan called me and apologized for not being there when he said he would. Not wanting to pry, I simply arranged for a haircut in his next available slot but when the same thing happened the next time, I knew there was trouble. Nissan said it plainly, "Odelia is having seizures again."

Two weeks later I was asked to deliver a talk to the class which Odelia's mother had addressed, and I shared with them the bad news — Odelia was very, very sick and she needed our help. I began the class by reading her story from the book and then we spoke about the idea that every small thing one does can accomplish great things. As the class was about to end, Shaul, one of the coordinators of the group, asked me to read the story once more. It was difficult to read it again but I made it through as the audience sat and listened — quietly, pensively, and sadly. The next morning, unexpectedly, we saw one another once more. It was to say goodbye to Odelia.

The funeral home was filled; it seemed that the entire community was there. Fathers and mothers together with their children had come to say good-bye to a young girl who had changed so many lives. She had inspired countless *Tehillim* groups and hundreds of others to accept upon themselves various improvements in their collective lives. The first *hesped* was emotional; the speaker described how a young girl could accomplish so much in such a short time. But nothing could brace the crowd for what they would see next. Nissan walked to the front of the room. Just watching a broken father was enough to cause the crowd to break down and sob. But then, in one of the sweetest, purest voices one will ever hear, he spoke.

In a mind-numbing display of *emunah,* Nissan began, *"Shema Yisrael — Hashem Elokeinu — Hashem Echad."* A stunned crowd burst into loud wailing as a calm, composed Nissan continued. And again his pure voice pierced the heavens, *"Hashem Melech — Hashem Malach — Hashem Yimloch Le'olam Va'ed."* As I sat in the second row and softly repeated the words, I wondered if I ever had, or ever would, feel such *kedushah.* And then Nissan, overwhelmed with love and emotion, burst out, "Odelia! Abba loves you."

Most of what Nissan expressed in the following few moments was difficult to understand, but that did not matter. Those assembled had experienced something they will not soon forget. Nissan finished and stepped down; the time had come to escort Odelia one final time. I walked behind the *aron* and followed Nissan and many others as they began the short walk from the front of the hall out to the waiting hearse. As we walked I tried to make out what Nissan was saying. He was crying and it was difficult to hear the words, but when I finally figured it out I was almost certain that he was not speaking. He was singing!

"Ve'atah Vanim Shiru Shiru Shiru LaMelech — Shiru Shiru LaMelech."

During the week of *shivah,* I went to be *menachem avel* and although I was not surprised, I was nevertheless very moved that Nissan himself was helping to get chairs for the many people who were standing. That is just the way he is. I shared with him the sentiments I, and so many others, had felt at the funeral but he dismissed it as if he had done nothing extraordinary. And then as we sat around he revealed a very special conversation that he had had with his children after the *levayah.*

He had come home and had explained to his other children that Odelia went away on a trip. When they asked where, Nissan and his wife explained that she had traveled to *Shamayim.* "But she didn't take any suitcases!" one of the children exclaimed. Nissan replied, "Don't worry, children. Odelia went up with more suitcases of mitzvos and *Tehillim* than you can ever imagine. They are going to have to call a lot of *malachim* to help her with all of her suitcases."

As I was leaving I uttered the words of appropriate comfort and as I was about to leave I built up the courage to ask Nissan why he was singing *"Shiru"* as he was escorting Odelia. His response is a reflection of his sincere faith and belief. "That was the song Odelia loved to hear when we put her to sleep."

Laylah tov, Odelia, laylah tov.

Gevurah /
Courage

Rewarding a Rebbi

YOSEF STERNBERG HAD JUST LEFT FOR A DAY TRIP TO another city, Lodz. He promised his wife and children that he would be back later that day. But when he returned he was horrified at what he found. His home had been ransacked and there wasn't a trace of his wife or his children. Terrified, he quickly ran from house to house along his street, but nothing and no one remained. He tried to compose himself but his heart was torn to pieces. He had dreaded this day — and now it had finally come. The Nazis had taken them away. The more he looked, the greater his desperation. He felt in his heart that he would eventually find them, but knew that if he wanted to find them, he himself had to figure out how to survive. With that intense desire motivating him, Yosef went from place to place and eventually joined the men and boys of the Mirrer Yeshivah, which he had attended as a *bachur,* and fled the country with them.

Years passed and after the war Yosef joined the thousands of others who searched for some, or any, of their remaining relatives. He traveled from city to city, hoping to stumble upon someone who knew something about his family's whereabouts. After a few months of unsuccessful searching, Yosef decided that he would be best off making his way to Eretz Yisrael. Perhaps there he would find peace.

A year passed and then another. Yosef tried to reignite his desire for life but could not let go of the family he had left behind. He thought about them continuously and if he ever stopped thinking about them for a moment, his conscience was wracked by guilt. His heart and soul were tormented. Finally he unburdened himself to his rebbi, the great Rav Yitzchak Zev Soloveitchik, the Brisker Rav. His rebbi reassured him that not only was he permitted to remarry but he strongly encouraged him to do so. The Rav himself suggested a young widowed woman whose first husband had been a prominent *talmid chacham.*

Eager to move forward with his life, Yosef accepted the proposal, met the woman, and soon married her. The Rav was overjoyed that he had been instrumental in helping his *talmid* find some measure of happiness after all he had gone through. The new couple seemed happy and well suited, but after five years, they still did not have any children. Although Yosef and his wife tried to be positive, those close to the couple knew their pain was deep.

Seventeen years passed. Many of their friends urged them to go to the Rav for advice, but Yosef adamantly refused. And then, to their indescribable joy, the couple found out that they were expecting a child. A year later a baby boy was born. Yosef immediately ran to his rebbi to share the wonderful news and the Rav was filled with *simchah.* On his way out Yosef met a friend, one of the many who had been imploring him over the years to get a *berachah* from the rebbi. After embracing Yosef and wishing him mazel tov, the friend asked, "Do you feel there is a particular *zechus* (merit) to which you can attribute this?" The answer was shocking.

"For many years you and many others urged me to go to our rebbi to receive a *berachah* for children. And you probably wondered why I refused to go. After all, what is the big deal? Why wouldn't I go? Well, now I can tell you. When I first came over from Europe, my life was in shambles. I could not let go of the family and the world that I had left behind. Finally I turned to our rebbi for help. He encouraged me to remarry and he himself arranged the *shidduch*. He was elated that he had helped me, thrilled to have been instrumental in removing some of my pain. Had I gone to him to ask him for a *berachah* for children, that would have implied that we were unhappy. And it is possible that this would have caused the rebbi pain, since he was partially responsible for some of that anguish, having arranged the marriage."

At this point Yosef looked at his friend and as tears filled his eyes he cried out, "How could I have caused my rebbi pain just because I wanted a *berachah* for children?

"I want you to know," he concluded, "I think it was that *zechus* which enabled us to merit having children."

This amazing story typifies the difference between this sensitive talmid and the overwhelming majority of even the most well-meaning individuals. I once called an adam gadol to ask his advice concerning a talmid of mine. It was a heart-rending situation and after he guided me as to what to do, he asked me if occasionally I could call with some good news as well. Gedolim take their responsibility seriously. They are nosei be'ol im chaveiro — carry their brethren's burden. It is a difficult load to carry and whenever possible we must do our best to help them shoulder that burden.

Mistakes of Magnitude

*T*HERE IS NOTHING QUITE LIKE IT. YOUNG MEN, MANY too young to be placed on the performing stage, face enormous pressure when preparing for their bar mitzvah. They often invest hundreds of hours of preparation for the day when they will be placed on a stage in front of the entire shul — and sometimes the entire community — to put on the performance of a lifetime. Sometimes boys perform very well on the day of their bar mitzvah. There are boys who *lain* the *parashah* without mistakes, follow that with a flawless rendition of the *Haftarah,* and top it off with a *derashah* delivered like a seasoned orator.

And then there are others who stumble through their *laining,* making enough mistakes to create a rumble through the crowd echoing the sentiment, "Who taught this kid his bar-mitzvah lessons?" His *Haftarah* may be full of various reading errors, and his *derashah* might seem elementary. The third group falls somewhere in between the other two — certainly not excelling but by no means failing.

A few years ago a young boy in Ramat Elchanan attempted to put on his best performance at his bar mitzvah. His name was Pinchos Adler. Pinchos had practiced for months before his bar mitzvah and had utilized every ounce of potential he had. His performance wasn't perfect but he was very proud of himself. There had been some precarious moments throughout the preparation, and at times he had been on the verge of tears, unable to "get it." But now it was over. And he was relieved and by and large satisfied with his performance.

The next week, in the same shul, the anticipation ran high. Meir Froelich was known to be the best boy in his class. He was the one everyone called the night before the test. There were not enough seats in the *beis midrash* for those who wanted to gather around this outstanding young man. He would surely excel on the day of his bar mitzvah. Truth be told, anything short of excellence would be highly surprising.

But the unexpected happened. Not only was Meir not perfect, his performance was average at best. His *laining* was laden with mistakes and his *Haftarah* replete with inaccuracies and oversights. And his bar mitzvah *p'shetel* was filled with incoherent thoughts! It was almost shocking!

Of course there were the perfunctory, "Wow, you did a wonderful job …" remarks, accompanied by the boisterous applause of *"Yasher Koach!"* But for those who were close to Meir, especially his parents and rebbeim, his performance was disappointing. As for Meir's father, it wasn't that he was dissatisfied or let down by how his son had performed; rather, he was curious. He had heard him *lain* and recite his *derashah* that very morning and Meir was nothing short of perfect. It was almost as if Meir were making those mistakes on purpose! So as they walked home from shul that Shabbos afternoon, Meir's father broached the subject. Meir's response was memorable.

"Please don't be upset with me, Abba. You're right. I did do it on purpose. Let me tell you why. Last week my friend had his bar mitzvah in this shul. He's not so smart but he tried his best. And his best was filled with many mistakes. Next week another one of my friends is having his bar mitzvah and he too will try his best but I know that he will most probably do an average job. If I had done a perfect job then everyone would have thought that the other two boys were weak and that I am smart. But I realized that if I also would have a mistake-filled performance then my friends wouldn't look so bad. People would probably figure that this is just the way the bar mitzvah boys perform nowadays."

Meir looked up at his father with the most innocent, pure eyes. "Abba, I hope I didn't disappoint you. Please don't be upset with me."

Meir's father wiped away his tears as he held his son tightly. "Meir, you couldn't have made me any prouder."

A Well-Deserved Honor

ONE OF THE MORE INTRIGUING ASPECTS OF THE Simchas Torah davening is the bidding which is held for the various honors. Every shul has their reliable "bidders" — the movers and shakers who tender proposals for any one of the honors they wish to obtain. But in yeshivos it often works quite differently. The honors are awarded by means of bids which are composed of *blatt* of Gemara.

Moshe Bittersfeld was spending the year in Israel, at Yeshivas Tiferes Binyamin. Being a loyal and caring student, he often called his high school rebbi back home, just to check in. Shortly after Simchas Torah, he decided to call his beloved rebbi to tell him the good news — he had bought *Chasan Torah.* Rebbi was overjoyed. But when he learned that Moshe had bid 1570 *blatt,* he was shocked and thrilled at the same time! Obviously, Moshe had made tremendous growth since his senior year in high school. "Wow, you must have really wanted to be the *Chasan Torah.* I'm really proud of you."

"Actually, Rebbi, it wasn't for me. It was for my friend, Yoni Fleisher."

In Yeshivas Tiferes Binyamin in Yerushalayim, there is an emphasis on transforming the typical young American yeshivah boy into a mature *ben Torah.* Often the boys, as well as their parents, enter the yeshivah with specific plans for the future. While these plans for the future are admirable, and inevitable, they can pigeonhole the young man and stunt his growth. Often a young man in yeshivah undergoes an incredible transformation that his parents, and he himself, cannot possibly have foreseen. Conflict sometimes arises between parents and their child in yeshivah; the child wants to remain and continue learning and the parents feel that the young person has "had enough" of the Israel experience. And sometimes this conflict escalates to the point of serious strife.

Yoni Fleisher and his parents were excited when Yoni went away to yeshivah, but when he began to gently bring up the idea of staying a second year in the program, his parents were just not interested. They informed him that they were delighted with his growth but felt it was time for him to come back home and "get on" with his life. However Yoni, who for the first time was really feeling the excitement and passion of *Yiddishkeit*, did not want to hear of going home. Not now, not when he was just starting to experience something unique and special. But Yoni's parents held their ground and adamantly refused to discuss the matter any further. He was coming home and that was final.

Soon it was Pesach, and the Fleishers were eagerly anticipating their son's homecoming in June, at the end of the school year. When the doorbell rang, they went to answer and were shocked to see their son Yoni at the door — he had surprised them! Their joy was soon changed to concern, however, when Yoni explained why he had come home. His desire to stay in Israel for the coming school year was so intense that he had made the decision to come home for Pesach and stay home until he had earned enough money to pay his own way, so as not to burden his parents.

And that is precisely what he did. His love of Torah was so overwhelming that his parents had no choice but to go along with his plan. And his love of Torah so impressed his friend Moshe that Moshe decided to buy him a gift — the gift of *Chasan Torah*.

A Soldier's Grave

*I*T WAS A SCORCHING JUNE DAY AND YEHUDIS AND HER SISter Joanne walked slowly up the steep incline of Har Herzl as they solemnly made their way to their brother's grave. Their brother, Daniel Haas *hy"d,* a *chayal* in the Israeli army, had been killed in an ambush in Lebanon in 1982. And today a special memorial was being held to honor the memory of those killed in that battle.

There were two other days when Daniel's memory was commemorated — the day on which he was killed, Rosh Chodesh Av, and Yom Hazikaron, the day all fallen soldiers are memorialized in a very large ceremony held atop this very same mountain. On that day thousands of broken family members come together to cry for their loved ones — children, husbands, brothers, fathers — men who have given their lives for their people. Among the mourners are families that have been shattered, and parents who have offered their own personal *akeidah* — and only through unconditional *emunah* have remained true to their faith, and strong enough to publicly declare, *"Keil Malei Rachamim* — G-d, Full of Mercy ..."

The gathering on this June day was smaller, more intimate; the war in Lebanon was being commemorated, and those who died in battle were being honored — honored by a *Kaddish,* a chapter of *Tehillim,* and an endless flow of tears. And even the intense heat of the *chamsin* could not keep these two sisters from visiting their brother Daniel's grave on this day. As they trudged uphill they noticed an elderly Sephardic Jew breathing heavily and sweating as he struggled up the steep climb in the blistering heat. Suddenly, he stumbled and fell. Quickly, the two women ran over to help him and then called to a soldier who was nearby to tend to the elderly man. And as the soldier began to help the elderly man, the two sisters continued on their way to their brother's grave.

Once they reached Daniel's grave they began to recite *Tehillim.* They soon noticed that the elderly man they had just helped was now standing in a nearby row, staring at them. At first they assumed that he was appreciative that they had helped him. However, immediately following the *Keil Malei Rachamim* and *Kaddish* he approached them and asked who they were and why they were standing at this particular *chayal's* grave. They told the gentlemen their names and explained that they were this soldier's sisters.

The old man looked completely bewildered. "But that's impossible. I know that this *chayal* was a *chayal bodeid,* a lone soldier, who had no family members in Israel when he was killed."

The two sisters responded that when Daniel had been killed there was no family in the country, but soon afterward they had moved to Israel. As the conversation continued, the sisters asked the elderly Sephardic man how he knew Daniel. He explained that his son had been Daniel's commanding officer in Lebanon. He then pointed to the grave at which he was standing. It was his son's.

"When Daniel was killed, my son told me that Daniel did not have relatives in Eretz Yisrael, and every year my son used to arrange for a *minyan* to come and say *Kaddish* for him." By now the man was crying. In a tear-choked voice he asked, "What do you do on your brother's *yahrtzeit*?"

Yehudis described the *shiur* that was delivered, the Torah that was learned, the *seudah* they would serve, and of course the *Kaddish* that was recited. When he asked her why he had never seen them before at this yearly memorial ceremony, she patiently explained that they would always hold a larger memorial service on Daniel's actual *yahrtzeit*.

The elderly compassionate man could not stop crying, "But I never knew —"

By now Yehudis and her sister were overcome with emotion as they listened to this complete stranger describe his yearly ritual. "Ever since my own son was killed in battle I have continued the tradition of saying *Kaddish* on this day for this *chayal bodeid*. I never knew you were here — I never knew —"

Emotionally drained, he now looked at the two women and pleaded with them, "Do you promise me you will continue to make sure *Kaddish* is said for him? Promise me — Promise me you will continue —"

When the two sisters promised, this simple, elderly Sephardic Jew walked over to the *kever*, looked up to Heaven and with his arms raised upwards he cried out, "*Ribbono Shel Olam*, Master of the World, You know how faithful I was to this *niftar*. Only You know how I arranged for *Kaddish* to be recited by this *kever*. Today I am giving this responsibility over to these two sisters. They promise to make sure that *Kaddish* is said." And then he looked at them once more and made his way down the hill.

A few months later the man passed away.

The family will never forget the kindness of a simple, elderly Jew who cared for a *chayal bodeid* as if he were his own son.

And — in the *Olam HaEmes* — neither will Daniel.

Hashem yinkom damo.

And how many chayalim bodedim, lonely soldiers, who have not perished but are alive and well — and very sad and lonely — have no one looking after them.

Of Hurt and Heart

I N THE SMALL VILLAGE OF RADIN, WHERE THE CHOFETZ Chaim lived, it was not easy to obtain a set of *arba minim* during one particular year. The community leaders had already tried many times to get at least one set. There was tremendous anxiety over whether they would be successful, and this anxiety was shared by everyone in the village. So far, everyone's valiant efforts had proved fruitless. What would they do? As if this were not cause enough for concen, it seemed that the venerated Chofetz Chaim himself would not have the holy items for Yom Tov.

Some frenzied last-minute cables were sent to outlying areas and finally there was good news. A *lulav* and *esrog* set would arrive the next day by train — just in time for the first day of Yom Tov. The news spread quickly throughout the town and the elation grew. They were going to have an *esrog* and *lulav* after all! Children ran through the streets spreading the news and husbands ran home to inform their wives.

Perhaps they had been spoiled in the past, with each family possessing their own set. After all, some towns were not fortunate enough to have even a communal *esrog*. And now they had come to appreciate what they had always taken for granted. It was decided that the Chofetz Chaim would be presented with the set and the community members would line up in shul one by one to perform the mitzvah.

The first day of Succos arrived and the entire population of the village came to shul early, eager to make the *berachah* over the *minim*. The Chofetz Chaim, like everyone else, stood in line. After everyone was finished saying their *berachos* over the *lulav* and *esrog,* it was decided that the Chofetz Chaim would hold the set during the reciting of *Hallel*. But when the leaders of the community presented the *lulav* and *esrog* to the great sage they were startled by his response — he declined the honor.

The communal leaders were stunned. Why would the Chofetz Chaim refuse to hold the *lulav* and *esrog* during the recitation of *Hallel?*

The Chofetz Chaim looked at the growing crowd and spoke from his heart. "I am honored that you have chosen a simple Jew like myself to be the fortunate one to own the set of *arba minim* and to use them during *Hallel*. But while initially shaking the *lulav* is a mitzvah, after one has fulfilled that duty, any additional shaking is only a custom. And what right do I have to perform a custom, as time honored as it may be, at the expense of another Jew. No doubt there will be some who are jealous that they do not have their own sets and flaunting mine will only cause them additional pain."

They looked at the *esrog,* the citrus fruit that represents the heart of a human being, and now — ironically, as they began *Hallel* with nary an *esrog* in hand — they understood more than ever what the *lulav* and *esrog* were all about.

From Bloodshed to Bucharest

"*R*EBBE! THE TOWN IS ON FIRE! THEY'RE MUR-DERING *Yidden* in the streets!" Those chilling words pierced the early morning silence in the city of Yas, where Rav Yaakov Yosef Twerski, the Rebbe of Skver, resided. The people had heard rumors of the atrocities that had taken place in nearby villages, but could not imagine that this would happen in their town. But now the unimaginable was happening and the fear was all too real — the Nazi murderers were making their way through the town, systematically eliminating anyone in their way.

The soldiers marched into homes, searching for Jews who might be hiding. They emptied each and every house, apparently focusing on finding the men of the community; the women and children who were found were sent out and ordered to stand on the road. By early afternoon the Nazis arrived at the Rebbe's home. They immediately ransacked the house and, finding the Rebbe, pounced on him, tearing at his clothing and dragging him through the street by his beard and *payos* like a rag doll. Despite the indescribable pain, the Rebbe did not allow even the smallest cry to issue from his lips. He was dragged to the edge of the road where the women and children were standing. Most didn't speak. Mothers held their young ones close by as the leader of the soldiers barked orders at the terrified group.

The Nazis knew all too well that the Jewish people looked up to their rabbis and considered them their spiritual and emotional leaders. And so, the sadistic beasts used to make an example of the rabbis. Rav Yaakov Yosef Twerski was no exception. They brought the 45-year-old Rebbe to the front of the crowd so that all could see him, and then one of the guards smashed him over the head with the barrel of his revolver. The Rebbe fell to the ground with a thud. Blood spurted from his head and his yarmulka fell off. He opened his eyes, the blood blinding his vision, and reached with trembling hands for the precious yarmulka, replacing it on his head. When he staggered to his feet, the enraged soldier struck him once more — this time even harder.

Again he fell to the ground as the villagers watched in horror; their beloved Rebbe was being tormented by a group of savage beasts. The Nazis mocked and taunted the great man who couldn't even see them, so much blood was pouring from his skull. Again, with amazing courage and strength, he felt his head uncovered and reached out to grab hold of his bloodsoaked yarmulka. He clutched the drenched yarmulka once again, placed it on his head, and in a heroic act of defiance stood up proudly.

The community watched, knowing all too well what would happen next. The furious soldier, eyes bulging in rage, brought his revolver down in a thunderous blow on the Rebbe's head. And again the Rebbe fell to the ground in a heap. Once more his head was bare and this time he knew that if he would dare to replace his yarmulka he would be killed in an instant. Instead he thought of an ingenious idea. If they wanted to make a fool of him he would allow them to do so, but not at the expense of his head remaining uncovered. With trembling hands he reached into his pocket, removed a white handkerchief and wrapped it around his head. With the bloodstained handkerchief atop his head the Rebbe looked quite absurd, and this somehow pacified the soldiers for a moment. Incredulously, they spared his life. The men were then taken captive and brought to the police station while the women and children were let go. The casualties were great as many of those who "got in the way" were simply disposed of.

The day after the pogrom in Yas, a picture appeared on the front page of the newspaper depicting the "Rabbiner" who looked like a clown — to the Nazis. But to all of his own people, the Rebbe had managed to make a glorious moment out of a tragic scene, and no one would ever forget it.

His life somehow miraculously spared, the Rebbe and his family soon thereafter made their way to Bucharest, Romania, where they settled and created a home which, after the war, served as a haven of hospitality, refuge, and protection for many distraught and downtrodden Jews. Those who had lost their belief in humanity had it restored in the sanctuary of the Rebbe's home.

One particular person who found refuge in the Rebbe's home also found much more; young Aharon was found walking aimlessly through the streets of Bucharest. He had lost his entire family and had been starving for days. Someone who saw him suggested that he go to the Rebbe's home — and he did, being desperate enough to try anything. He stood outside the house peeking in when he heard the warmest words he could remember in a long time, "*Bochurel, kum arein und vasht zich* — Young man, come in and wash."

He washed, sat down, and was served a piping hot meal. He could not believe that someone was actually feeding him, and ate ravenously. More than his body, his soul was warmed and revived by the atmosphere of this home, as he experienced a warmth for which he had truly been starving. As he finished eating, the rebbetzin looked at him and asked if he would care for more. At this point the young man burst into tears. That very question reminded him of the mother he no longer had, of the love and caring that he so desperately missed. He sobbed bitterly, feeling more than ever the pain of his loneliness. His entire family had been ruthlessly murdered and he doubted that he would ever feel that sort of affection again. As he continued to cry uncontrollably, the worried rebbetzin called the Rebbe to speak to the young man. She had tried to calm him but it was to no avail. The Rebbe then put his hand on the boy's shoulder. Aharon looked up and saw that it was the Rebbe himself who was providing the comfort, and fell into the man's arms. As the Rebbe held him, he whispered the most memorable words this young man would ever hear. "It's all right, *bochurel*. From now on you will eat from my bread and you will drink from my wine." And the Rebbe held him tightly and continued, "And from now on *bochurel*, you will be my son."

A promise he would always keep.

A Korban for Shabbos

WHEN A PARENT LOSES A CHILD, THE PAIN IS overwhelming, devastating. These days, thanks to advances in medicine, this hardly ever happens; but years ago, many children would not make it past their childhood years. And even when they did, disease and malnutrition would often claim them before they reached the age of 20.

Rav Yosef Chaim Sonnenfeld and his rebbetzin had already lost six children when their son Shmuel Binyamin fell ill. The situation quickly deteriorated and one Erev Shabbos Shmuel Binyamin passed away. His father quickly arranged for someone to "guard" the body until after Shabbos and he made his way back to his home. As he approached the house he prepared to face his family. Although he wanted to spend time sharing his pain with his wife and children, he could not afford himself that luxury, for it would soon be Shabbos. With indomitable strength he put on his Shabbos clothes, gave them the sad news, and then went on to wish his entire family a "Gut Shabbos." Although his pain was deep and intense, Rav Yosef Chaim refused to allow it to show. With unbelievable courage, he steeled himself into carrying on as usual.

After davening he greeted everyone in shul with his customary "Gut Shabbos." The congregants, although they knew that Shmuel Binyamin was very sick, did not suspect that he had passed away, such was the Rav's fortitude. Throughout the rest of Shabbos, Rav Yosef Chaim conducted himself in his usual manner — with normal *zemiros* and normal davening — not once hinting at or discussing the tragedy that had just taken place.

After *shalosh seudos,* Rav Yosef Chaim walked slowly to shul to daven Maariv. The moment Maariv was over he fainted. The impact of what had happened now hit him. The *levayah* was immediately arranged and those who were close to Rav Yosef Chaim felt that a man his age, with all that he had endured, would be better off not attending the funeral. They felt it would endanger his life to attend such an emotional event. But Rav Yosef Chaim insisted on escorting his son. He was once again bringing a sacrifice to Hashem — his very own *Akeidah* — and he knew it was preferable for the owner of the *korban* to be present throughout.

Guessing With Guests

We often find that great acts are really very simple ones. A hand extended, a phone call made, a visit — these are simple tasks that everyone is capable of, and that can change someone's life. What makes these deeds so special is the fact that the one doing them recognizes a need of a fellow human being and acts to meet that need. It is quite simply a mind-set — always looking for opportunities to help others. One example of this is the mitzvah of hachnasas orchim, hosting guests in one's home. The following two episodes are related, and exemplify the patience and unassuming greatness of two extraordinary hosts.

I T WAS ALREADY WELL AFTER MIDNIGHT WHEN YECHEZKEL Rothstein, a middle-aged man from Yerushalayim, arrived in Bnei Brak. He walked from house to house, trying to find one with a light on inside, since he did not know anyone in Bnei Brak and needed a place to stay for the night. After a while he chanced upon the home of the Steipler Gaon. He tapped lightly and almost immediately the door was opened by the Steipler's daughter. She directed him to the famous Lederman's Shul where she was sure that the man would find someone to assist him further. He thanked her for her time, and apologized that he had come by so late.

He arrived at the shul, but it was empty. With nowhere to sleep and a long night ahead of him, he decided to make good use of the time and opened a Gemara to begin learning. Attempting to learn, he found it quite difficult, as the hour was late and the shul was eerily quiet. Suddenly he looked up and saw none other than the Steipler Gaon himself standing in the doorway. He was breathing heavily and leaning on a cane. It had been nearly an hour since

Yechezkel had left the home of the Steipler and he was shocked to see the elderly Rav here in the shul. "I've come to invite you to stay in my home."

Yechezkel was astounded. The Steipler, already in his 80's, explained that when he had discovered that a guest had come to his door, he was upset that the man had been sent away. So he himself went to retrieve the "homeless" man and invite him to stay in his own room for the night! On the way back to his house, the Rav would not afford himself the luxury of stopping to rest on the bench along the way. After all, his guest was waiting.

The next morning after davening he insisted that Yechezkel return to his home for breakfast; after all, "Receiving guests is greater than welcoming the Divine Presence of the A-mighty Himself."

When this story became known and many expressed amazement at the *mesiras nefesh* of the elderly sage, he simply dismissed it, "Next thing you know they will be flabbergasted when I put on *tefillin*."

Perhaps what best epitomizes the selflessness of the Steipler Gaon is an incident related to the written correspondence the Rav had with Rav Mordechai Gifter. In a stirring eulogy that Rav Gifter delivered for his esteemed colleague, he spoke about the letters they used to write each other, a correspondence that ended eight years prior to the Steipler's passing. Rav Gifter explained that every week they would write to each other, but once a few weeks passed until he received a letter back from the Steipler. The Steipler apologized for not having written but explained that he had not been able to find a messenger to deliver the letter and as such had to bring the letter to the post office himself. And the difficulty he experienced while walking prevented him from getting to the post office sooner. Rav Gifter was astounded. Here was a man surrounded by so many people, individuals who were anxious to do anything and everything they could for him — many of them his own grandchildren. But he refused to allow himself the benefit of asking someone to do something for him, even

delivering a letter. When Rav Gifter read this he sadly decided to end their written correspondence.

A man who carried the burden of Klal Yisrael on his shoulders did not feel it was below his dignity to carry his own letter to the post office.

The Steipler revealed his own admiration for the exemplary *hachnasas orchim* of Rav Yitzchak Grodzinski, a famous protector of the deprived and unfortunate in the city of Warsaw before World War II. Once, a poor, famished mute man appeared on his doorstep. The man was unable to communicate, but no words were needed to understand his plight. While most people ignored him and blamed his lack of communication on his unstable emotional state, Rav Yitzchak welcomed this impoverished man into his home. That in itself is noteworthy, but what Rav Yitzchak did next best personifies his unique dedication and commitment to the mitzvah of *hachnasas orchim.*

Rav Yitzchak asked the man if he was hungry. The mute fellow nodded in affirmation. Then Rav Yitzchak asked him very gently if the food he wanted to eat began with the letter *aleph.* When the man signaled that it did not, Reb Yitzchak — displaying Herculean patience — asked him if it started with the letter *beis.* And this continued throughout the entire alphabet! He would say the letter and the man would respond either in the affirmative or the negative.

When the letters had finally been appropriately identified, Reb Yitzchak went into the kitchen and emerged with every possible food he could think of that began with those specific letters. The voiceless man could not articulate his profound thanks for this wonderful host, but the glowing expression on his face said it all.

Thunder and Lightning

I T WAS 1929 AND THIS WAS THE EVENT OF THE DECADE. After years of planning, collecting donations, and building the royal palace of Torah in all its grandeur, Yeshivas Chachmei Lublin was ready to occupy its new building. Rav Meir Shapiro, the Lubliner Rav, had the vision to build a yeshivah where young men would have a place to learn, to eat, and to sleep — all within the same building. Those wishing to enter into the hallowed halls of the yeshivah were required to pass a very stringent entrance exam — they had to know 200 *blatt* of Gemara! Only the very best boys were accepted.

The elite of the Torah world came to partake in the *Chanukas HaBayis* of this revered institution. Over 50,000 people flooded the gates of Lublin to join in this historic occasion. The crowd waited for the event to begin, but it was delayed because Rav Meir Shapiro was meeting with another Torah giant, discussing a certain urgent matter, and the festivities could not move forward until the meeting was over.

Rav Yisrael of Chortkov arrived at the yeshivah and was greeted with appropriate honor and respect. But he immediately asked for a private audience with Rav Meir. The two entered Rav Meir's private chamber and began to talk. "Reb Meir, while this is an incredible event I am very concerned about something. You are aware that when the first set of *Luchos* were given to *Am Yisrael* they were given in a grand fashion. There was thunder and lightning and the loud, blaring sound of a shofar. Because of all that, there was an *ayin hara* and the *Luchos* were ultimately destroyed." He then turned to Reb Meir. "I'm worried about an *ayin hara*. The greatest Torah scholars have gathered here to celebrate the opening of the most beautiful yeshivah ever built. It is frightening to think of the ramifications of the *ayin hara* in this situation."

Reb Meir looked at the Chortkover Rebbe and asked him, "Don't you think that Hashem knew that the glorious spectacle, the magnitude of *Matan Torah*, might result in an *ayin hara* causing the *Luchos* to be broken? So then why did He not just give them quietly without any fanfare?"

The Rebbe was quiet as he looked at Reb Meir, eagerly waiting for an answer to the piercing question just posed.

Reb Meir's face glowed with the fire of Torah. "There is no question that Hashem was aware of the possible dangers. But the Talmud, in *Zevachim* 116a, states that the Giving of the Torah was seen by the entire world, and the *Kiddush Hashem* that it made on all those present was worth it — even if it meant the *Luchos* would be destroyed later! So it seems that Hashem was willing to chance His own handiwork being destroyed as long as the Giving of the Torah would make a *Kiddush Hashem* and an indelible impression on those who witnessed it."

In a legendary display of commitment to Torah, Reb Meir concluded, "I too am willing to accept upon myself the possible *ayin hara*. I am willing to sacrifice and be *moseir nefesh* for the honor and glory of Torah."

The Chortkover felt the sanctity of Reb Meir's words, and his dedication to Hashem and His Torah. He then turned to Reb Meir, "So let us go out to the crowd and begin."

A few years later Rav Meir Shapiro was taken from this world at the young age of 47.

The Luchos were broken …
but the Kiddush Hashem remained forever.
Yehi zichro baruch!

My Brother Meir

THE YANKELOVES LIVE ACROSS THE STREET FROM US and somehow, I always knew they were special people. They seemed not to care about "things" but about spirituality. I always admired them, but never expressed that admiration. I remember clearly when their oldest son, an outstanding young man, celebrated his *aufruf* in shul. His father got up and began his *derashah* not with a joke or a story but with a declaration, "My son is in love with G-d and His Torah."

That says it all! I thought to myself back then. What more could a father possibly hope for than to be able to declare that his son loves Hashem and Torah? But as I got to know the Yankeloves over the years, I began to realize how much effort it takes to become this type of family — to be able to overcome all challenges, no matter how difficult, by maintaining their faith in Hashem and their love for one another. But perhaps what makes this family so unique is that they attribute their successes to everyone but to themselves.

I once heard that a *neshamah* is able to choose which family it will join. But one thing we know for certain is that the Almighty chooses which parents and which family is best suited to help that *neshamah* make it through the world. This most certainly holds true with the Yankeloves. But I have written more than enough in my own words. Chavi, their daughter, says it in a much more meaningful way. She gave this speech to her classmates in the Bais Yaakov of Baltimore. It is a lesson to us all.

"The story which I am about to tell is one through which my family and I have grown tremendously. My story is a very personal one. It is a narrative of trials and effort, and now after so many years, I feel ready to share my experiences of growing up with an autistic brother.

"When I was 2½ years old, my mother gave birth to a beautiful baby boy, my darling Meir. It is very difficult for me to describe Meir's personality because my memories of his early years are very few. However, my parents often told me that Meir was a happy child, full of life and vitality — and very bright.

"But when Meir was around 2½, tragedy struck in our home. Meir ran a high fever for two days; the doctors reassured my mother and told her not to worry. But the sparkle in Meir's eyes had disappeared. It was replaced by a forlorn, distant, glazed look. He no longer responded to his name, and simple motor skills like holding a fork became impossible for him. His communication skills were gone and he was unable to share his pain and frustration. My parents were devastated. They felt as if they had lost their Meir. And finally a specialist diagnosed Meir as low functioning, autistic, and retarded.

"For two years my parents searched for a cure for autism. But in the deepest recesses of their hearts they knew that the mental damage he had incurred was almost certainly irreversible. Then came the most painful yet pivotal moment in our lives — acceptance. We had to accept that Meir would not be cured. We knew we must strengthen ourselves if we were to endure. We had to learn how to give endlessly to Meir without so much as receiving a thank-you. We had to accept that my mother would not be able to attend our poetry recitals and class plays. And we had to accept that often our mother would be unable to join us for our Shabbos meals because somebody had to watch Meir. And finally, we needed to learn to accept the fact that at times we would have to take from the kindness of others.

"While Meir was living at home, the unending kindness we received made us appreciate that we were *Yiddin*. Often high school girls would come over to take Meir to the local playground, in order to give my mother a break. My neighbors would come over Shabbos morning when the men were at shul so that my mother could prepare the Shabbos meal. They sang to Meir and showered him with incredible amounts of love. And anytime our family celebrated a *simchah*, my whole neighborhood would help to prepare it as if it were their very own because they knew that my mother could not do it alone.

"If I were to make a list of the kindnesses done for my family the list would go on forever. Over the years we have learned to give and we have learned to take. And we have always had one constant in our lives — to remain strong as a family unit.

"My mother would function on three to five hours' sleep a night because she would stay up with Meir. And yet there was always a warm supper waiting for us. We always had a feeling that she was there for us when we needed her. I was never forced to watch Meir and was always encouraged to go out and have a good time with my friends.

"Last year, around Succos time, Meir became too difficult to manage and he was placed in a residential home in Rockville, Maryland. Last year was a very painful one for me because — I know this may sound strange — I honestly missed my Meir. Our daily hugs were a highlight of my day. I missed the constant noises he made and I couldn't stand how quiet my house had become. I knew I could not just go out and do *chesed* for others; I needed to heal and adjust to my new existence before I could help others. Once again I had reached a pivotal stage — acceptance.

"It's been a little over a year since Meir has been placed in a home. I visit him occasionally but I have to admit that it is very painful for me every time I see him. I now realize how much Hashem has given me and what a sad life he has. I have been blessed with a functioning mind, the ability to communicate with others, and the facilities to enjoy the world around me.

"I daven that Hashem should watch over Meir and all others like him in the way only He can, because they are innocent and incapable of defending themselves. My *berachah* to all of you is that you should be able to use your capabilities to your fullest potential. May we strengthen each other to build this world into a healing place for everyone."

Mitzvos

Ready – Aim – Fire!

*A*S A YOUNG MAN, YAAKOV YISRAEL WAS confronted by many major challenges and obstacles. He was one of the many Orthodox Jews who were coerced into joining the Russian army, which meant that Yaakov Yisrael had to spend time with soldiers who were violent and vicious men. Their sinister attitude toward him had filtered down from the commanding officer, who made no effort to hide his dislike for Yaakov Yisrael and his annoyance over all the problems this Jewish soldier had caused.

From the food that he refused to eat to the special days he made himself unavailable for work and duty, Yaakov Yisrael threw a monkey wrench into the scheduling, order, and regulations which are so fundamental to army life. Constant adjustments were required to accommodate this one Jewish soldier and his fanatical religious belief. But since the resilient Yaakov Yisrael combined his staunch, unfaltering convictions together with a sensible low profile, more often than not he was able to stay out of harm's way.

The additional guard duty he accepted upon himself coupled with some extra sharing of responsibilities enabled him to obtain furloughs for Shabbos and Yamim Tovim. But when Officer Karlenkiev watched this soldier rest while others were working, it made his blood boil. And finally he decided he would do something about it. He would make life miserable for the Jew.

The next Saturday, Karlenkiev made it his business to cross paths with the Jewish soldier. As was customary for his Shabbos duties, Yaakov Yisrael was keeping guard duty without violating any of the thirty-nine Shabbos prohibitions. Suddenly Karlenkiev appeared. Without explaining why, he ordered Yaakov Yisrael to fire his gun at a target located fifty meters away. It was not a day designated for target practice and there was no valid reason for Karlenkiev to have issued the order other than to disturb the Jewish soldier's day of rest.

As the startled Yaakov Yisrael mulled over his options, the spiteful commanding officer added that he should continue shooting until he hits the bull's-eye in the middle of the target. This demanding feat was no easy task for a seasoned marksman, let alone a novice like Yaakov Yisrael. This further complicated the dilemma, as Yaakov Yisrael reasoned that perhaps he had some minuscule chance of hitting the mark while shooting with his good right hand, which would be a major desecration of Shabbos, an *issur d'Oraisa*. But he had decided to shoot with his left hand. This would mean that he was shooting with a *shinui*, and therefore creating less of a desecration of the Shabbos, as it would only be an *issur d'Rabbanan*. But shooting with his left hand, he knew, would likely greatly lower his changes of ever hitting the mark. Thus he was left in a quandary — one *issur d'Oraisa* or many *issurei d'Rabbanan*.

At first he attempted to defy the order. But Karlenkiev promptly informed him that disobeying a command from a superior officer could result in a severe punishment, possibly even death! Left with no choice, Yaakov Yisrael prepared to shoot.

He deliberated and then quickly resolved to fire his gun with his left hand. True, in all probability he would not succeed and would be forced to shoot many times. However he determined that it is his responsibility to do everything within his power to reduce the gravity of his sin. He knew that he most probably would be forced to discharge his firearms many times but he hoped and prayed that the A-mighty would have his bullet meet its mark.

Yaakov Yisrael aimed his gun and prepared to shoot. Karlenkiev noticed that the Jew was not shooting with his stronger hand, instead he was using his weaker one! *What a fool!* he thought to himself. *Doesn't he realize he'll be forced to shoot many times until he hits the mark?!*

But when the gun discharged, all present were shocked to discover that the bullet had indeed hit the center of the target!

Yaakov Yisrael tried to hide his smile. He was certain that the Hand of Hashem had guided his hand to shoot the gun so that the bullet landed exactly where it needed to.

The only one more surprised than Yaakov Yisrael was the menacing officer who had orchestrated the plot against him. Karlenkiev stared at the Jewish soldier as it dawned on him that this was no religious fanatic, rather someone who was guarded and blessed by a Higher Being.

From that moment on, Yaakov Yisrael was treated like a hero. Karlenkiev watched out for his well-being and, ironically, became his greatest proponent. However, since he now would no longer work at all on Saturdays, the other officers felt that it would weaken the morale of the other soldiers to have an individual around who was not fulfilling his duty. Thus the only logical solution was to give him an honorable discharge from the army.

The Jewish soldier eventually made his way to Eretz Yisrael, where he grew in Torah and mitzvos to become a leader of many — for Yaakov Yisrael was Rabbi Yaakov Yisrael Kanievsky, the Steipler Gaon.

All because of a gunshot — the shot heard 'round the world.'

Mentchen ... and the Moon

Like it does today, the outside world lured the Jewish youth of the early 1900's; but unlike today, they were not lured to permissiveness and glamour, but rather to many dangerous "isms." Communism, Socialism, and Secular Zionism, in addition to the Jewish Haskalah movement, were just some of the dangerous progressive groups that lured the young away from the traditions and Torah lifestyle of their parents. Tragically, hundreds of souls searching for meaning found their way to the meeting places of these factions. No family could assume that they would remain untouched by the new free-thinking movements.

Reb Shimshon Pincus, in his recently published "Shaarei Emunah," shares an episode in which he and Rav Hillel Zaks took a trip to Be'er Sheva to visit Reb Hillel's cousin, a granddaughter of the Chofetz Chaim, a woman who had lived almost her entire life in Russia, and who was drawn to an "ism" — the Haskalah movement.

I
T WAS FASCINATING TO MEET HER. SHE SHARED MANY incidents regarding her grandfather which she remembered from her childhood. The two cousins caught up on the years and miles that had distanced them. Finally she related a telling conversation which took place between her grandfather and herself.

The year was 1917. The world was at war. And she too was waging her own internal battle. She had been raised in the spirit of the age-old traditions of Torah. But then she was introduced to the laissez-faire attitude and liberal thinking of some of her newest friends. A conflict raged inside of her. Finally one day she entered her grandfather's home, summoned up her courage, and decided to ask him a question that had been gnawing at her. She knew that this man was not just her grandfather, he was one of the most important people of the generation. And yet, she bravely persevered.

"How could it be, Zeidy, that you sit here in this *finsternish* — darkness? Don't you realize that there is an entire *lichtige velt* — enlightened world — out there?"

The Chofetz Chaim gazed at his granddaughter for a long moment. Finally he spoke in his gentle voice. "My dear grand-daughter, do you see those planes that are flying outside in the sky? One day soon those planes will reach the moon.

"And do you hear those bombs that are exploding all around us? It won't be long before there is a bomb that will be potent enough to destroy an entire city." Now he turned to his pre-cious granddaughter. "But we — *mir machen mentchen* — we are making individuals into people! And to make people one does not need the exposure of the *lichtige velt*. It is precisely here in the *finsternish* where people are made and individuals are created."

She finished the story and the visit soon concluded. The story does not have a "happy ending," as this young woman never rediscovered the beauty of Hashem's Torah.

But the message of the Chofetz Chaim will remain with us forever — especially for those who are in the "mentchen" business. This daunting task can be accom-plished only in the beauty, purity, and "lichtige velt" of "finsternish."

Truth and Lies

SOME OF REB MICHOEL BER WEISSMANDL'S TRAVELS had brought him to countries far away from his home in Slovakia. In these places he was often exposed to groups of people with customs and practices very different from his own. Having dedicated his life to saving those who were trapped in the Nazi inferno, he sought support and relief from anyone willing to help. One time his travels took him to a remote village near Tangiers. The contrast between this chassidic Jew from Europe and the traditional Sephardic members of the community could not have been more apparent.

Reb Michoel Ber had not intended to be there for the Yom Tov of Succos, but Providence had other plans. As the Yom Tov approached, he wondered when the four species would be sold. In his hometown, the Jews spent weeks searching for the perfect *lulav* and *esrog*. But surprisingly, in this village the focus seemed to be elsewhere. He could not imagine what type of Torah-committed Jews would not preoccupy themselves with the time-honored mitzvah of the *arba minim*. But now he was here and he really had no choice. This is where destiny had led him and this is where he was meant to be. He asked others when the "market" for the Succos needs would begin. They assured him that Erev Succos was the time designated for *lulav* and *esrog* selection.

Although he was somewhat comforted by this assurance, he was still anxious. Would they have the exact *esrog* he was looking for, from the most authentic orchard — and with no blemishes, blots, and imperfections? His apprehension caused a degree of unease as the Yom Tov drew nearer. Finally, the morning of Erev Succos arrived. He wanted to ask when the market opened but instead decided to just follow the crowd. Davening ended and the group of colorfully robed congregants moved to the back of the ancient shul. And then suddenly the *gabbai* appeared with a large, gray burlap sack. Right there in front of everyone, he emptied the sack. Reb Michoel Ber watched in disbelief as a pile of bruised and blemished *esrogim* rolled out onto the wooden table. There was no panic and no sense of urgency. One by one each of the congregants chose an *esrog.* They picked it up and looked at it in a slapdash fashion. Satisfied that they had an *esrog,* a moment later they walked away. Reb Michoel Ber stood there dumbfounded. He could not believe what he had just witnessed. This is Succos?! Is this the way one chooses the *arba minim*? Is this the way one treats a mitzvah?

Downtrodden, he spent the day wishing he were elsewhere, dreading the upcoming Yom Tov. He returned to the shul for Minchah and with a heavy heart waited for the next "surprise," which no doubt would soon be forthcoming. And sure enough it was not long in coming. Soon after Minchah a middle-aged man walked toward the *amud* to assume the position of *chazzan.* Hushed conversation filled the room and then one of the prominent members of the shul walked over to the would-be *chazzan,* whispered something in his ear, and took the *tallis* from the embarrassed fellow, who sheepishly walked away from the *amud.*

Shocked by what he had seen, Reb Michoel Ber could not begin to imagine what the man had done, of what he had been guilty. He asked the fellow next to him who, although he did not want to say, merely indicated that the would-be *chazzan* had done something inappropriate — and very, very wrong. At first Reb Michoel Ber was surprised but then he realized that these people were not exactly outstanding Jewish citizens. After all, these were the same individuals who had chosen their *esrogim* from a bag which had been carelessly emptied onto a table. Who can begin to imagine what type of *aveirah* this fellow had committed that caused him to be removed from his position as *chazzan*?

Although Reb Michoel Ber knew that it was not anyone's business what the man had done to deserve such censure, he could not help but wonder. Had he spoken publicly in a heretical manner? Had he acted immorally? Was he corrupt in his way of life? Did he keep any of the mitzvos of the Torah? And then he overheard another curious bystander spill the beans. "*Hu diber sheker* — He told a lie."

It was then that understanding dawned on Reb Michoel Ber. This was a society completely different from the one to which he had grown accustomed. It was one that placed great emphasis on the tenets of honesty and truth. In this village and tradition, the mitzvah of taking an *esrog* required a kosher *esrog* — that's all — and the people had met that requirement. But living a life of honesty, integrity, and candor was considered of paramount importance.

> *No. He was not in his hometown for Succos. And cer-*
> *tainly there were many years when he had secured a nicer*
> *esrog. But he surely had learned an invaluable lesson*
> *which he would remember forever. We are not capable of*
> *placing a value system on observance of mitzvos, for we*
> *don't know which one holds greater reward. But we are*
> *able to strengthen and intensify our commitment to those*
> *tenets which are essential to our being. For if we are not*
> *truthful then we cannot possibly know who we are and*
> *we can never become what we are meant to be.*

Better Late Than Never

HAVING GOTTEN HIS TEFILLIN FROM ONE OF THE most prominent scribes of his time, Reb Michel Prager was quite proud of them. He would always point out how dear they were to him and how rewarding it was to wear them. Throughout his lifetime he had been faced with numerous challenges and difficulties, but never did he miss the opportunity to wear his *tefillin.* As a *chassidishe Yid,* Reb Michel's davening played a major role in his life, and knowing that his *tefillin* were so special made it all the more gratifying.

Although he knew that there were some opinions that encouraged checking *tefillin* every so often, Reb Michel was careful not to have the sealed boxes opened for fear of exposing them to air and dust, and perhaps ruining them. And so, the *tefillin* were never checked. One day, however, seventy-two years after he first put on the *tefillin* for his bar mitzvah, someone inadvertently switched their *tefillin* with his, and this man gave what he thought were his *tefillin* to a *sofer* for checking. The *sofer* carefully checked all the words, scrutinizing them to ensure their validity. Suddenly, he let out a gasp, "*Gevalt,* these *tefillin* are missing an entire word!"

He continued to check the *shel yad* portion of the *tefillin* and found a missing word in them as well, rendering the entire pair *pasul*. The man who had brought the *tefillin* to be checked was quite upset, but soon realized that these were not his *tefillin* at all. Upon closer examination he was able to determine that they were Reb Michel's *tefillin*. It was unbelievable! Reb Michel's *tefillin* were *pasul*!

How would they break the bad news to the elderly man? He was 85 years old and the shock, horror, and disappointment of *never* having fulfilled a mitzvah of which he had been so proud could possibly cause him enough grief to endanger his life. Several of the elderly members of the shul conferred and decided that they had no choice but to tell him. A doctor was brought along just in case Reb Michel experienced any medical problems.

"Reb Michel," one of the elder gentlemen said, "we have something important to tell you." Slowly they spelled out the story — how the *tefillin* were switched, how Reb Michel's *tefillin* were taken to a *sofer,* and how Reb Michel's *tefillin* were found to be *pasul*. They didn't have to explain further; Reb Michel understood that he had never properly fulfilled the mitzvah of *tefillin*. Not even once. At first Reb Michel sat there frozen. They worried. *Had he heard them? How was he going to react?* They were wondering what else they should do when suddenly Reb Michel stood up and started smiling.

At first Reb Michel began to laugh and then he started to sing and dance. Instead of joining him they watched with pity, assuming that he was "losing it." This was someone who took more pride in his *tefillin* than in any other mitzvah. Who could blame him now for losing control? He sang and danced around the room, skipping with joy. To see an 85-year-old act this way was quite unusual and, under the circumstances, very sad. But no one dared to interfere. After all, he was entitled. Finally he finished.

Suddenly he looked up and noticed everyone staring at him. He then explained: "Do you know what this means? Had my *tefillin* never been checked, I never would have had the opportunity to fulfill this precious mitzvah. *But now I will.* For this, I am very grateful."

And then, with tears streaming down his eyes, he began to unwrap a pair of kosher *tefillin* and put them on his head and on his arm. With a smile on his face and tears running down his cheeks, 85-year-old Reb Michel Prager fulfilled the mitzvah of *tefillin* for the very first time.

Lechavod Shabbos Kodesh

MANY CUSTOMS HAVE DEVELOPED THROUGH the centuries relating to Shabbos, each designed to enhance the day in some small but meaningful way. One of the most beautiful of these customs is the declaration, *"Lechavod Shabbos Kodesh!"* Whether one practices Sephardic, Ashkenazic, chassidic or Litvisher customs, this thought-provoking ritual has taken hold. Some people actually say this phrase before taking their first bite of the Shabbos meal, while others will make the pronouncement preceding every morsel of food they eat. In certain homes, it is recited on Erev Shabbos as the food is being prepared.

In 1948, Rav Shach was living in Yerushalayim but learning in the Lomza Yeshivah in Petach Tikva. It was difficult for him to travel back to Yerushalayim each week, so often he would remain in Petach Tikva, where he had been invited to stay in the home of Rav Avraham Hillel Goldberg.

Rav Goldberg and his family were honored to host this outstanding *talmid chacham* and provided him with his own room so that he could enjoy the privacy he needed in order to learn. At one point, while Rav Shach was in his room, Mrs. Goldberg was inside the kitchen preparing for the Shabbos meal, trying to ensure that everything was just right for the special guest they were hosting. For a short while her little baby had been crying softly but then the crying grew incessantly louder. Mrs. Goldberg just wanted to finish up the last few items before she tended to her infant. Suddenly the baby's cries stopped; checking to make sure everything was okay, she ran to the baby's room.

As she peeked in she saw her little baby in the right hand of the great *tzaddik,* while he held his Gemara in his left. And as he walked back and forth he hummed the melodious, sweet sounds of learning Torah, and gently calmed the crying baby with the words,

"Shh — *Lechavod Shabbos kodesh* — Shh — *Lechavod Shabbos kodesh."*

She thanked the Rav for soothing the baby and then offered to take the infant. But Rav Shach insisted that he wanted to hold the baby. "Everyone has to help in the preparation for Shabbos, but I cannot help in the kitchen. Instead I can assist by allowing you to cook in peace. Please let me hold him — please."

And with the baby in one hand and the Gemara in the other, Rav Shach continued with the sweet sounds of *Lechavod Shabbos kodesh.*

The Cost of a Lulav

*Searching for a lulav and an esrog is an arduous task
that often takes many hours. One must select not only an*

esrog that meets the halachic requirements, but one that is beautiful in the eyes of its owner. Nowadays in Israel, and elsewhere as well, there are a plethora of mochrim (sellers) and each one has his following of buyers. It is sometimes difficult to get "in," but once one does he will find himself jostling with other buyers to find just the right esrog or lulav.

A S RAV YAAKOV YISRAEL KANIEVSKY, THE STEIPLER Gaon, set out to buy his lulav in Bnei Brak, he was escorted by one of his students, one who had accompanied him for the past few years. This student knew the ins and outs of the business and therefore many dealers had called him to request that the Steipler buy his set of arba minim from them. The young man had chosen one particular dealer, and he and the Rav were on their way to that store.

When the Steipler walked in, all eyes turned to him. Although there were quite a few individuals there when he arrived, he was immediately ushered into a back room so he could examine the *lulavim* in peace. The nervous dealer had chosen what he thought were the absolute best *lulavim* in stock and set them out on a table. The Steipler picked up the first one, examined it, and placed it down on the table where the others were. He then picked up the next one and did the same; each one he selected seemed to have its fault. Finally he reached the last one on the table, inspected it, and after scrutinizing it closely, put it down. He then went back to the very first *lulav* he had looked at, one that he had quickly dismissed, and decided to purchase it. The seller, though somewhat perplexed by the Steipler's behavior, was thrilled to have been able to sell the *lulav* to the Steipler.

After the Steipler walked out of the shop, his student turned to him and wondered aloud why his rebbi had settled on that *lulav* when here there were so many other stores and *lulavim* to choose from. The Steipler was not one to compromise on mitzvah observance. Why had he settled now?

The answer he gave to his questioning student contained an unforgettable lesson. "It is true. There are many, many shops from which to choose a *lulav* and an *esrog*. I am certain in fact that I could have bought one that was much nicer than the one I chose. But at what cost? Had I walked out the door without a *lulav*, then not only would those who were in the outer room have questioned why I had left empty-handed, but word would have spread on the street that the Steipler could not find a kosher *lulav* in this dealer's shop. This in turn would have caused him to lose many customers. And that is too high a price to pay for a *lulav*."

The Shabbos Guest

EVERY SHABBOS, THE YOUNG MEN FROM THE YESHI-vah in Pressburg would eat their meals at the homes of members of the community. After davening, they would emerge from the *beis midrash* en masse and walk through the town to their respective hosts' homes. Every week, one of the young men would wander off by himself for a while, and then catch up with the group a few blocks away. This young man, Chaim, was well respected among his peers as a caring, generous individual, always ready to help a friend in need. Chaim's "disappearing act" intrigued his friends, and they decided to follow him one week to see where he went.

The next Shabbos morning, the boys followed Chaim into a particularly poor part of town. Chaim walked to a basement apartment and knocked gently on the door. An old woman answered and Chaim wished her a warm "Gut Shabbos." Seeing the smile on her face, they assumed that this was his grandmother. They managed to get away before he could see them, but when he rejoined the group, they confessed that they had followed him. "So," they asked, "who is that woman? Your grandmother?"

A bit embarrassed that he had been "caught in the act," Chaim shyly responded that the woman was not even related to him. That piqued their curiosity even more. "Then, Chaim, why do you go to wish her a Gut Shabbos every week?"

By this time a bigger crowd had gathered, with everyone eager to hear Chaim's story. "The truth is that this woman is a widow, and she has very little family around. So I figured I would go to wish her a Gut Shabbos. She seems so happy when I come and it is such an easy thing to do — How could I not?"

The stunned friends hung their heads in humility. Amazed that their young friend had the sensitivity to look after an old widow, they knew then that this boy would become something special.

Rav Yitzchak Shloime Blau remembered this story fondly because he was a little boy at the time and the old woman was his grandmother. "And although I was only 6 or 7 years old, I remember waiting outside for him every Shabbos and then running inside to tell my grandmother, 'The *bachur* is coming! The *bachur* is coming!'"

Chaim's friends were correct in predicting that this young man was destined for greatness. Young Chaim grew to become the great Rav Yosef Chaim Sonnenfeld, Rav of Yerushalayim!

For Cholent and Chatting

"GO AWAY!"

The knocking persisted but Yankel Rosengarten had no interest in seeing who was at the door. Six months had passed since the elderly Gerrer chassid had lost his wife. Since that time he basically did nothing; he sat in his apartment all day long and wallowed in self-pity. No one could convince him to leave his apartment. The knocking persisted; he hoped that if he ignored it long enough, the person would go away.

Yankel and his beloved wife had had a wonderful marriage; they did everything together and adored each other. She had fallen ill two years ago, and he never left her side. Their bond, if possible, became even stronger. It got to the point when, as her death neared, he felt he could not live without her.

The knocking persisted. He became angry as he rose to answer the door and give this intruder a piece of his mind.

When he opened the door he nearly fainted.

It was Rav Leizer Shach!

Yankel stammered, excusing himself, and apologizing for not answering the door sooner. Rav Shach reassured him that it was fine. They sat for a few moments and an awkward silence filled the air. Finally Rav Shach spoke. "I know how you feel. I'm also a widower. And sometimes it is very depressing and sad. Aren't you a Gerrer chassid? Perhaps you know a *niggun* we could sing together."

Yankel looked up, nodded, and again hung his head. He began to hum a little tune to himself and Rav Shach started humming with him, unsure of where the song was heading but simply joining in so the man would not feel so alone. The song picked up in intensity and before long this depressed, elderly man was glowing with a spark that had been buried deep inside of him for a long time. After a few moments the *niggun* died down and again they sat in silence.

"Can I ask you for a favor?" Rav Shach began. "I make a wonderful *cholent* and I would love to have some company with whom to eat it. Would you allow me to send it over to you? I will come by on Shabbos morning and we will spend some time together. I would love to eat the Shabbos meal with you."

By now Yankel was embarrassed. "I'm sorry. I could never intrude on the Rosh Yeshivah's time like that." Yankel was adamant and thanked Rav Shach, but refused to accept his offer.

The Rosh Yeshivah persisted, "I'm afraid you don't understand. I really enjoy being with you. It cheers me up and I really need it. Could you please let me come?"

Yankel smiled and accepted the proposal. They spent their Shabbos meal together, and for the next few years Yankel turned to his new companion for friendship, encouragement, and warmth. Two years later Yankel Rosengarten passed away — a happy man who was forever grateful that when everyone else had given up on him, one great man did not.

Weeping and Wicks

*I*T WAS THE 21ST DAY OF THE MONTH OF KISLEV, 1944, A mere four days before Chanukah, when the Satmar Rebbe, Rav Yoel Teitelbaum, was taken from Bergen Belsen to freedom in Switzerland as part of the famed "Kastner Transport."

Upon their arrival, the refugees were confined in the Swiss city of Caux to insure that they were free of disease. The Rav gave the refugees encouragement and strength, as they prepared for their first Yom Tov to be celebrated in freedom in nearly five years.

Rav Botchko, Rosh Yeshivah in the nearby city of Montreaux, mustered all of his influence to convince the authorities to allow the Rav and a small entourage to join him in Montreaux for the kindling of the first Chanukah light. The Rav was allowed to leave the internment center and spend the evening in the home of Reb Michoel Tzvi Danenbaum, a respected layman in the community.

When the Rav arrived, he was offered food and drink but politely refused to partake of it, instead turning his attention to the menorah that had been set up in his honor. He went to the menorah and, instead of using the wicks that had been prepared, he carefully reached into his pocket and took out a small wick, woven of tattered threads. He replaced the menorah's wick with his own, as he explained what had happened. "Several weeks ago, we were still in

Bergen Belsen, and I had no idea where we would be for Chanukah, so I began saving threads for wicks. When we were liberated a few days ago, I made sure to take these wicks along with me."

The crowd watched in silence as the Rav began to sway. He remained in that position for a few moments as tears flowed down his angelic face. And then in an emotional, heartbroken, thin but strong voice he began to make the *berachos* on the lighting of the menorah. He recited the first two *berachos* to the response of a resounding "Amen."

As he began to recite the *berachah* of *Shehecheyanu,* he could hold back no longer. Tears began streaming down his cheeks — tears of gratitude that he and those with him had been saved, and tears of pain for those left behind, the millions still suffering. Wracked by sobs and suffused with tears, he attempted to make it through the *berachah,* each word a struggle. "*Shehecheyanu* — that You kept us alive ... *lazeman hazeh* — for this time ..."

Emotionally spent, he held the Chanukah light in his hand, its flame shining proudly. He moved the *shamash* to the menorah's wick, and it caught. The flame had been lit and they began to sing *Maoz Tzur* as they never had before and never would again: "... *Chayai meireru bekoshi* — They had embittered my life with hardship." Truer words were never said.

> The Satmar Rav had insisted on lighting the wicks he had brought with him from Bergen Belsen because they symbolized the struggle of the Jewish nation — not only during the horrifying years of the Holocaust, but for our entire history. It is an eternal struggle, a struggle for survival, for the triumph of light over darkness, of good over evil. We must vanquish the dark, endless night — the bitter exile — and hope to soon be able to witness the ohr haganuz, the concealed radiance of Hashem's Goodness.

Just a Little Tired

*A*CONTEMPORARY OF THE NODA BIYEHUDAH, AS well as a brilliant *talmid chacham* in his own right, Rav Yaakov Shimshon of Shepetkov journeyed to his beloved Eretz Yisrael in the year 1794. He had always dreamed of making this trip and now his dream had finally come true. In addition to helping establish the Jewish settlements in Eretz Yisrael and spreading Chassidus there, Rav Yaakov Shimshon found it necessary to leave the country in order to raise money for his brethren there.

On one of his voyages, the ship set sail and the weather soon grew stormy. The ship rolled with each huge wave, the thunder and lightning were fearsome, and many of the passengers grew severely ill. Some were thrown overboard by the crashing waves, and many clung to life and whispered their last prayers. Sounds of wailing trailed off and were swallowed up in the deafening roar of the leviathan storm. But amazingly, almost miraculously, Rav Yaakov Shimshon survived and made it safely to Europe.

The storm had taken its toll on his elderly body, however, and many who saw him were shocked at how frail he looked. Not knowing about the storm, they assumed that his ragged appearance and weak physique were the result of life in Eretz Yisrael. This fueled the then-popular myth that life in Eretz Yisrael was harsh and too severe for most people to endure. When Rav Yaakov Shimshon heard the murmuring in the streets he was highly distressed. Suddenly, he disappeared from public gatherings. For three weeks no one heard from him. He spent that time recovering from his ordeal and regaining his strength. He did not want the townspeople spreading false rumors about life in the Holy Land; he was literally saving these townspeople from the sin of the spies who spoke ill of life there. Only after he recovered would Rav Yaakov Shimshon allow himself to be seen in public.

Fruit of the Land

RAV YOCHANAN TWERSKI, THE RACHMISTRIFKA REBBE, was soft spoken, kind, and full of humility. Despite his self-effacing manner, his greatness shone in many ways. Both the common folk and the scholars flocked to hear his wisdom and bask in his holiness. Descended from great ancestors, Reb Yochanan was the youngest of eight great brothers, all children of Reb Muttel of Hornosteipel. His father had once mentioned that his son Yochanan had within him the spark of the great Tanna, Rebbi Yochanan ben Zakkai. When this was brought to the Rebbe's attention, he dismissed it by admitting that his name was Yochanan and agreeing to the fact that his father was certainly *zakkai,* innocent of all wrongdoing; so in fact he was a "Rebbi Yochanan ben Zakkai" of sorts.

His greatness, cloaked in simplicity, and boundless love for Torah and mitzvos was visible to all. When he visited other Rebbes, his followers would escort him. It was on one of these visits — when he went to see Reb Yitzchak of Skver, one of his brothers, a respected and revered Rebbe in his own right — that his chassidim discovered Reb Yochanan's sensitivity to mitzvos.

Reb Yochanan's brother had a custom of honoring his guests by bringing out the finest wine he had from Eretz Yisrael and proposing a *l'chaim.* However, when Reb Yochanan visited, he asked his brother for a different wine, one from *chutz la'aretz,* from outside Eretz Yisrael. His disciples were perplexed at this unusual request. Why had Reb Yochanan refused the wine originally offered and asked for a different bottle?

When he saw the questioning looks on the faces of his chassidim, he explained. "I personally am not a wine connoisseur. In fact, I really don't care much for wine at all. And because of that I am afraid that when I drink the wine I will think negatively about the fruits of Eretz Yisrael — and that is something I wish to avoid."

Missing ... but Not Forgotten

THOSE WHO LEARNED IN THE MIRRER YESHIVAH IN Brooklyn, New York remember him well. There was certainly something a little bit different about Alan Yakow. He was fairly bright and managed to progress from one level *shiur* to the next, but his behavior and manner always bespoke mild but very evident personality problems. Everyone wondered why he was allowed to stay in the yeshivah, and how he was able to progress from *shiur* to *shiur;* it was because the yeshivah and its rebbeim showed extra care and compassion to this young man. Even his classmates knew that something was different about Alan, and because of it they treated him accordingly.

As the years went by and the yeshivah grew, there remained one constant that was familiar to the current and former students — Alan Yakow. His own classmates moved on to other yeshivos, to married life, and then to their careers. But as his classmates and the others in yeshivah found their calling and continued with their lives, Alan found his calling through the yeshivah. As he grew older, his personality and behavior remained an issue, yet he loved the yeshivah and became a self-appointed "fundraiser" of sorts.

One of his projects was to raise money to buy new candelabra lights for the *amud*. He approached anyone and everyone to help raise the "much needed funds." Those who pitied him supported his cause and gave whenever he asked. They would then be rewarded with a page in a "journal" and at times a "raffle ticket," although no one ever knew if these were real or imagined rewards. Although he was never given much credit for his efforts, no one dared to question his sincerity. Alan was 100 percent committed to his one and only true love — the yeshivah.

Alan also took upon himself the photography of all of the yeshivah's special occasions, creating photo albums for each event, which he would sometimes sell as a way of raising money for the yeshivah.

Throughout these years, and more often as he grew older, Alan would sometimes need to be admitted to a hospital for treatment. As he aged, his mental challenges became progressively more difficult, to the point where, sadly, he did not return from his hospital stay. Slowly, people noticed his absence, and eventually the word spread that Alan had been admitted into a mental hospital for treatment and was no longer able to live on his own. The yeshivah community was saddened for quite a while, missing Alan's presence, but eventually he was forgotten.

∽ၹ∾

Twenty years later, hundreds of people gathered at the Brooklyn funeral home for the funeral of the father of Reb Reuven Schepansky, one of the yeshivah's rebbeim. The funeral was attended by many dignitaries and Roshei Yeshivah. The overflowing crowd came in great numbers to give their *kavod acharon* to a wonderful individual. As the eulogies concluded and the crowd began to filter out, several people noticed that another funeral was about to take place. It was the *levayah* of Alan Yakow. When the large crowd heard the name of the deceased they were stunned. Although they had not heard from or seen Alan in more than twenty years, they knew about his commitment to the yeshivah. And the large crowd of Mirrer "yeshivah *leit*" made their way back into the funeral hall.

It is simply remarkable. Everyone had forgotten about Alan Yakow and his silly projects. But the sincere dedication, honest commitment, and unbridled love Alan had for the yeshivah was not forgotten. It was remembered by the One Who never forgets. And He made sure that they would be there to remember Alan Yakow one final time.

Coming Up Short

R AV SHLOMO FREIFELD WAS A PHYSICALLY IMPOSING figure, but his heart was even bigger. There are myriad stories which describe Reb Shlomo's unique ability to relate to each and every person he met — each on his or her own level. With the intellectual, Reb Shlomo could discuss complicated topics in philosophy; for the street kid, he had a different language. But there was one common thread — the indescribable warmth that emanated from him. Every person with whom he came in contact felt as though he was the only one on Reb Shlomo's mind. His smile, warmth, and sense of humor allowed him to relate to even the most detached of our youth. And in his own inimitable style, he was able to utilize his wit to teach some memorable and timely lessons.

Generally, Reb Shlomo did not get involved in the day-to-day money matters in the yeshivah. That job was given to other devoted employees. It was only when a crisis arose that Reb Shlomo would get involved. Sometimes, these situations involved a financial crisis — especially when the yeshivah was running out of operating funds. On one of those occasions, Reb Shlomo went to the bank and approached the teller, introducing himself as Rabbi Freifeld.

The young Chinese-looking woman behind the teller's window had been looking down counting money, and when she looked up at the sound of a new customer, she caught her breath, taken aback by the imposing figure who was standing in front of her. "Wow, Rabbi — You big!" she remarked. Reb Shlomo smiled warmly at her, amused by her reaction. Then she directed him to the manager's office.

The man pulled out the yeshivah's file and sat for awhile reviewing the paperwork, scowling the entire time. Reb Shlomo stood there quietly as he waited for the banker to complete his analysis of the financial crisis. Finally, the manager shook his head and looked at Reb Shlomo, "I'm sorry, Rabbi. Whatever way I look at it you keep on coming up short." Reb Shlomo's response was a slowly growing grin.

"What's so funny?" The man was quite respectful of the Rosh Yeshivah and wondered what could possibly be funny at a time like this.

Reb Shlomo smiled again and this time shared his wisdom with the kind banker. "What just happened over the last few moments really encapsulates my life. While I was downstairs the woman at the teller's window was amazed at how 'big' I am. And yet when I came upstairs all I kept hearing was how 'short' I am." The financier listened as Reb Shlomo began to put his twist on the matter. "When I am down here in this world, where so many people are 'small,' they look at a simple person like me and are amazed at how 'big' I am. But as soon as I get upstairs and reach heaven, they will see the 'real me' and will see how 'short' I truly am."

> Most of the people who knew him would agree that Reb Shlomo was not correct in his self-assessment. In fact, he was not only "big" in the eyes of small people, but also in the eyes of the great leaders of our generation. But he still considered himself as "small" — even though he was a person who could relate to everyone, was deeply loved by all, and left an impact on so many.

Mesiras Nefesh /
Self-Sacrifice

Jarring Judgments

LTHOUGH FIFTY YEARS HAVE PASSED SINCE THEIR memorable last meeting, Rav Chaim Dov Keller, the Rosh Yeshivah of Telshe Yeshiva in Chicago and one of Rav Eliyahu Meir Bloch's closest *talmidim*, remembers vividly the last encounter he had with his beloved rebbi. He originally wrote about his last visit in "The Jewish Observer." This story is rooted in that original article. I can never fully capture the emotion and feeling that Rav Keller's gifted pen was able to convey. And as such I will revert back to some of the original wording in his moving account.

It was painful to behold: Rav Eliyahu Meir Bloch, the Telzer Rosh Yeshivah, a man who had already endured so much suffering, was now in yet another difficult situation. He was in the hospital being treated for an illness which would eventually take his life. It was a few short days before he would return his *neshamah* to His Creator. He was a man who exuded *regesh,* emotion. It literally permeated every fiber of his being. When a joyous occasion would come, Rav Elya Meir, as he was affectionately called, would sing and dance with boundless energy and emotion. And when tragedy would befall him, he would shoulder the burden with undying faith and *gevurah*. No matter how trying the situation, Rav Elya Meir was able to find the good.

But now in the hospital, his pain was so evident, although he never complained. Rav Chaim Dov and his father-in-law, Rabbi Leizer Levin, came to visit the Rosh Yeshivah but he was not in his room. "After a while he entered, dragging his slippered feet, leaning heavily on his stepson, Reb Mordechai Glicksman. Perspiration beaded his forehead and he had considerable trouble breathing. I winced at the sight. Rav Elya Meir, who had greeted all with genuine warmth, could not gather the strength to say *Shalom Aleichem*, not even nod. He merely acknowledged our presence with his eyes. With great difficulty he was helped to an armchair and sat there breathing heavily."

And then after a few moments he managed to utter two labored words — "*Ah shvera mishpat* — such a harsh judgment."

Reb Chaim Dov was somewhat surprised. This was not the usual manner in which his Rebbi had addressed the most challenging moments of his life — and there had been many. His wife and their four children, along with the rest of the inhabitants of Telshe, Lithuania, had been killed in the Nazi massacre. When he was informed of their deaths he was in the middle of learning, writing his *chidushim*. When he heard the horrific news, he wrote, "I am not able to concentrate as I should… for the news which I feared has now reached me — the terrible news of the death of my family at the hands of the cursed Nazi murderers. May Hashem avenge their blood and have mercy on His people …

"Should someone look at these writings, let him not judge me as callous and cruel for having delved into the words of the Torah after hearing such terrible news … I feel that I can never come to peace with myself without the toil of Torah…Having learned of my awful tragedy, my first call of duty must be to labor in Torah … Of what importance are the woes of one individual when compared to the duties of the *klal* … "

This was a man who never complained about his own personal discomfort. Why was he complaining now? It seemed so out of character. But then Reb Elya Meir looked deeply into his *talmid's* eyes and shared with him an unforgettable lesson. "It's not the pain. For as long as I can remember, I've never known what it meant to sit and do nothing. I would either be learning by myself or with others, writing, speaking or even fixing something around the house. But just to lie in bed and do nothing, that is a *shvera mishpat*."

But as their final visit came to a close, Reb Chaim Dov was given one last glimpse of his rebbi. Not as a "helpless, terminally ill man" but rather as the man who described himself as one who *"can never come to peace with myself without the toil of Torah."*

Once again we turn to Reb Chaim Dov's last impression of the rebbi he loved so much. "After some conversation I mentioned an observation on a passage in the *Ketzos HaChoshen*. And then, as soon as I mentioned the *Ketzos*, the Rosh Yeshivah underwent a remarkable change. His eyes lit up, his face evinced its old warmth, a smile crossed his lips and his voice became strong and clear. 'I made the same observation in one of my *shiurim*,' and proceeded to discuss the *Ketzos* with a *lebedikeit* which so entranced me that, to my everlasting regret, I could not concentrate on his words." It was incredible, "as if the old Reb Elya Meir had been revived …"

Indeed he had.
The Rosh Yeshivah was finally at peace with himself.
Yehi zichro baruch.

The Warmth of a Jew

There are times when we meet someone and instinctively feel that there is something special about this person. This is how one feels when meeting Mrs. Sarah Hildenfeld.

Special indeed — one cannot help but wonder how she was able to overcome even the most difficult of situations and raise six outstanding children.

*I*T WAS NOT AT ALL EASY. SARAH HAD LOST HER HUSBAND when the oldest of their children was not yet 10 years old. How would she manage? To whom could she turn in her time of need? It was tricky enough raising children in the slums of Tel Aviv. All the more so when one wanted to ensure that those children are raised in the spirit of Torah. But Sarah met her challenge head-on. She tackled each and every challenge that came her way. She did her best to deal with the elements and trials that often seemed endless.

She shared a one-bedroom apartment with her children, and her daily schedule revolved around her children; she always ensured that they were happy. One problem which faced them every summer, however, was the stifling Tel Aviv heat. The tiny apartment had little ventilation, so it became quite hot during the summer months. The children rarely complained — they had become used to the situation — and appreciated the little relief they got by playing in the courtyard in the fresh air.

That courtyard was also the play area for the Hildenfelds' neighbors' children. Sarah was comfortable having her children play with the neighbors' children; they were not religious, but were well behaved, modestly dressed, and refined. But when these neighbors moved, Sarah faced a difficult problem. The new neighbors did not require their children to dress modestly or act modestly — quite the opposite. Sarah wondered how to handle this situation. How could she deny her children the pleasure of playing in the courtyard, in fresh air, but by the same token how could she allow her children to come under the influence of these undesirable friends? In fact, she wondered if she even wanted them looking down into the courtyard and watching these children — considering their unacceptable behavior and mode of dress.

She decided that she needed to talk to her children about this issue. As she spoke to them, they listened respectfully, and answered with tremendous feeling, "Mommy, whatever you feel is the right thing to do, that is what we will do. We won't play out there anymore." Their soft-spoken yet determined response bespoke their own dignity and honor. Then the two oldest children did something more, an act which proved how responsible and mature they were: They moved their only bookcase directly in front of the window, the only window in the house. Even though it would make the apartment even stuffier, they were willing to endure that in order to uphold the level of *kedushah* that their mother had instilled in them.

> *A poor widow with six children, in a hot one-room apartment, creating a life filled with Torah values — special indeed.*

The Maftir and the Miracle

ANY INDIVIDUALS GO TO GREAT LENGTHS TO obtain specific honors during davening. This is a time-honored practice that has existed for many generations. There are many honors available during davening, with specific ones being associated with *"segulos,"* or signs of good luck. One of the more distinguished honors is *Maftir Chanah*. On the first day of Rosh Hashanah we read about Chanah, a childless woman, heartbroken and inconsolable. She pleads desperately and pours out her heart to Hashem, begging Him to remember her plight. Ultimately she is blessed with a son, Shmuel HaNavi. Reciting this *Haftarah* on the second day of Rosh Hashanah has become a great *segulah,* and this was especially true in certain chassidic circles in Europe where the Rebbe's *berachah,* together with this *segulah,* had helped many childless couples.

Moshe Lieberfeld was one of those who had heard of this tradition and had traveled to the court of a chassidic Rebbe where those who had bid for and obtained *Maftir Chanah* were ultimately blessed with children. The trip was not easy but Moshe felt it was important to take off from work to try this *segulah.* Moshe and his wife had yearned for a child for many years. They had endured much disappointment and heartache. His friends had suggested that he make the journey and buy *Maftir,* and he felt that he owed it to his wife. He owed it to himself. If Hashem had blessed him with the means to afford the trip, then he felt he had to try and obtain the *kibbud.*

Moshe arrived at the chassidic court to find a busy scene. The *aliyos* were being sold, and the sales were made quickly. The prices ranged from a few thousand to over $10,000. But for *Maftir Chanah* the cost would certainly escalate. The bidding began and many made offers. Before long the price for *Maftir* had soared. It went to 15, then $20,000. Finally the field was narrowed down to the two highest bidders. Back and forth they went until finally *Maftir Chanah* sold for $36,000! And the winning bidder was none other than Moshe.

He was overjoyed to have secured the *aliyah,* and anticipated the moment when he would be called up to the *bimah* and would hear the heartrending story of Chanah. He hoped that the Rebbe would invoke the mercy and compassion of Heaven and miraculously intercede on their behalf. It had cost a large sum of money but was a small price to pay for the Rebbe's intervention.

The moment finally arrived. Davening in the presence of the Rebbe had been decidedly uplifting. And then, as *Maftir* drew nearer, Moshe began to think about the fellow who had bid against him. What was *his* plight? How had he and his wife suffered? What were *their* troubles? He thought deeply about the dreams that his rival bidder must have had — the last-gasp hopes of that couple. And then he realized what he had to do. He went over to the *gab-*

bai and whispered something in his ear. The *gabbai* gave Moshe an astonished glance. But when he noticed that Moshe was insisting, he nodded in the affirmative. A moment later the *tzibbur* was shocked. Moshe was not called up for *Maftir Chanah*. Instead, his runner-up was summoned.

Shocked and overwhelmed that he was called, Moshe's replacement cried his way through the *Haftarah*, eternally grateful that he had been given this opportunity of a lifetime. And miraculously, a year later Moshe was blessed with a baby girl.

> *Rav Shimshon Pincus related this story and deliberately omitted the name of the Rebbe in whose court it took place. Instead he chose to highlight the incredible ability of the common, or so-called common, individual. And when we are able to be "mevater" and to give up that which is most dear to us in order not to hurt someone else, then the everyday commoner is capable of moving Heaven and earth.*

Counting With Courage

HE DID NOT SEEM LIKE A YOUNG MAN WITH A PROBLEM, but he was.

After a few months of learning more and more about Torah and its observance, Shiko, an Israeli living in Baltimore, Maryland, had made a pledge to become fully observant. Although many of his Israeli friends had not as yet made the same leap of faith, Shiko was moving forward at full steam. With a smile that matched his sincerity, Shiko was not hard to like. He was respectful, kind, considerate, and eager. Very eager.

He spent each spare moment trying to discover more and more about his religion, the religion about which he knew so little. It was shocking for him to realize that he had been born in a country where so much holiness abounded, and yet it had been all but hidden from him. He was aware of the *Kosel* but had no idea of who Avraham Avinu and Moshe Rabbeinu were. His life journey had brought him to Baltimore, and it was there that he had settled.

Then, in Baltimore, he was introduced to the popular Yoni Alon and his group that convened every Thursday night. Once he became comfortable and familiar with this crowd, Shiko's thirst for learning grew by leaps and bounds. Meeting once a week in the Beit Edmund Safra Synagogue in Baltimore, the halachic *shiur* was peppered with an Israeli flavor. Delivered in *Ivrit,* it attracted many outsiders, sometimes up to one hundred people. While a small table was spread with chumus, techina, and other salads, to provide food for the bodies, there was no shortage of "food" for the many souls who hungered for Torah knowledge. Many have found their way back to their roots. One of them was Shiko.

As Shiko learned, he began practicing mitzvos; davening was very special to him. With deep emotion, he concentrated on every word, sometimes ending *Shemoneh Esrei* of Minchah and Maariv well after the *minyan* was over. Such was the scenario on the night of the sixteenth day of the *Omer.* And this is where his problem comes in.

He had always davened longer than the rest of the congregation but remembered to count the Omer afterward. However, this time he forgot which night it was and instead of counting the sixteenth he inadvertently counted the fifteenth, the wrong number.

It was not until the next night, well after the *minyan* had finished Maariv, that he realized his error. Unaware of the ramifications, he approached the Rav to discuss the matter with him. He wanted to know if — since he had indeed counted, even though he had counted the wrong number — he could still continue counting with a *berachah*. Shiko waited anxiously as the Rav listened to make sure that he fully understood the question being posed to him.

The Rav gently and patiently explained to Shiko that since he had counted the wrong day it was as if he had not counted at all.

In other words, Shiko would no longer be allowed to count with a *berachah*. Shiko listened intently to every word. He walked away and placed his head in his hands and began to cry.

After a moment he collected himself and approached the Rav one more time. And with a last gasp of hope he wondered, "If I would make it up by fasting, would I then be allowed to count with a *berachah*?"

The Rav looked at Shiko in amazement. He had a feeling that he had already "made up for" everything he had to.

The Tastiest Kugel

One of the most meaningful things a mother can do for a child is to make his or her favorite Shabbos treats. Sometimes it is a cake or cookies and other times it is an exceptional kugel. But whatever it may be, the unlimited love a Jewish mother has for her children drives her to provide whatever individual attention they need. This is a story Reb Moshe Prager told about one such mother, a mother faced with an impossible dilemma — a dilemma in which she prevails as only a Yiddishe Mama can.

THE HUNGER WAS UNBEARABLE. RATIONING OUT THEIR allotment of food into seven portions, one for each day, was a daunting task. Many devoured the entire allotment at once, their hunger too great to overcome. Some of those would starve to death during the week. Parents knew that they had to dole out the food slowly, over the anguished cries of their starving children. It is painful just to imagine it. And yet this was the daily scenario every parent faced in the ghetto.

One particular mother had gone even further; she had saved up her own bits of bread in order to make a special *kugel* for Shabbos for her sick child. She had even found some potato peels and spices to enhance the treat, and had such joy knowing that she could provide something special for her precious son. Then she had a thought: Instead of using the drops of oil she had saved for her Shabbos lights, she would put them into the *kugel,* and the result would be an even more delicious treat for her child.

At the same time she also knew that, halachically, the most preferable use for that oil was to light the Shabbos candles. And, also, if she used the oil for the *kugel,* she would not be able to say the special prayers over the Shabbos candles, asking Hashem to heal her child. She thought about the two options, and then resolved to do what her heart told her. She took the small jar and emptied it into the *kugel.*

As the sun began to set on Friday afternoon, she stood before her empty candle holders and wept bitterly. She had no oil left with which to fill the holders. All she had left was a prayer, a special *tefillah,* one which surely shook the Heavenly Throne. *"Ribbono Shel Olam,* Master of the World, I am so sorry. I have no oil left with which to light Your special Shabbos candles. But I beg You to accept them without any light. Please forgive me for stealing the light from Your Shabbos candles. And if You cannot forgive me for stealing the oil to provide a tastier *kugel* for my sick child, then at least listen to the sounds of my child singing the beautiful songs of Shabbos as I feed his emaciated body this *kugel."*

That Friday night at their Shabbos meal, as this broken mother gave her child a taste of Gan Eden, they began to sing together softly, *"Mizmor Shir LeYom HaShabbos ..."*

Listening closely, one might have been able to hear the Shabbos Queen singing along in praise of a heroic Jewish mother.

Three Brave Soldiers

THE MORNING OF DECEMBER 7, 1941 BEGAN THE WAY most mornings did for Alfred Gross and his brother Sidney. The two strapping young men were daily attendees at the small *minyan* in Duquesne, Pennsylvania. They took their *minyan* seriously this day as they had every day since their childhood. Their father had passed away in 1922 and their mother bravely raised them and their siblings alone. She was a strong woman, and strongly principled as well; it was well known in Duquesne that if you were to talk during davening then you would be subject to the glaring gaze of Mrs. Sarah Gross. And it was under her watchful eye that these two young men grew up, firmly committed to the traditions of old, although living in a city far from the center of Jewish life. On the morning of December 7, 1941, however, the world changed forever.

Until that day, Americans kept their hearts and minds fairly distant from the European war, exhibiting only a slight interest in the battles. The growing sentiment was: As long as it doesn't affect me, why get involved? But when the Japanese attacked Pearl Harbor, America was forced into war. (Word had it that Pearl Harbor was such an obscure entity that when some heard of the attack they responded, "I didn't know her. How old was she?")

It wasn't long before the dreaded telegram arrived at the Gross' door. The grim cable informed the two brothers that they had thirty days to report for duty. They were being drafted into the army. It was quite difficult closing the business, but they really had no choice. The war would wait for no one.

After completing basic training, Alfred was sent to Burma, while Sidney was stationed in the South Pacific. It was not easy for their mother to part with her two children. They might have been two broad-shouldered, brawny soldiers, but to her they were still her little boys. As they departed from their mother she cried softly, whispering a special prayer to herself, *Ribbono Shel Olam, I'm sending away tzvei Yiddishe kinderlach. Please send me back tzvei Yiddishe kinderlach.*

Alfred, stationed in Burma, was by and large out of harm's way, but the same could not be said for his brother. Sidney's regiment faced the daily threat of the ruthless Japanese soldiers. The Nazis were known to be sadistic barbarians, and the same can be said regarding the savagery of the Japanese soldiers. The fanatical soldiers razed village after village. The kamikaze tactics represented their imbalanced, extremist attitude to the war. In fact, it was common for the Japanese to attack villages of innocent, defenseless women and children, slaughtering them for no reason at all.

As Sidney's battalion reached an area near Manila, he came across a smoldering village with smoke still rising from the scorched ground. He surveyed the scene — the destruction of a village that had once existed. Sidney had heard that there was a religious Jewish family living somewhere near Manila and hoped to find them. As he searched the area, he came across a small straw hut with a woman and her young child standing outside cooking on a tripod. He was shocked to discover that this was the family he was seeking! They had escaped from Europe, made their way to Shanghai, and eventually had reached the Philippines, where they had narrowly escaped death. Sidney spent some time with them; the young child was impressed by the muscular American soldier who, amazingly, could speak Yiddish. They even wound up spending Pesach together, and formed a relationship that would be remembered for a long, long time. Sidney spent the rest of the war in the South Pacific area, dodging death and simply trying to survive. He tried his best not to bring attention to his Jewish ways, thereby avoiding possible confrontations.

And then one day the long-awaited news arrived: The war was over. The Allies had won! An atomic bomb had been dropped on Hiroshima and Nagasaki and the Japanese had surrendered. Sidney was going home! He sent word to his mother and the rest of the family that he would be arriving on a Sunday and was anxious to see them all. Sidney's mother was overwhelmed with joy that her sons were finally coming home. Not a day had gone by when she had not prayed for them. But on the Thursday before their homecoming one of the other children noticed that their mother was not eating. When asked why, she simply explained that for the past three years she had fasted every Monday and Thursday as a *zechus* for her sons!

But the children seemed confused. "Mommy, the war is over — We won — The boys are coming home — Why are you still fasting?"

Mrs. Sarah Gross looked at her children and with tears filling her eyes, explained, "Children, I did not fast so that we should win the war. I fasted because I sent away *tzvei Yiddishe kinderlach*. And when I see that my *tzvei Yiddishe kinderlach* have remained true to the traditions they were taught, then I will stop fasting."

That Sunday Sidney and Alfred Gross returned to their hometown of Duquesne and were greeted by the folks they had left behind. When they arrived home, their mother could tell that they had held strong to their beliefs throughout the trials and tribulations of war. Then, out of pure relief and gratitude to Hashem, she cried true tears — tears of relief, of joy. And, ultimately, tears of thanks — for she had merited to see her *tzvei Yiddishe kinderlach* once again.

The next morning, Mrs. Sarah Gross ate on a Monday morning for the first time in three years. And her many grandchildren, great-grandchildren, and great-great-grandchildren are forever thankful for the uncompromising love and dedication of their *bubby.*

The Soloist's Sacrifice

WHILE SHE GENERALLY DID NOT LIKE TO PERFORM in public, the young Shiff girl had a voice that was the talk of all those who knew her. On those occasions when she had the opportunity to sing, she was able to bring her audience to tears. The beauty of her voice and the talent she possessed was nothing short of professional. But for a religious young woman in Vienna, Austria in the early 1900's, professional singing was not an option. She came from a prestigious, traditional Torah home and becoming a singer was not considered an appropriate career choice. But one day she chanced upon an individual who happened to be involved with some of the most famous theaters in the country and he offered the young woman the chance of a lifetime — her one shot at fame. Thrilled at the opportunity, she decided to discuss the matter with her parents.

The Shiffs were well aware of their daughter's love for music and her unusual talent, but when they heard about the offer made to her, they knew that it could not be. This was not the appropriate future for their daughter. Desperate in his efforts to explain this to the young woman, her father brought her to Rav Shlomo Baumgarten, who tried to convince the talented girl to abandon this career. But in her dreams she was already standing in front of sold-out crowds. The chance to use her voice, the fame and fortune it would bring, proved a tremendously strong pull; she just could not see herself rejecting the offer made to her. Rav Shlomo, sensing that he had not swayed the aspiring singer, suggested to her father that he visit Rav Yitzchak Meir, the Kapichinitzer Rebbe, who happened to be in Vienna at the time.

Immediately, father and daughter set out to visit the Rebbe. As soon as they arrived, the frantic father poured out his heart. The Rebbe then spoke to the young woman. "Tell me, *mein Yiddishe tuchter,* my dear Jewish daughter, why do you want so badly to go into this line of work?"

The young woman answered honestly. "It is because of the fame that I will find. I'll be known throughout the world."

The Rebbe closed his eyes, deep in thought, contemplating the sentiments the young lady had just expressed. After a moment or two, he opened his eyes and began to speak. "Listen closely, my dear daughter. It is the dream of every young Jewish woman to be blessed with a child who will illuminate the world through his Torah learning." He then looked at her and in as serious a tone as she would ever hear, he offered her the proposal of a lifetime. "I promise that if you now sacrifice your chance at fame, there will come a time when you will be blessed with a child whose Torah will light up the world. He will become the *poseik hador,* one of the greatest halachic authorities of his time. Your fame will come — but it will be through him."

The young woman wiped away her tears and thought deeply about the magnanimous promise the Rebbe had just made. She was a fine, young Jewish girl — and so, after considering the offer, she accepted.

Rav Dan Segal found this amazing tale in the *Sefer Kehillos* of Austria and decided to pursue the rest of the story. He discovered that this young woman who declined the offer of fame and fortune, following the Rebbe's advice, married and had a son by the name of Shmuel. He is Rav Shmuel Wosner, the *Av Beis Din* of Bnei Brak, the author of the *Shevet HaLevi,* and one of the outstanding halachic authorities of our time.

When Rav Dan approached Rav Wosner to ask if the story were true, he became quite emotional and with tears in his eyes responded, "It all makes sense now, because when I was younger my mother always used to encourage me to learn well and be an *ehrliche Yid.* She would always say, 'You cannot imagine what I sacrificed for you.' "

This beautiful story is just one example of the sacrifices that every Yiddishe Mama makes for her children. Small or large, those sacrifices come naturally to women whose only worldly desire is a good future for their children — a life of Torah and yiras Shamayim. It is impossible for children to fully appreciate this mesiras nefesh — but all children, no matter what age, should always strive to do their best, to in some way make their mothers' sacrifices worthwhile.

Fair Is Fair

These two stories, though very different, have a common theme: Jewish men exhibiting true mesiras nefesh — giving to a fellow human being with a full heart, and without any consideration of their own sacrifice.

DUE TO THE THREAT OF SUICIDE BOMBINGS AND other terrorist attacks, the Israeli army was forced to enter the volatile city of Jenin to flush out the terrorists. The soldiers involved in this action were aware that entering into a hostile environment such as Jenin entailed a great risk — their very lives were at stake. Nevertheless, when the time came for the troops to be dispatched to the dangerous region, two soldiers appeared at the door of Brigadier General Weiss. Eli Cohen was 19, although he appeared even younger. His slight build was certainly not typical of Israeli soldiers, but his brave and confident demeanor were impressive. The other soldier, Benny Lapidot, was old enough to be Eli's father. The paunch above his waist revealed that he was more of a grandfather than a soldier, but he too was dressed in his uniform and prepared for battle. They were sent to the general because they had had a disagreement.

Eli felt that only the young soldiers should enter Jenin on this dangerous mission where they might very well be killed. After all, the young had no wives or children for whom to care. Eli spoke passionately, like a child pleading for a chance to do something important for a big reward — only he was not a child and Jenin was not a reward.

As Brigadier General Weiss listened intently to Eli's pleas, he was touched, though not surprised, that a Jewish soldier would feel this way and want desperately to fight for his nation and protect his fellow Jews. But Benny, after listening to Eli, also pleaded to be allowed to fight in Jenin. After all he was older and better suited for a battle that would require more than just physical prowess. It required maturity and experience, both of which Benny and his fellow "older" soldiers possessed. But most importantly, Benny argued that these "kids" had not yet experienced the beauty of life, marriage, and having children. As he so sadly put it, at least I have a son to say *Kaddish* for me if necessary.

Brigadier General Weiss carefully listened to each side and determined that both were right. A mix of both young and old, a blend of youthful energy and seasoned wisdom would make up the squadron that was to be sent into the perilous terrain of Jenin.

And so, both Eli and Benny entered Jenin. They went from house to house, risking their lives as they walked through every door. And then suddenly — in one horribly sickening moment — Eli and Benny were no longer alive. These two brave *korbanos* were killed in a booby-trap explosion. And while Benny's four sons stood over his *kever* and proudly recited the *Kaddish*, their mother looked on and wondered how she would ever be able to manage, and how she would explain it to her 3-year-old son, who could not understanding why everyone was looking at him with such pity.

Eli's father and mother stood weeping over their only son's grave. Their son had died and now he would never feel the pleasure of holding his own child in his arms. He would never know the joy of sharing every moment of his life with a wife. He would never bring his child to school and would never smile at his daughter's new Shabbos dress.

And years from now, when Jenin and its selfless heroes were no longer remembered, there would be One Who would always remember Eli's and Benny's unforgettable disagreement.

Yizkereim Elokeinu letovah … im she'ar tzaddikei olam.

Hard times had fallen on Reb Shmuel Gruskin. He had done the best he could to provide for his family but was much too proud to ask for handouts, and so his Friday-night *seudah* would be downgraded from gefilte fish to tuna fish! His job as a rebbi at Yeshivas Ohr Yisroel did not pay enough for his family to live on, and the extra tutoring he had undertaken had petered out. He felt very bad for his family but there was really not much else he could do. Luckily for him, though, he had a friend named Reb Moshe Labowitz.

Reb Moshe, who had been a close friend of Reb Shmuel's for many years, had only recently discovered just how desperate the situation had become in his friend's house. And Reb Moshe made a commitment to buy fish for his friend for every single Shabbos. Even though Reb Shmuel was quite proud and did not want to accept the offer, Reb Moshe refused to take no for an answer. This "agreement" lasted for a number of years — until Reb Shmuel discovered that his friend's financial situation was really no better than his own. Horrified that he had been accepting handouts from another needy Jew, he informed his friend that now under no circumstances would he consider accepting the fish for Shabbos.

But Reb Moshe was not relinquishing his right to buy the fish. And so the two friends went back and forth on the issue. Was providing for a fellow Jew considered one's own private Shabbos expenditures, which the Talmud (*Beitzah* 16a) clearly states are not included in the amount of money the A-mighty designates yearly for every person? They finally decided to bring the halachic question to Rav Chaim Kanievsky.

When Rav Chaim heard about the "Argument" of the two friends, he could not help but smile as his eyes filled with tears of joy. *"Ashreichem Yisrael!"*

If these are the arguments we have, then it won't be too much longer ...

Kiddush Hashem /
Sanctifying
Hashem's Name

The Last of the Mohicans

AS I STOOD DANCING WITH MY CHILDREN IN SECTION 109 of the Continental Airlines Arena on March 1, 2005, I could not help but feel that this might be just what it will feel like when Mashiach arrives. I watched as a group of yeshivah boys in section 232 bounced back and forth, imbued with a sense of purpose. I wondered if any of them had finished *Shas*. Probably not — they would have been too young to have started seven-and-a-half years ago. But each one was celebrating Torah and the privilege of being a *ben Torah*.

I watched as two men near me, apparently from completely diverse backgrounds — one wearing a knitted yarmulka and the other a black hat — swayed to the music while holding onto each other, to each other's *neshamos,* bound by a timeless treasure, a priceless gift. I glanced over to see a large section of seats, separated by a black-mesh net, in which proud mothers, wives, daughters, and sisters came to celebrate the accomplishments of their children, husbands, fathers, and brothers, beaming with pride and thrilled to be part of the celebration. Their very pride and joy were a visible testament to who they were.

But perhaps what touched me most was the sight of my father-in-law, Rabbi Yehuda Lefkovitz, and his father, our "Pappa," Rabbi Moshe Lefkovitz, standing on the floor directly across from us. You see, they aren't just a father and son coming to watch as observers in this historic event of *kiddush Hashem*. No. They are much, much more. They are *chavrusos*.

Seven-and-a-half years ago, my "Pappa" and my father-in-law began learning Daf Yomi. For my grandfather this wasn't his first time. It was at least his third, although I am almost certain he has finished *Shas* throughout his other Talmudic travels. But this time they were not sure they would be able to finish. They couldn't have been. Because Pappa was 85 when they started the cycle. But that was no impediment for Pappa; it never has been.

Pappa comes from a different world, a world where *Yiddishkeit* was not taken for granted. He grew up in America in the early 1900's. It was a country almost completely devoid of Torah education and Torah learning. And although a city like Cleveland where he grew up had almost eighty kosher butcher shops, none of the children went to a full-time Hebrew day school. In fact many people themselves would head out to work immediately following shul on Shabbos morning. As the old adage went, *Es iz shver tzu zein a Yid* ...

And although Pappa was one of the few fortunate ones, he feared what might be, what might become of the Torah world. He was present as a young man when the dynamic Lubliner Rav, Rav Meir Shapiro, came to Cleveland. The Lubliner Rav was young at the time, perhaps in his mid-30's, but he was already a celebrity, a figure recognized worldwide. Spending a Shabbos meal in his parent's home with this *gadol* had made a distinct impression on Moshe. He remembered receiving a *sefer* from the Rav and learning one of his many beautiful *niggunim*, the composition of *Libi U'Vesari*. Moshe knew that a world of Torah existed in Europe. But what about him and his kind? What about Torah in America?

Perhaps this anxiety stemmed from when Moshe Lefkovitz was a young man. He was present when Rabbi Barnet Brickner got up to speak in front of a packed audience of Jews in

Cleveland. In those days things were different. Rabbi Brickner was the rabbi at Fairmount Temple, one of the largest Reform Temples in Cleveland. At a citywide gathering, Rabbi Brickner referred to the Orthodox Torah Jews of the world as a dying breed. Those stinging words burnt a hole in young Moshe's heart. The declaration regarding Torah Jewry had been spoken. Torah Jews were, in Rabbi Brickner's cutting, callous words, "The Last of the Mohicans."

So I watched and wondered what Pappa was thinking, watching the *gedolei Yisrael* celebrate at the largest celebration for *limud haTorah* since Har Sinai. I was proud: Proud of my father who, although not there, had finished his fourth cycle. Proud of my father in-law and Pappa, who had finished their first together. Proud of my older brother, who was also making his first *siyum*. Proud to just be a *Yid*. But what was Pappa feeling?

On the way home I found out. He wouldn't and perhaps couldn't fall asleep. "A man lives 93 years for a night like tonight." I couldn't tell if he was crying although I knew that his children who were present were. So were his grandchildren and great-grandchildren. But Pappa? His tears were mixed with laughter, perhaps the laughter that David HaMelech refers to …

Az yimalei sechok pinu …

He thought of the over 120,000 individuals who had participated in tonight's life-altering event, and he thought of Rabbi Barnet Brickner and his seriously flawed prophecy of so long ago. Last of the Mohicans, indeed.

What Will They Say?

We are often faced with dilemmas about how to act or react in challenging situations. In the following two stories we witness the responses of two great leaders who used the phrase, "What will they say?" as a means of motivating themselves and others to do the right thing.

RAV YOSEF CHAIM SONNENFELD, THE LEGENDARY Rav of Yerushalayim, normally returned home from Shacharis by 10 a.m. On most days he would come home from shul still wearing his *tallis* and *tefillin,* greet the usual crowd of people waiting for him, answer their questions, have a short breakfast, and spend the rest of the day learning. But today he was very late. The group waited patiently and then decided to go and look for their "lost" Rav.

As they traced the route that the Rav normally took from his small home to the shul, in the distance they noticed a man wearing *tallis* and *tefillin* standing near a well. Upon closer inspection they realized that the man was none other than their Rav; and two water buckets joined by a wooden plank were draped across his shoulders. Apparently, he was drawing and carrying water for someone. But for whom, and why?

Standing next to the Rav was a shabbily dressed little boy and his younger sister. Their shoes were completely torn and their sad eyes told a story of woe. As the group approached their revered Rav, one of his followers offered to take the buckets from him. "Rebbi, how can you carry these around the streets? It is just not befitting a man of your stature." Rav Yosef Chaim, undaunted, although he had clearly heard the man's comment, continued drawing the water, lugging the buckets back and forth, and placing them on a nearby wagon.

To his questioners he explained, "When I passed by the well this morning I saw this little boy and his sister trying to haul these buckets. I asked them why they were doing such a dangerous job and they informed me that their father had been in bed for the last six months, incapacitated by a debilitating disease. Their mother, who had drawn the water until now, was almost due to give birth and could no longer do the job. So the responsibility had fallen into their laps. Leaning in and reaching down could have caused the young children to fall into the well. So I decided to do it myself."

The group listened, but were themselves worried; after all, Rav Yosef Chaim was an elderly man. He was weak and somewhat feeble. And besides, they thought, someone of the Rav's stature should not be doing such a menial chore. "Rebbe," they begged, "what will they say on the streets when they see you doing this?"

Rav Yosef Chaim looked at the men and then back at the children. "And what will they say in heaven when they see that I don't do it?"

And with that the elderly Rav of Yerushalayim hauled the last buckets of water, placed them on the wagon, and helped the children bring them home.

What Will They Say? (Part II)

THE YOUNG MAN STOOD THERE FIDGETING. HE WAS NOT sure what the Chofetz Chaim was going to say to him and he certainly did not know what he was going to answer. But one thing he knew for certain. Torah Judaism and all that came along with it were no longer for Tzvi Staubler. Much of his life was meaningless and empty, and he felt like an outsider most of the time. He was just not interested in the Torah life anymore, and even though his parents and friends tried to talk to him, he remained unmoved and implacable.

One can just imagine his surprise when he received a message that the Chofetz Chaim wanted to see him. He walked into the room and although somewhat intimidated in the presence of the Torah giant, he was determined not to compromise. He was no longer interested in being a "frum" Jew. Period.

The elderly *tzaddik* spoke to the rebellious youth, but no matter what he said, nothing seemed to make an impression. Finally the Chofetz Chaim looked at Tzvi and took a different tack, "You know, Tzvi, I knew your grandfather. He was a wonderful person. I also remember when your father got married and when you were born."

The defiant young man seemed to let his guard down just a bit. They spoke for a few moments about his grandfather, the relationship the boy had had with him, and how much he had loved him. The Chofetz Chaim reminisced about his childhood relationship with Tzvi's grandfather. And then he continued, "It won't be long before I too am going to die. And when I do I am probably going to see your grandfather. I imagine he is going to ask me if I ever saw his *einikel*, his grandson. And of course I will tell him that I had seen him."

At this point Tzvi's guard was breaking down as he feared the inevitable conclusion of this conversation. He had loved his grandfather so much and pictured the scenario the Chofetz Chaim had described, cringing at the thought of his *zeide* seeing him now. "And when I tell your *zeide* that I have seen you, he is going to ask me how you are doing." By now the Chofetz Chaim's soft eyes were filling with tears. "Tzvi, what will I tell him?" The question hung in the air as Tzvi's soft, muffled cries could be heard. "I'm sorry, *Zeide*, I'm so sorry — "

Part of the greatness of the Chofetz Chaim was his uncanny ability to find the perfect word or gesture to bring back so many who were lost and needed love and encour-

agement to find their way home. Sometimes it was a soft word. Sometimes it was sincere tears, and sometimes it was just the warmth he generated. The Chofetz Chaim yearned to bring these souls back to Yiddishkeit — back to lives of beauty and meaning.

Of Boxcars and Blessings

ELI BERGMAN WAS 11 YEARS OLD BUT, YOUNG AS HE WAS, he knew that he was "out of his element" in his school. His parents had moved to a town where most of the families were not as religious as they were. He longed to live in a more religious community, where he could fit in, where his peers would be more like him, where he wouldn't feel so out of place all the time. The boys in his school were nice, but it was just not his type of crowd. Try as he might, he could not feel comfortable. His father felt the sadness in his son, and felt somewhat guilty that his job kept the family in this particular place. Finally, at his wit's end about what to do, he decided to go to a very special person for advice.

Rabbi Bergman, Eli's father, decided to go to Israel to ask the Steipler Gaon for advice in this delicate matter. The venerated sage received his guest warmly. Rabbi Bergman detailed what his community was like and how his children were doing in their social lives. The Steipler listened closely to Rabbi Bergman's description and inquired about the schools in the nearby areas. Eli's father described the schools in a less-than-flattering light. He watched the expression on the great leader's face and was certain that the advice would be that they should move. Shockingly, the Steipler responded, "If there is not a good school where you live, then build one and not only will the school thrive but your children will excel as well."

He built the school, and Eli thrived.

Yoel Rebibo lived in Netanya in the late 1940's. At that time, Netanya was literally a wasteland, almost completely undeveloped and barren except for a few neighborhoods. Living there was difficult, especially for religious Jews, and Yoel longed to live in a town with a larger population and livelier environment. Looking for guidance, he traveled to meet with the Chazon Ish, Rav Avraham Yeshayah Karelitz, in Bnei Brak. He stated his question bluntly, "Should I move to Petach Tikva or perhaps to Bnei Brak? Staying in Netanya seems impossible — my children are accosted by the nonreligious children to such a degree that it almost feels as if we are living among Jewish anti-Semites!"

The Chazon Ish's response shocked Yoel. He instructed him, "Begin a new school and build it from the ground up. The sweat and tears you put into building the school will help your children grow and fulfill the dreams you have for them." Yoel stood dumbfounded.

The Chazon Ish then recounted a story to illustrate his point: "One day during the First World War, when I was a young man learning in the Novardoker Yeshivah in Humel, a band of soldiers entered the yeshivah and ordered the young men to come with them. We were forced to go on a work detail.

"On the fast day of Asarah BeTeves a boxcar filled with heavy logs pulled up. We were instructed to take the wood from one boxcar and load it into the adjacent one. The burden was too great to bear. Ten young men were required just to carry one colossal log, and as they began to buckle under the pressure it started to rain so heavily that they were told to stop working; indeed, a heaven-sent rain exempted them from this horrible task.

"Think about it," the Chazon Ish turned to Yoel and concluded. "What fools those soldiers were. Instead of moving the immense logs, they could have simply attached the boxcar containing them to the rest of the train." He now smiled at Yoel. "There is a great train of Torah education moving forward in our lifetime. Instead of transferring the children to a 'train car' that already exists, why not just add your own 'car' to the train?"

Soldiers and Recruits

The numbers of Jews returning to their roots continues to grow. Many people and organizations give endlessly of themselves to work with these individuals, and deserve a tremendous debt of gratitude. But we must also remember to recognize the parents and grandparents who imbued their beloved offspring with a spark of appreciation for Torah and Judaism. While some of their progeny went on to create flames from those sparks, for others the sparks lay dormant — waiting for a moment of understanding, of revelation, for the flame to grow.

*I*N THE EARLY 1950'S, MANY JEWS WERE BROUGHT TO ISRAEL from Yemen. These fervently religious Jews walked off the planes with their *payos* flying in the wind, thrilled to have been saved from certain doom in their native country and to finally be in Israel. But soon after they landed, many of the young Yemeni Jews became totally different. They cut off their *payos,* stopped observing mitzvos, and started a "new life," happy to be unburdened of the "old-fashioned" ways.

Seeing their children behaving this way, the parents and grandparents were crushed. They shed endless tears, hoping that somehow things would change.

Rabbi Yaakov Galinsky was sent to Rosh Pina to help improve the disastrous situation. He had hoped to use his charisma to lure the youth away from the enticement and temptations of society. But, sadly, he was largely unsuccessful. Upon meeting an elderly man who had seen one of his very own grandchildren slip into the trap of modernity, the man passionately exclaimed, *"U'mipnei chata'einu galinu le'artzeinu* — Because of our sins we have been exiled to our land." The irony of losing their younger generation to the modern world precisely when they entered the Holy Land was not lost on any of the older generation.

Rav Galinsky felt helpless and turned to the Chazon Ish for help. "Rebbi, what is going to become of these people? What will happen to their children? Will they be lost forever?"

The Chazon Ish listened to the pleas and empathized with those who were losing their children, but knew that change would not happen quickly. "We are soldiers and we must do what we are commanded to. It will not always work out as we hope, but we are obligated to do everything within our power to save these *neshamos* from being lost forever. We must never ever give up!"

Many of those young men and women were lured away by the permissiveness of the material world. The temptations were too much to handle. But the prayers of the parents and grandparents of that generation of Jews must have reached their destination, for eventually they had an impact. Today we are witnessing a breathtaking phenomenon, a movement unlike anything we have seen before — men, women, boys, and girls returning to their roots.

The task is daunting. But we cannot give up hope for those who have lost their way. They're counting on us and they're searching to find their way home.

Blind Faith

The transformation of Kiev, Ukraine over the past twenty years has been miraculous. A country whose Jewish identity had been buried deep, which was nearly devoid of any Jewishness, was suddenly aroused to the tune of thousands of Jewish souls longing for the chance to allow their neshamos to soar.

INYAMIN RIBIAT HAD SPENT THE PAST FEW YEARS IN Yeshivas Orach Chaim in Kiev, as a counselor/rebbi and much more. During his time there, he befriended many young men, one of whom was named Sergei Kotechenko. Sergei had grown up in a remote Chechnian village, on a farm. By some twist of fate, he ended up in Kiev and visited the yeshivah. He became enamored of the religious life, and joined the growing group of young men learning and becoming religious. Sergei was one of the best — his learning and observance of mitzvos increased day by day. It was amazing to watch Sergei change from a gruff farmhand to a religious young man. One cold morning, Binyamin found out just how far this young man had come.

It was 3:30 a.m. on a Sunday morning when Binyamin was roused from a deep sleep. The yeshivah boys had stayed up late the night before for a lively Melaveh Malkah, and Binyamin was not happy to have his sleep interrupted. However, when he heard the reason he could hardly be angry; Sergei realized that he did not have his *tefillin*, and needed them for Sunday-morning davening. Binyamin was at once pleased and puzzled, but nevertheless got into a cab with Sergei to go to the *beis midrash* where Sergei's *tefillin* were stored during the week. During the cab ride, Sergei told Binyamin the real reason for his panic — his eyes were bothering him to the point where he needed to go to the hospital immediately, and he did not want to go without his *tefillin*!

After retrieving the *tefillin*, the two headed straight for the hospital. Sergei insisted that Binyamin return immediately to the yeshivah, and Binyamin promised to come by in a few days to check on his young friend.

Three days later Binyamin returned to the hospital. Upon entering, he was nearly overcome by the odors and the filth. He had hesitated visiting Sergei, because he knew that in this anti-Semitic environment, a visit by a religious person could have negative repercussions, but he so much wanted to see the boy that he decided to go nevertheless.

As he walked down the hospital corridor, he was reminded of photographs of hospitals from the turn of the century — primitive medical equipment, rusting furniture — certainly not what Binyamin was used to from living in America. When he entered Sergei's room, the nurses began screaming at him, "What are you doing to this boy, you crazy people?" Shocked by this outburst, Binyamin looked to Sergei for an explanation. What he saw was even more shocking — the boy looked positively ashen, hollow eyed, and weak. "Sergei," he said, "what happened to you?"

"I haven't eaten in three days — there was no kosher food here, and when I asked for vegetables, all they gave me was one rotten tomato."

Binyamin stared in disbelief. Could it really be true? Had Sergei practically fasted for the better part of three days because he was not able to find kosher food? No wonder the nurses were angry! They looked at Binyamin as if he and all the other Jewish teachers were forcing this patient to starve himself.

"Why," he asked Sergei, "why did you do it?"

Sergei looked at him with fierce pride, "Binyamin, you always taught me to be proud of who I am and to stand firm for my principles. Well, I finally had chance to put this teaching into practice."

Binyamin glanced around the room and could not help but notice the *tefillin* and *siddur* proudly displayed on the windowsill. Sergei beamed with pride. Binyamin sent someone to quickly get some kosher food and he watched with satisfaction and pleasure as the boy ate ravenously. Sergei smiled weakly. He had made his friend proud.

And one can be certain that his Father in Heaven beamed with pride as well.

D'veikus BaShem / Cleaving to Hashem

Make a Wish

AT FIVE FOOT SEVEN, 135 POUNDS, SHMULY Abramson was a popular, charismatic, and energetic ninth grader. With a charming smile and amicable demeanor, Shmuly was well liked not only by his classmates but by his rebbeim as well. When he started feeling ill, everyone was concerned.

At first it was his stamina. Although he had adequate sleep and rest, he found himself constantly tired and sluggish. Then the headaches began. And when the headaches persisted, Shmuly and his parents began to suspect that his illness was more than just a lingering virus. A few weeks later extensive testing confirmed the worst fears. Shmuly had a brain tumor. His hopes and dreams were put on hold, his future was now uncertain. And as he and his family prepared for the long haul, Shmuly's unrelenting smile and cheerful personality would be challenged, as they never had been before.

The surgery went well. But afterwards Shmuly's head was swathed in bandages and completely immobilized! Soon thereafter his treatments began. His hair fell out and his body became emaciated. It became increasingly more difficult to maintain the smile that radiated from his face. But his resiliency allowed him to persevere. It wasn't easy; at times it was terribly difficult. The nausea, the sickness, and the vomiting wreaked havoc with his body. But the road to Shmuly's recovery was paved with love and support from his devoted and loving parents and supportive family, and with the encouragement of his rebbeim and friends.

One of the small amenities available during a patient's recovery is the numerous offers by many generous and big-hearted organizations. While Chai Lifeline is certainly one of the more prominent of the many such Jewish groups, the Make-A-Wish Foundation is one of those in the non-Jewish world that extends its generosity to those like Shmuly. From Paris, France to Disneyland, California, ailing children, together with their families, are taken across the world and allowed to spend a week or two away from it all. It is a much-needed break from the tornado of upheaval that has overturned their lives. Shmuly was now in twelfth grade. He had regained almost all the weight he had lost. His hair had all but grown in; a token bald spot on the back of his head remained as a small souvenir of his illness. But Shmuly had lost so much. He had been robbed of his healthy teenage years by a devastating illness and had lost many of his *bochureshe yuhren,* his teenage years of learning. Now Shmuly was looking to grow, to inject his life with a surge of *ruchniyus,* and was anxious to visit Eretz Yisrael. And so he applied to the Make-A-Wish Foundation for a trip to Eretz Yisrael.

But when he received their reply, he was shocked. They had determined that Israel was considered too dangerous a place for their applicants to visit. Shmuly tried to plead his case but it was no use. Rules were rules. There could be no challenging the ruling from the board of the foundation.

But the foundation was very gracious. They offered him anything else he would like. "Anything?" Shmuly asked with wide-eyed anticipation. "Well, of course, anything within reason." The response prompted Shmuly to conclude: If a trip to Paris with my family might cost about $15,000, then certainly they'll allow me to choose a beautiful gift.

He thought long and hard and then composed a magnificent letter, one that detailed his wish. He explained that he had missed many months of classes at school and that he wanted to grow in his learning of Talmud. He asked for a big, beautiful wall unit in which he would be able to display his ultimate wish — a set of *Shas*. One month later his wish was granted.

This is a boy who could have asked for anything in the world, and his choice was loud and clear.

> *Torah hi, velilmod ani tzarich — It's Torah and I must learn it.*

The Pride of Poland

IF ONE WERE TO GLANCE AROUND THE SECOND-GRADE classroom of Rabbi Baruch Brull, one would see an enthusiastic group of boys bubbling with excitement and the desire to learn. A closer look reveals that one of the boys is much taller than the others. As the class reads the *pesukim,* this boy sings along with perhaps even more excitement than the others. His name is Yaakov Wasilovic. He comes from Poland. But that is not the only reason he is different from the other boys in the class. There is one more reason. Yaakov is 16 years old.

When one looks at Yaakov it is hard not to notice the glow of his eager *neshamah.* His infectious smile and sweet personality endear him not only to his rebbi but also to the wonderful classmates who love to play soccer with him during recess, disregarding his age, background, and size. He came to America several years ago and was introduced to Talmudical Academy through a family friend. It has been quite literally a match made in Heaven.

Every November, the school holds its annual Book Fair, conveniently scheduled for the same nights that parents come to visit the school for their parent-teacher conferences. In that way, the parents can purchase some new books for their children after hearing a good report from the teachers! On the day of the conferences, the children and their teachers create a "wish list" — books that they hope their parents will choose for them. They then go home and give their parents their wish list, hoping that they will receive those books as a gift.

Yaakov Wasilovic had never seen a book fair. When he saw the massive piles of books in the gymnasium, he assumed a library had been brought to the school. He began browsing through the books to see which ones he would want to borrow.

The books on display ranged from the "Amelia Bedelia" and "Beezus and Ramona" series to many books on Jewish themes. Some were historical, others were short stories or novels. In addition the Book Fair displayed various English *sefarim* on Torah and *tefillah*.

Most of the children chose books that were age appropriate. So did Yaakov. He selected books on *Shemoneh Esrei* — three of them. He specifically chose these books because as a novice he did not know much about *Shemoneh Esrei* and he wanted to know more; he loved to *daven*, he just wasn't sure what it all meant. As the children finished choosing their books, his teacher explained to Yaakov that he could not have the treasured new gifts yet. Later that period, Yaakov was informed that he would have to wait until that night if he wanted the books, so he put them down and waited anxiously for the evening to come.

That night at the Book Fair, Yaakov retrieved the precious books he had chosen earlier in the day. He was ready, he felt, to check them out from the "library." One of the yeshivah's employees, Yosef Lefkovitz, noticed Yaakov standing in line and knew that Yaakov had not understood how the Book Fair worked. Yosef knew that Yaakov did not have the money to actually pay for these books, and did not understand that he could not just borrow them. Yosef discreetly approached the young boy and questioned him about the books he had chosen. Yaakov replied that he wanted to take these books out in order to learn about *Shemoneh Esrei.* Yosef realized that Yaakov was going to be quite embarrassed when he realized that he would have to pay for the books, and that his weak English skills would make him even more uncomfortable. Initially Yosef decided that he would carefully explain to the Polish boy the "ins and outs" of the Book Fair.

But then he reconsidered, thinking to himself, *He's such a sweet kid and the books aren't that expensive to begin with. Why not do my good deed for the month and buy the young man his books on tefillah?* With those thoughts in mind, Yosef took the books from Yaakov and told him, "I will check these out for you."

But Yaakov would not hear of it. He did not want or need anybody to do him any favors. That's just the way Yaakov is. He was not the "taking" type and was happy to check out the books himself.

Noticing that he was not making headway, Yosef realized that the best approach was to be straightforward and honest. He would explain everything to Yaakov — that this was not a library and that the books had to be purchased, and that he in fact was not only willing but also happy to sponsor the books for Yaakov. Yosef explained all of this to Yaakov, but Yaakov refused to accept it. The two continued the discussion, with Yaakov steadfastly refusing to accept the gift. Then Yosef came up with an idea.

"I'll tell you what. I'll pay for them and you can consider it a birthday present from me." Yosef was sure that Yaakov would accept this deal.

Suddenly Yaakov began to cry. His tears were accompanied by a shy smile. Yosef was perplexed: Was this young foreigner pleased or had he been hurt? Yaakov looked up and his smile began to spread. "What's so funny?" Yosef wanted to know. This young man was certainly difficult to figure out.

"Thank you very much." Yaakov's English was broken at best. "How you know? Today is my birthday!" And then he bent over and hugged his new friend. Yosef returned the embrace, knowing that this young man has quite a future. He has a Good Friend looking out for him.

The growth this young man has exhibited in just a few months has been astounding. He has used those books to work on his Shemoneh Esrei, and watching him daven is absolutely inspiring. He has a long way to go and there is a lot of work still to be done. But of one thing we can be certain — he will know to Whom to turn in his time of need.

Tenderness and Pain

FOR MOST OF THE LATTER PART OF HIS LIFE, THE Chofetz Chaim, Rav Yisrael Meir Kagan, lived in Radin, and the *kedushah* that radiated from him permeated the entire city. Such was his influence that on Shabbos the community and nearby areas were almost completely devoid of *chillul Shabbos*. If someone chose not to keep Shabbos carefully, out of respect for the Chofetz Chaim that person would never transgress the Shabbos publicly. In those days — the early part of the 20th century — there were very few cars, and the entire area remained quiet and peaceful. One was able to sense the serenity and sanctity of the holy day.

But a time came during World War I when the Chofetz Chaim had to visit another town, a town where there was rampant *chillul Shabbos*. The members of the Chofetz Chaim's entourage were concerned about how he would react when he witnessed the lack of Shabbos observance. When that moment came they were not in the least bit surprised. He cried bitterly. The shock of seeing so many Jews who cared so little about Shabbos brought the Chofetz Chaim to bitter tears.

As the next Shabbos drew nearer, his followers were prepared for the outpouring of tears. But this week it was even worse; the

Chofetz Chaim's pain had deepened, and he was crying even more than he had the previous week. His followers asked him why.

The Chofetz Chaim looked at those gathered around him and shared an invaluable insight. "The first time I saw the *chillul Shabbos* and the indifference of so many Jews it was very painful. And I couldn't help crying. But on the second Shabbos I was expecting to see it again, and this time when I witnessed the disregard for Shabbos it hurt less. I didn't experience the same anguish I had the first time. The pain I felt was not as strong. And that caused my neshamah even more grief."

And once again the Chofetz Chaim began to cry.

Four Thousand Times

WHEN REB ELIEZER YOSEF LEDERBERG FIRST STARTED to experience the pain, he dismissed it as just another headache. But when it would not go away he realized it was time to go to the doctor. The medical technology in Yerushalayim in the early 1950's was not at all advanced and often the lack of expertise resulted in a misdiagnosis. The doctors informed Reb Eliezer Yosef that in their opinion an operation was necessary, one that might possibly cause him much discomfort and blindness for only a few months, but most likely would render him completely blind.

Devastated by the news, Reb Eliezer Yosef spoke to the group of scholars in the Batei Warsaw neighborhood where he delivered his daily *shiur,* confirming the rumors which had been circulating regarding his health. Although he was just a businessman, Reb Eliezer Yosef would deliver *shiurim* to some great Torah scholars.

Everyone had an opinion on the matter; some suggested that he wait a bit, but most felt that he should go ahead with the doctors' recommendations and not put himself at further risk. But Reb Eliezer Yosef just wanted to know one thing — *How soon would he need the operation?*

The doctors told him within six months. Reb Eliezer Yosef realized that once the operation was performed, it was quite possible that he would never be able to look inside a Gemara again. The thought was unbearable, but if it was indeed true, he had work to do.

For the next six months Reb Eliezer Yosef spent every waking moment of every day focused on one thing — learning two *masechtos* by heart. He reviewed *Maseches Beitzah* and *Maseches Rosh Hashanah.* Over and over. Day and night. Only one thing consumed him — mastering those two tractates of Talmud. And while most people might have been preoccupied worrying about their health or visiting sites that they had dreamed of seeing all their life, Reb Eliezer Yosef was preparing himself for the challenges that he might be forced to face along the difficult road ahead.

The day of the operation came. His family wept, recited *Tehillim* and hoped for the best possible outcome. Reb Eliezer Yosef cried as well. He gazed one last time at his dear family, and at the words of his beloved Gemara, knowing quite well that this might be his last time. He thought of all the moments he had wasted during his lifetime — time he could have spent doing more, learning more. But now he had done all he could. He had mastered these two *masechtos* and knew that he would always have them, close to his heart and forever etched in his mind. He closed the Gemara and was wheeled into the operating room, where he was cast into a world of darkness.

When he woke up his eyes were bandaged and he was told he would not know, until the bandages were removed in a few days, whether the operation had blinded him. Finally the day arrived. A thick apprehension filled the air as the bandages were taken off. He opened his eyes and began to weep … he could see.

For the remainder of his life Reb Eliezer Yosef continued to teach the Torah he loved so much. Wherever he went, he would review the Gemara he had studied so diligently during those six months that his eyesight hung in the balance. And in 1955, when Reb Eliezer Yosef Lederberg passed away, his children opened his will and found an unusual request regarding the text he wished to have inscribed on his tombstone. He requested that it be written that he had learned *Masechtos Beitzah* and *Rosh Hashanah* over 4,000 times! And then the following words were to be engraved: "In his will it was written that this feat be engraved on his tombstone so that perhaps one day someone will read this and accept it upon himself to do the same ..."

We take so much for granted in our frail lives. Sometimes we have to be threatened with not having our precious gifts in order to appreciate them.

A Little Bit of Sunshine

We take it for granted — the beauty of Hashem's world. The colors, the sights, the smells of the natural world fill us with appreciation for His masterful work. Hashem created a beautiful world for us to enjoy. The following two vignettes speak of two individuals who appreciated that beauty in its full and true richness — at the end of their lives.

AS RAV YISRAEL OF HUSYATIN REACHED THE END OF his days, he had already lived an incredibly rich spiritual life, one in which he had spread the radiance and sanctity of Torah and Chassidus to many. He had recently celebrated his 90th birthday and the illness which would eventually take his life had put him into the Asusa Hospital In Tel Aviv. The illness sapped him of his strength and he began to wither away. His chassidim and children hovered around his bed, awaiting his beck and call, anxious to help in any way they could. They watched as he mumbled to himself, *"Malchuscha, malchus kol olamim,"* extolling the vastness of the A-mighty's kingdom, his heart overflowing with love for His Father.

The days wore on and finally, with labored breathing, he asked if he could be wheeled outside. He had spent the last few weeks holed up in a building, a creation of man. He desperately wanted to behold the beauty and glory of Hashem's magnificent world. When he was brought outside he just stared. He gazed at the flowers and trees and grass and soaked in the beauty and splendor of a world that most just take for granted. And then he began to cry as he whispered his last prayer, *"Hadur Na'eh … Ziv HaOlam … nafshi cholas ahavasecha* — Majestic, Beautiful … Radiance of the Universe … my soul pines for Your love. Thank you, Hashem, for allowing me once more to see Your beautiful World."

After I told the above story, a young man approached me and shared a similar story, but with a tragic ending.

Jeremy's father ran the emergency room at Sinai Medical Hospital, and one day a young woman was brought in. She was semiconscious; she had overdosed, swallowing a bottle of pills. She had been depressed for some time and fallen into a state of hopelessness. Tragically, she no longer had a desire to live.

The doctors worked feverishly to save her, but she went into shock. After a few hours she was placed in the ICU, clinging to life by a thread. The next twenty-four hours would be crucial. Jeremy's father spent the evening doing his rounds and went into the young lady's room. The girl was hooked up to many machines; he could not help but wonder what had caused her to harm herself so seriously. As he walked by he noticed that she was opening her eyes and he went to her side, hoping to speak to her, but she did not want to speak to anyone. Perhaps she was ashamed that she had tried to do something so foolish, or — sadly — perhaps she was upset that she had failed.

But Jeremy's father persisted, speaking to her softly. She quietly responded to his questions, and he was able to determine that she seemed, indeed, ashamed for having done something so foolhardy. "Do you think I am going to live?" she pleaded with him. He wanted to reassure her that she would be all right, but he was really not sure. Instead he just told her not to worry.

He left her room and felt the tears welling up in his eyes. Doctors were supposed to be used to this already. He decided not to go home that night, but to stay nearby in case she needed help. Early the next morning he went to check on her. She was barely awake but was happy that he had come by again. "Would you take me outside one last time?" He wanted to tell her to stop talking like that but instead informed her that it was against hospital rules to leave the building in the state she was in. "Please — just for one minute."

His instinct as a father took over and as he looked into her sad eyes he told her that he would return with a wheelchair in a moment. As he wheeled her downstairs he wanted to ask her how she felt but he was afraid that he knew the answer to that question. Finally they reached the "garden area" of the hospital and he wheeled her outside. He stopped and watched as this young woman who, a mere twenty-four hours ago had tried to take her own life, now wanted nothing more than to hold onto her every moment, every breath. She looked around at the beautiful garden which surrounded her, breathing the air and smelling the flowers. And then suddenly she started to cry — and she could not stop. A few moments later she asked him to bring her back inside. And as he wiped his own tear-filled eyes he could sense her desire for life and her regret for having tried to give it up.

His shift was over and he desperately needed to go home and rest but he didn't want to. He wanted to stay and help this girl get better. But he knew that he had to go home and rest for a few hours. He stopped by to let her know that he would be back soon but she did not indicate that she had heard him or that she cared.

Later that evening Jeremy's father returned to the hospital and immediately headed for his patient's room. An eerie silence filled the corridor and when he looked into the room he saw that she was gone.

He came home that night and hugged each of his children and told them how much he loved them, and shared with them the story of a girl who had such a beautiful life ahead of her — a life she would never live.

The Strongest Man in the World

MOSHE STUBENFELD WAS THE TYPE OF PERSON you would ask to help you build a succah; he was physically strong, but even more important, he was happy when he was helping others. And he would never accept thanks; it did not occur to him that helping people was anything out of the ordinary. In his hometown of Warsaw, in 1941, he led the *Chevrah Kaddisha* and performed many other community tasks in a quiet, unassuming way.

But during that year, Moshe felt compelled to take a more active role in helping others. He had to make himself more visible and accessible to the weak, starving population of the Warsaw Ghetto. So many people needed so much help. It was not unusual to pass starving, emaciated bodies lying on the ground, both the elderly and the very young. The beast of hunger did not discriminate.

As the Nazis began to liquidate the ghetto they relished the opportunity to mock and scorn their victims, or even to shoot them on the spot. When they spotted Moshe they decided they had found their amusement for the day. Clearly he was very strong and no doubt could handle prolonged torture. They ordered him to pick up a horse-drawn wagon and they watched, laughing, as he struggled to complete the task.

Thankfully, they could not read his mind. Because as the rage built within him, he struggled mightily to hold himself back from punching the soldiers. He imagined pounding his fist into their faces and inflicting pain and punishment — retribution they deserved in the worst way. But Moshe knew that if he would dare to react in such a manner not only would he be put to death instantly, but the consequences of such a disobedient act could be the death and pain of many others. And so he displayed his strength by what he did not do. Some might have been surprised at his "cowardliness" and meek behavior, but Moshe knew this was not a time for him to flex his muscles or to show his strength. Now he had to show self-control.

But his tormentors were just getting started. As the crowd grew so did their glee in watching the Jewish Hercules demonstrate his muscle and might. Stunt after stunt, Moshe proved equal to the task and then finally, inexplicably, they left him alone. Their amusement for the day was done. But Moshe knew that this was not it. They would find him again and next time he had a feeling that just shaming him would not be enough.

The next day was Shabbos and the people of Warsaw did their best to ignore the daily tragedies and try to celebrate Shabbos as it was meant to be. They donned their finest garments to help make the holy day just a little bit nicer than the rest of their miserable lives.

It was time for Minchah, as the sun was setting soon. Moshe was on his way to shul when he saw the same band of soldiers that had started up with him the day before. When they spotted Moshe once again, they chased him down. "Come on, strong man, perform for us again." *Please, let them leave me alone*, he thought. But it was not meant to be. They pointed to the wagon he had carried the day before and commanded him to do it again. But Moshe was determined not to be mocked again. He refused to do what they asked.

The Nazis began to threaten him with force, and soon were beating him. But Moshe still refused to carry the wagon. He would not lift a finger. He knew very well the fate that awaited him, so he decided to daven Minchah — one last time. The sun was setting as the wicked beasts were inflicting their punishment, but he was not going to give in. And so he began to pray.

Tehillas Hashem yedaber pi …

The beatings escalated and he was marched in front of a large crowd. Now the Nazis ordered him to pick up a pile of bricks, "Show us how strong you really are, Jewish swine!"

But Moshe ignored their fanatical screams. Instead he chose to spend his last few moments the way he wanted. *"Mechayei meisim berachamim rabbim …"*

"Pick it up, Jew!" The beatings continued.

"Mi chamocha baal gevuros, u'mi domeh lach …"

"Coward! Weakling!" Moshe was now covered in blood — but refused to fight back.

"V'neeman Atah lehachayos meisim …"

"Aren't you embarrassed to behave like this in front of your people? You're a disgrace!"

And with his last ounce of strength he cried out, *"Atah echad veshimcha echad."*

And if one listened closely he might have heard a cry from Heaven: *U'mi ke'amcha Yisrael goi echad baaretz.*

Let's Get Started

*T*HEIR REBBE, RAV YOEL TEITELBAUM, THE SATMAR Rav, had invited them to join a nightly *shiur* in *Maseches Berachos*. It was just a few years after the war, and they constituted quite a ragtag bunch — Shmiel, Yankel, Leibush, Berel, and a few others — Holocaust survivors trying to get on with their lives after having lost everything. They came together every evening at 7 o' clock. When they had received the invitation to participate in the *shiur* they were quite flattered and appreciative that the Rebbe had invited them. But it soon became apparent that there was something odd about this *shiur*.

It began promptly at 7 o'clock. They would sit down and open their Gemaras. But then the Rebbe, instead of diving into the text, would ask each of these men about their day — their job offers, daily errands, whom they had seen in the street, seemingly mundane matters. After an hour or so, the Rebbe would open up his Gemara and as he was about to begin learning, would look at the clock and announce with disappointment, "*Oy vei — es iz duch shpeit.* Oh, it's late! Perhaps tomorrow we will be able to begin."

This bizarre routine repeated itself day after day — every single day — throughout the course of the year. The chassidim who regularly attended the *shiur*, although they enjoyed the discussions immensely, could not understand the apparent charade that was taking place, until an entire year had elapsed. And when the year finally ended the Satmar Rav opened his Gemara at the beginning of the *shiur*. He looked around the room and focused on each of the dedicated men in the group. They were no longer just a ragtag bunch. Recalling from where they had started just a short while ago, he now was sitting in the company of reenergized, revitalized, faith-filled chassidim. Their fragile lives had been mended and they were on the way to a new beginning, not by forgetting the past but by building with it. He smiled and then in one sentence summarized his intent, "*Biz yetzt, huben mir gerlernt daf aleph* — until now, we learned *daf aleph*. *Itzter lumer lernen daf bais* — now let us learn *daf beis*."

Interestingly, each masechta begins with *daf beis*, not with *daf aleph*. Why begin a "book" with page two? What is the missing first page all about? The Satmar Rav's *shiur* provided an eye-opening answer. Much spiritual preparation is necessary before one begins learning, and time must be spent getting oneself ready for that venture. In the case of these men, the Rebbe spent a year on "*daf aleph*," until he felt that they were spiritually ready to begin their lives again, and to start learning the Gemara on *daf beis*. This is what "*daf aleph*" did for these men. With the Rebbe's help, it lifted up broken, dispirited individuals and — through warmth and understanding that only he could give — provided the strong message that it was time to go forward with their lives and rebuild. When the Rebbe felt they had mended their shattered souls, he was ready to begin.

Who Knows? Just Maybe ...

It is a small anecdote. Almost too small to call it a story. It is the story of Rav Yehoshua Leib Diskin, the Rav of Yerushalayim, and his fervent hopes and dreams. But it encapsulates the hopes and dreams of our entire nation.

THE YOUNG MAN APPOINTED TO WALK RAV YEHOSHUA Leib to shul waited patiently outside the Rav's home. After a few moments the door opened and Rav Yehoshua Leib, carrying his *tallis* and *tefillin,* emerged. But instead of heading down the street toward the shul, he began to climb the stairs outside his home, one step at a time, until he reached the top. Rav Yehoshua Leib was already an elderly man; it would take much effort for him just to walk to shul. Why, then, was he climbing the stairs outside his home?

The scenario grew even stranger, for when Rav Yehoshua Leib reached the top of the steps, he seemed to be looking for something. No longer able to control his curiosity, the young man waited for the venerated sage to come back down and then asked him what he was looking for.

Rav Yehoshua Leib looked directly into the young man's impressionable eyes. "You know, the first two *Batei Mikdash*, which were man made, had to be built during the day. But the third one will descend in a heavenly blaze — and that can happen even at night. I was just looking to see if it came down last night." And then the Rav added plaintively, "It didn't."

The stunned *talmid* did not move. He just stared in disbelief at his disappointed rebbi who was already on his way to shul. He still had much for which to daven.

U'venei osah bekarov beyameinu.

Glossary

abba — father

Acharonim — "later" commentators on the Torah

Aibeshter — the One Above; G-d

aishes chayil — a woman of valor

aleph-beis — the twenty-two letters of the Hebrew alphabet

aliyah — being called to the Torah

almanah (pl. *almanos*) — widow

amud — podium

arba minim — the four species used on Succos

aron — coffin

aron kodesh — holy ark in the synagogue, where the Torah scrolls are kept

atarah – silver collar on a *tallis*

av beis din — chief judge of a rabbinical court

aveil — mourner

aveiros — transgressions

avodah — service in the Temple

avodas Hashem — the service of G-d

baal korei — one who reads the Torah at services

baal Mussaf — the one who leads the Mussaf prayer service

baal teshuvah — a penitent returnee to Jewish life

baalebatim — householders

baalei tefillah — those who lead the prayer services

bechinah — test

beis din — rabbinical court

Beis HaMikdash — the Holy Temple

beis midrash — study hall

bekesha — long jacket, usually worn by Chassidim

bentch — say a blessing

bentching — saying Grace After Meals

berachah — blessing

bimah — table in synagogue from which the Torah is read

bircas habanim — parental blessings

Bircas HaMazon — Grace After Meals

bircas hedyot — layman's blessing

Birchos HaShachar — blessings said at the beginning of the morning prayers

blatt — folio page

Bnei Yisrael — the Children of Israel

bochur (pl. *bochurim*) — young man

Borei Olam — the Creator of the World; i.e. G-d

bris — circumcision

bubby — grandmother

chaburah — group

challah — braided bread used at Shabbos or festive meals

chasan —bridegroom

Chasan Torah — the person called to the Torah to complete the annual cycle of Torah reading on Simchas Torah

chashivus — importance

chaval — a pity

chavrusa — study partner

chayal (pl. *chayalim*) — soldier

chazzan — leader of prayer services

cheder — elementary school

chein — grace

chesed — kindness; acts of beneficence

chevrah kaddisha — burial society

chiddushim — Torah novellae

chillul Hashem — desecration of the Divine Name

chinuch — education

chizuk — encouragement

cholent — stew of meat, beans and potatoes traditionally eaten on Sabbath day

cholov Yisrael — milk produced under the supervision of a Jew

Chumash — Five Books of Moses

chuppah — canopy under which the marriage ceremony takes place

daf — page (of Talmud)

Daf Yomi — worldwide Torah study project in which all Jews study the same folio page of Talmud every day

daven(ing) — pray(ing)

derashah — sermon or discourse

doar — post office

d'var Torah (pl. *divrei Torah*) — a Torah thought

d'veikus baHashem — the ecstatic state of cleaving to G-d

emunah — faith

esrog — citron, one of the four species taken on Succos

ezras nashim — women's section (of a shul)

gabbai — synagogue sexton; attendant of a Rebbe

gabbai tzedakah — attendant in charge of collecting and or distributing charity

gadol (pl. *gedolei*) *hador* — Torah giant of the generation

gadol b'Torah — one who is great in Torah

gaon — genius

gedolim — Torah leaders

Gemara — loosely, a synonym for the Talmud as a whole

gevurah — inner strength

gut voch — a good week

gut yahr — a good year

hadassim — myrtle branches

hadran — prayer recited at the conclusion of a tractate of Talmud

Hakafos — the dancing around the *bimah* in the synagogue on Simchas Torah

halachah — Jewish law

hashgachah pratis — Divine providence

hasmadah — consistency in Torah learning

Havdalah — ceremony marking the end of Shabbos and festivals

heiliga — holy

heimish — with an old-world flavor

hesped (pl. *hespedim*) — eulogy

illuy — genius

im yirtzeh Hashem — G-d willing

ima — mother

Ivrit — Hebrew

kabbalas panim — groom's reception before the wedding ceremony

Kabbalas Shabbos — Shabbos eve prayers

Kaddish — prayer sanctifying G-d's Name, often recited by mourners

Kaddish Yasom — *Kaddish* said by an orphan

kallah — bride

kapota — black frockcoat

Kapparos — ritual performed on Erev Yom Kippur

kasha — question

kashrut — Jewish dietary laws

kavannah — concentration

kavod acharon — final honor

kedoshim — holy martyrs

kedushah — holiness

kefirah — heresy

kehillah — community, congregation

kever — grave

kezayis — halachic unit of measure equivalent to the volume of an olive

kibbudim — honors

Kiddush — blessing recited over wine expressing the sanctity of Sabbath and festivals

kiddush Hashem — sanctification of G-d's Name

kiruv rechokim — teaching non-observant Jews about Judaism

kitel — shroud-like garment worn on certain solemn occasions

Klal Yisrael — Jewish people in general

kneidlach — matzah balls

Kol Nidrei — prayer which begins the Yom Kippur service

kollel — academy of higher Jewish learning, whose students are mostly married men

korban (pl. *korbanos*) — sacrifice

Kosel HaMaaravi — the Western Wall of the Temple in Jerusalem

krechtz — moan, sigh

kriah — tearing one's garment in mourning

ksav yad — manuscript

kvittel — a written petition to a tzaddik

l'chaim — "To Life!"; traditional toast

laining — reading from the Torah scroll

leichter — candelabra

levayah — funeral

levayat hameit — escorting the dead

lichvod Shabbos — in honor of the Sabbath

lulav — palm branch; one of the four species taken on Succos

maavir sedra — review the weekly Torah reading

machlokes — difference of opinion; dissention

machzor — prayerbook for the high holy days and festivals

Maftir — the last person called up to the Torah reading

maggid — preacher; teller of tales

maggid shiur — Torah lecturer

malkus — lashes

maseches — tractate

mashgiach — spiritual guide in a yeshivah

maspidim — eulogizers

matanos l'evyonim — charity to the poor, distributed on Purim

mayim acharonim — water used for rinsing the fingers at the end of a meal

mechallel Shabbos — person who does not observe Shabbos

mechilah — forgiveness for past wrongs

Megillah — lit. scroll; commonly applied to the Book of Esther

mekadesh shem Shamayim — to sanctify the name of Heaven

mekubal (pl. *mekubalim*) — mystic; one who is well-versed in Kabbalah melamed (pl. melamdim) — teacher

melaveh malkah — meal eaten Saturday night in honor of the departed Sabbath

menachem aveil — to comfort a mourner

menahel — principal

menahel ruchni — spiritual guide in a yeshivah

mentch — lit. a person, usually denotes one of good character

mesechta — tractate

meshulach (pl. meshulachim) — solicitor for charity

mesiras nefesh — self-sacrifice

mesorah — tradition

Mi She'beirach — prayer recited at public Torah reading (for the welfare of a particular person)

miklat — bomb shelter

mikveh — pool for ritual immersion

milchamah — war

minhag — custom

minyan — quorum of ten men for prayer service

mishloach mannos — gifts of food sent on Purim

mishnah — the teachings of the Tannaim which form the basis of the Talmud

Mishnayos — See Mishnah

mohel — one who performs circumcision

Motza'ei Shabbos — Saturday night

Motza'ei Yom Kippur — the night following Yom Kippur

mussar — ethical and religious teachings; chastisement

mussar sefer — book on self-improvement

nachas — satisfaction, pleasure

Ne'ilah — concluding prayer service on Yom Kippur

nechamah — comfort

neshamah — soul

niftar — passed away; one who passed away

niggun (pl. niggunim) — tune, melody

nisayon — a test

olam — group of people

Olam Haba — the World to Come

oleh — one who is called to the Torah

parshah — portion of the Torah read each Shabbos

pasuk — verse

payos — sidelocks

peirush — explanation

perek — chapter

pesichah — opening the holy ark

pikuach nefesh — a matter of life and death

piyut — liturgical poem recited during the prayer service of a specific occasion

posek (pl. poskim) — halachic decisor

rabbosai — gentlemen

rachamei Shamayim — Heavenly mercy

rebbeim — teachers

refuah sheleimah — a full recovery

Ribbono Shel Olam — Master of the World, i.e. G-d

Rishonim — early commentators on the Torah

Rosh Chodesh — the beginning of a new month

rosh hakahal — head of the community

rosh kollel — the head of a kollel

sandek — one who holds the baby during circumcision

seder — period of learning in a yeshivah

sefer (pl. sefarim) — book

Sefer Torah — Torah scroll

segulah — spiritual remedy

seudah — meal

shaliach tzibbur — one who leads the prayers

shalosh seudos — third meal on the Sabbath

shamash — synagogue caretaker; attendant to a Rebbe

Shamayim — Heaven

Shas — the six orders of the Talmud

she'eilah — question of a halachic nature

Shechinah — Divine Presence

Shehecheyanu — blessing said on a holiday, new garment, new fruit, etc.

shekel (pl. shekalim) — Israeli currency, like dollars

shelichim — messengers

Shema Yisrael — prayer recited twice a day, affirming one's faith in G-d

shemirah — guard duty

Shemittah — the Sabbatical year when agricultural work is forbidden in Israel

Shemoneh Esrei — the 18 blessings recited three times a day

Sheva Berachos — the seven blessings recited at weddings and the ensuing series of celebrations; the celebrations themselves

shidduch — marriage match

shirah — song

shiur (pl. shiurim) — lecture; lesson

shivah — seven-day period of mourning

shmuess (pl. shmuessen) — ethical discourse

shochet — ritual slaughterer

shomer — watchman

shomer mitzvos — one who is observant of mitzvos

Shomer Shabbos — one who observes the Sabbath

shtender — lectern

shtetl — town, village

shtiebel (pl. shtieblach) — lit. room; shul, usually used by Chassidim

shtreimel — fur hat worn by Chassidim on Sabbath and festivals

siddur — prayer book
simchas hachaim — joy of living
sippur — story
siyata d'Shmaya — Heavenly assistance
siyum — celebration marking the
    completion of a course of study
succah — booth in which a Jew dwells on
    Succos
sugya — topic; conceptual unit in Talmud
tafkid — job, calling
taharah — ritual cleansing of the dead
tallis — prayer shawl
talmid (pl. *talmidim*) — student
talmid chacham — Torah scholar
tatty — father
techiyas hameisim — resurrection of the dead
tefillah (pl. *tefillos*) — prayer
Tefillah Zakah — penitential prayer recited
    prior to *Kol Nidrei*
tefillin — phylacteries
teshuvah — repentance
tichel — head kerchief
tisch — lit. table; a Chassidic gathering around
    a Rebbe's Shabbos or festival table
tzaddik — righteous person
tzaros — troubles
tzedakah — charity
tzeischem leshalom — a parting wish to
    one setting out on a journey
tzibbur — congregation
tzitzis — fringed four-cornered garment;
    the fringes themselves

Ulpan — Hebrew study program
Vidui — confession said before death
vort — Torah thought
Yahrtzeit — the anniversary of a person's
    passing
Yamim Noraim — High Holy Days
yarmulka — skullcap
yasher koach — lit. may your strength be
    renewed; thank you
yasom (pl. *yesomim*; f. *yesomah*) — orphan
yeshivah gedolah — yeshivah for older
    students
yeshivah ketanah — elementary school
Yeshivah Shel Maalah — the yeshivah on
    high, in Heaven
yeshuah — salvation
Yetzias Mitzrayim — the Exodus from Egypt
Yid — Jew
Yiddishe treren — tears shed by a Jew
Yiddishkeit — Judaism
Yiras Hashem — fear of G-d
Yizkor — prayer recited in memory of
    departed relatives
yungerman (pl. *yungerleit*) — young
    married man
z'man — semester
zeidy — grandfather
zechus (pl. *zechusim*) — privilege; merit
zemiros — songs sung at Shabbos and
    festival meals
zocheh — worthy